SURVIVING BEYOND FEAR

SURVIVING BEYOND FEAR: WOMEN, CHILDREN AND HUMAN RIGHTS IN LATIN AMERICA

Edited by
Marjorie Agosin

Assistant to the Editor
Monica Bruno

WHITE PINE PRESS

Publication of this book was made possible, in part,
by grants fromWellesley College, the Ford Foundation,
the New York State Council on the Arts,
and the National Endowment for the Arts.

ISBN 1-877727-25-3

Printed in the United States of America.

Book design by Watershed Design.

First Edition

1 2 3 4 5 6 7 8 9 0

Published by White Pine Press,
10 Village Square, Fredonia, New York 14063

Acknowledgements

The inspiration, vision, and conceptualization of this anthology, *Surviving Beyond Fear,* has been made possible thanks to the generous support of the Ford Foundation which, for the past few years, has made special grants to Wellesley College for the purpose of conducting seminars in a variety of disciplines for the college honors students.

During the years of 1988-1991, under the sponsorship of the Ford Foundation, a group of honor students, under my supervision, conducted a weekly seminar on the subject of Gender and Human Rights in Latin America.

Extensive research from scholarly sources as well as non-government organizations, personal interviews with human rights workers, health professionals, activists, and writers were conducted on several of the topics addressed in this anthology. The researching of the material served a very powerful purpose in our curriculum and, therefore, human rights became a central dialogue in our daily lives, as well as in our socialization as women. Issues of freedom, censorship, and justice were dealt with and discussed outside the classroom.

The idea of this anthology emerged during the seminars and the tenacious research of the students paved the way for the articles included, although I hold total responsibility for the final selection and editing of the anthology.

This anthology represents a unique collaboration between a faculty member—myself—and students from several disciplines, including

Spanish, psychology, political science, history, and physics. As an educator, these multi-faceted gatherings brought me great joy, as well as an enhanced sense of purpose at the academic as well as the personal level. Ultimately, the participation in these seminars has increased our understanding of the pain of others, as well as the possibility of exercising our privileged position in our society for purposes of justice and dignity.

I would like to acknowledge the full contribution of the students that participated in this project:

Monica Bruno
Susana Rosario Cardenas
Juliette M. Donato
Primavera del Carmen Garrido
Elsa del C. Jimenez
Samira Yasmin Khera
Jennifer Joy Lucas
Faith Sheiner Najberg
Mercedes Maria Oris De Roa
Maria Raquel Vallarino
Paula M. Vega

Special thanks to professor Lois Wasserspring who gave three lectures on the subject of women and political participation in Latin America. Monica Bruno, a member of the seminar as well as an independent studies student, deserves a special word of recognition for editing and typing the manuscript. Also, Jennifer Lucas for editing several of the articles included and to Ximena Bunster for permitting us to use the title of her extraordinary essay as the title of this anthology..

A word of gratefulness for the two faculty members at Wellesley College who directed the Ford seminars for the entire college, Katie Park of the history department, and William Coleman of the chemistry department. A special thanks to the dean of the college, Nancy Kolodny, for seeing this project through to completion, the president of Wellesley College, Nannerl Keohane, whose vision and commitment to these issues make Wellesley College an institution of nurturing and commitment, and to the members of the Spanish department for their continuing support of my work.

This anthology exemplifies the best qualities of Wellesley College students and reflects our motto: Not to be ministered upon but to minister.

SURVIVING BEYOND FEAR

Contents

Children and Human Rights

SURVIVING BEYOND FEAR

Introduction

International human rights law was officially created in 1945, after the horrific crimes committed by the Nazis during World War II. These massive violations of human rights led to a strong conviction that effective international protection of human rights is an essential condition of international peace and caused the nations of the world to consider the promotion, implementation, and protection of human rights to be a fundamental issue and one of the principle purposes of the new United Nations organization. To achieve these goals, the UN Charter required member nations to respect human rights and provided for the creation of a commission to protect and advance these rights.[1]

On December 10, 1948, the Universal Declaration of Human Rights was approved by the General Assembly of the United Nations. The declaration proclaims that all human beings are free and equal in dignity and rights, without regard to sex, race, color, class, language, political opinion, or religious belief.

The countries that signed this declaration have the obligation to guarantee freedom to their citizens and to fulfill all the basic human rights outlined in the document. However, despite the rapid growth of international human rights law during the last four decades and the adoption of other global laws for the protection of human rights, such as the 1975 Helsinki Accord; the UN Declaration on the protection of all persons from being subjected to torture and other cruel, inhuman, or degrading treatment; and the Declaration of the Rights of the Child, massive violations of human rights continue to occur throughout the world, and progress to halt these violations has been slow and inconsistent.

The subject of human rights and its relationship to political violence, especially in Third World countries, gained importance in the 1970s when the general public began to recognize the concept, making it a key political issue. Nevertheless, in Latin America, where authoritarian regimes have dominated and controlled the lives of the civilian population over the past two decades, respect for human life and human rights has not been evident. Forced disappearances, torture, and mass executions have been the techniques of terror that these governments implemented to maintain fear among the population and establish state control. In the late 80s and early 90s, most countries of Latin America have moved toward democracy, yet, in most cases, the military apparatus has remained intact.

Although the human rights documents cited above have brought no significant material improvement in the status of international human rights, they do provide an important point of reference for governments, institutions and people wanting to promote these rights. The basic question then is how these rights can be enforced in countries whose governments continue to violate them.

This anthology represents a unique contribution in the field of human rights in Latin America by focusing on two very fundamental and neglected areas: women and children. This is, I believe, the only collection of essays that explores issues of gender and its relationship to human rights, and the essays included represent the research and activism of individuals working in countries whose human rights record is deficient. Robin Morgan, in her introduction to *Sisterhood is Global,* explains the neglect and lack of research in the area on which this anthology focuses:

> Because virtually all existing countries are structured by patriarchal mentalities, the standard for being human is being male, and female human beings, *per se*, become "other" and invisible and this permits governments and international bodies to discuss "the world's problems"—war, poverty, refugees, hunger, disease, illiteracy, overpopulation, ecological imbalance, the abuse or exploitation of children, and the elderly—without noticing that those who suffer most from "the world's problems" are women.[2]

Morgan presents alarming statistics that illustrate the relationship between gender and human rights: while women represent half the global population and one-third of the labor force, they receive only one-tenth of the world's income and own less than one percent of the world's property.

> In developing countries, almost half of all single women over age fifteen are mothers and are responsible for more than 50% of all food production. Concerning the issues of refugees throughout the world, women and children constitute more than 90% of all refugee populations.[3]

The situation of women and children has seldom been treated as a separate category and given the attention that it deserves. The vast literature on human rights, including classroom textbooks and scholarly articles, seldom focuses on these groups, ignoring the fact that problems of overpopulation, disease, malnutrition and exile are women's problems and failing to realize that women and children suffer disproportionately from these crises. For example, in Latin America, when a woman's husband is "disappeared" she is unable to collect his pension.[4]

Health problems affect women who give birth and women who are the sole caretakers of children. Pregnancy and childbirth are the causes of a large percentage of women's deaths; each year, half a million women of childbearing age die because of complications related to pregnancy and labor.

Non-Government Organization (NGO) initiatives, as well as the United Nation's Decade for Women, intended to substantially improve the situation of women. At the second meeting of women affiliated with the UN in Copenhagen in 1980 and at a final meeting in Nairobi in 1985, the role of women worldwide and the progress achieved was evaluated. As a result, a new document was drafted demanding the elimination of all forms of discrimination against women. This accord was approved by the United Nations General Assembly on December 13, 1979. To date, 94 countries have ratified this document, which states that, despite the Human Rights Declaration of 1948, women continue to be discriminated against in social, economic, cultural and political arenas. The signatory nations condemned discrimination against women and agreed to a series of measures designed to eliminate it. Gender discrimination is defined as "all distinctions, exclusions, or restrictions based on sex" that have as their objective or result the lessening or revocation of the recognition, enjoyment, or exercise by women of human rights and fundamental liberties in all areas.[5]

The specific situation of women and human rights in Latin America is complex. As mentioned above, during the last two decades, much of Latin America has been ruled by dictatorial regimes. The fascist ideology of the military leaders opposes equality of the sexes; ". . . therefore, the struggle for women's rights is considered by many Latin American dictatorships as a frontal attack to their social organizations and the demands for women's rights are at best ignored and at worst repressed."[6]

A quick assessment of women's legal rights throughout the continent reveals widespread discrimination against women. Cecilia Medina has done extensive studies in twenty Latin American countries and has shown that human rights in Latin America have not been implemented with regard to women.[7] In nine countries, the community property that arises as a result of a marriage is legally administered by the husband. Nine countries confer the *patria protestas*, that is, the right a parent has over the person or property of a son or daughter, to the father, or gives the father's opinion priority when the *patria protestas* is granted to both parents.[8] The true extent of discrimination against Latin American women is revealed in the area of criminal law: The fact that a woman's sexuality can be exercised only within the legal bond of marriage and an adulteress can be penalized with incarceration underscores female submission to their husbands in the sexual arena.

Human rights abuses against women are systematically overlooked by international organizations. For example, Amnesty International does not keep their otherwise careful and valuable records on political prisoners by gender. "We don't try to keep track of patterns," explained one Amnesty International spokesperson. There are several reasons for this, but virtually all the established human rights organizations have been singularly uncurious about whether and why women suffer human rights violations in ways that differ from men.

In an unpublished essay, renowned anthropologist Ximena Bunster and North American political scientist Cynthia Enlow have pointed out that most publicity of human rights abuses focuses on male political prisoners and victims of torture. They also state that "many of us have been encouraged to think of human rights violations as a form of repression raised by militarism, usually in alliance with free enterprise capitalism." The conventional assumptions, such as the general belief that political prisoners are male, are significant, because by assuming that most victims of human rights violations are men, we fall into the trap of imagining that most revolutionaries and opposition leaders are men. When women are made invisible in discussions of government abuses and torture, dissident politics is implicitly masculine and the crucial role women have played in opposing repression is marginal.

One fundamental aspect concerning women and human rights that is seldom addressed is the issue of torture.[9] Women are arrested, abused, and raped as punishment for their political activities or for their relationships to their husbands or lovers. Also, the torture of female political prisoners is closely linked to gender and sexuality, since torture strips women of their virtue in the eyes of society at large, transforming them from "good mothers" into prostitutes. Authorities refer to women protesters as the "crazy" mothers of subversives and terrorists, diminishing the authenticity and value of their struggles. Children are also manipulated in this oppressive process. One of the most common ways to try to break a woman activist is to threaten to abuse her children, making it clear to the woman that she has lost the ability to protect them.

This anthology documents the mobilization around human rights issues, focusing on the struggles of ordinary civilians mobilizing toward truth, justice, and acknowledgement of military crimes. Like all anthologies, it is not a comprehensive review of women, children and human rights struggles around the world, but the essays chosen speak about those countries where women's mobilizations have had a major impact and where human rights have been grossly violated.

After careful consideration and years of study, as well as my personal involvement in the human rights movement in Chile, I strongly feel that Latin American women have transformed the repressive society in which they live and have created a new female political imagination, a new way of *hacer política,* (making politics).[10]

The essays in the first section, Women's Political Mobilization Around Human Rights, address the ways in which ordinary women succeeded in becoming extraordinary human beings through social and political mobilization, helping to restore democracy to their countries. This first section does not deal with transitional politics in the new Latin American democracies, but rather examines the relationship between citizenship and gender. As we will see in the essays, women created human rights associations through a desperate need to find their missing relatives. These organizations transformed the political consciousness of their founders, who began to think not simply of human rights but also of female political mobilization. We cannot assume that female human rights organizations necessarily espouse feminist ideology, but there is a common link because the women began to develop a specific political consciousness dedicated not only to the search for the missing but also to the struggle to preserve the rights of work, education, and health care for everyone, not just for the privileged.[11]

The essays in this section of the anthology illustrate how women in several Latin American countries defied repression in their homelands. They began to protest and to become active participants in a silent society that not only denied its citizens the right to assemble but also the right to speak. The mobilization of these women can be linked to additional political issues related to gender. We can also see how these citizens have reconceptualized the definition of human rights as a universal phenomenon linked not only to political violence but to the pursuit of freedom, justice, employment, housing and many other issues.

Women's Political Mobilization Around Human Rights

Women's human rights groups in Latin America began to form around the issue of political disappearances. Individual actions by relatives, as well as legal actions by the courts, proved ineffective; therefore, women in several countries began to unite. The first group was the Chilean Association of the Detained/Disappeared formed in 1974, followed by the Mothers of Plaza de Mayo in Argentina, the Comadres in El Salvador, and the Group for Mutual Support in Guatemala. In 1981, organizations representing twelve Latin American countries formed the Latin American Federation of the Detained-Disappeared (FEDEFAM) as a collective response to the clandestine, illegal kidnappings carried out by repressive Latin American governments.

These groups are linked by the fact that they were formed by women under adverse conditions; the search for the missing as well as the demand for justice have been a common goal and bond, although each group has its own, unique symbols. The Mothers of Plaza de Mayo wear white scarves with the names of their missing children written on them when demonstrating in the Plaza de Mayo in Buenos Aires. The Comadres of El Salvador also wear white kerchiefs. The Chilean Association of the Detained/Disappeared chose the creation of *arpilleras,* tapestries with a political content, to denounce the circumstances faced by Chilean women.

As the authors of the essays in this anthology point out, opposition to military rule provided these groups with an opportunity to link women's issues to the struggle against dictatorship. The struggle for human rights was linked to women's rights, and protest against military authoritarianism became a critique of authoritarianism within families. The treatment of female political prisoners (which often involved rape and other forms of sexual abuse), the cynical manipulation of family ties to enhance the effectiveness of torture, the destruction of families, and the parceling out of the children of the "disappeared" all revealed the hypocrisy behind the state's glorification of motherhood. The scholar Jane Jarquette has clearly demonstrated how women are uniquely affected by human rights violations and how issues such as the treatment of women in detention centers led feminist groups to study the situation of women in their own homes. As a result of this new insight, women's organizations in Chile adopted the slogan "Democracy in the Country and at Home."

Jennifer Schirmer's essay serves as a general introduction to women's human rights groups and their role as agents of change in their countries' transition from dictatorship to democracy. Even though Chile, Argentina and Guatemala are the countries discussed, they serve as models for the study of other groups of female social resistance. Ximena Bunster has called this form of political mobilization "nurturing politics," based on the ideals of caring, loving, and preserving the unity of the family. Sara Rudich describes this as "a women's politics of resistance," a politics connected to mothering that incorporates cultural symbols of femininity in its resistance to repressive practices by governments.[12]

Schirmer, an anthropologist and professor of women's studies at Wellesley College, discusses the role of women and human rights groups under the most repressive dictatorships: Chile and Argentina in the Southern Cone and Guatemala in Central America. Her study explores the evolution of women's human rights resistance groups and the issue of disappearances. The overall objective of these movements was to search for the missing as well as to attract the attention of the general public and exert pressure on the government. The hunger strikes by the Chilean Association of the Relatives of Disappeared Persons and the demonstrations by the Mothers of Plaza de Mayo have alerted the press and made the public aware of the need for the vindication of human rights and justice. Schirmer also points out that, paradoxically, human rights violations have allowed women to create new modes of resistance and to emerge as leaders in a political arena that has traditionally denied the role of women in the political agenda.

It is important to understand that the key element in the concept of disappearance is the direct participation of the authorities: the government officials, armed forces, and intelligence officers. These groups are responsible for both the crimes themselves and the attempted cover-up after the fact. Women's human rights groups have played an integral role in documenting cases, supporting the relatives of the missing and enlisting the assistance of international organizations.

The second essay in this section, by César Chelala, an Argentine physician and human rights activist, is a more personal testimony on the early struggles of one of the most visible human rights groups in Latin America: the Mothers of Plaza de Mayo. Personal accounts have been important in the gathering of information about human rights violations, and Chelala interviews two of the founding members of the Mothers of Plaza de Mayo. The interview is moving and insightful, revealing the anguish, courage, and tenacity of the women who founded this movement. Chelala also focuses on the connection between the mothers' public and private lives. It is also revealing, as Chelala points out, that the Argentine military government, under the leadership of Saúl Ménem, has given amnesty to the members of the Argentine military junta. Once again, the Mothers, the victims, are the ones that continue to clamor for justice and the acknowledgement of their children's disappearances. Their weekly marches around Plaza de Mayo have become of great political, as well as ethical importance.

Historian Marifran Carlson presents the poignant testimony of Leonor Alonso, a political prisoner abducted with her daughter, María, and tortured at the infamous School of Naval Mechanics. This testimony also reveals how her granddaughter, born in captivity, was retreived from the family that illegally adopted her and returned to her grandmother. This essay is particularly powerful because readers are able to grasp, first-hand, the relationship of the interviewer with the life story of the victim. As with the Chelala essay, we can understand the courage, strength and the spirit of survival of these women. Leonor Alonso is an active member of the Grandmothers of Plaza de Mayo, and her granddaughter, Elena Gallinari, was the first child born in captivity to be found by this organization.

Patricia M. Chuchryk, a sociologist, explores how human rights groups were formed in Chile, as well as the opposition they faced from right-wing organizations. Her essay complements the general conceptualized study of women's human rights groups and focuses on the formation of two major groups inside one country. Important theoretical issues are addressed, such as the role of the Mothers as political subjects, women's place in the traditional family ideology and the role of Chilean women and democracy.

Ximena Bunster's essay is, I believe, the only study to date that deals with female political prisoners and torture. She examines how male torturers use psychological and sexual abuse to undermine the female prisoner's role as a mother, so fundamental in Catholic, patriarchal societies. Torture in Latin America and under most repressive governments has been practiced in secret and often supervised medically to intimidate and to inflict pain on political opponents. Despite international pressures, torture has tragically persisted and has continued to play a key role under Latin American dictatorships. Bunster's essay also helps us reflect upon the relationship between gender and political subjects and the discrediting of the female by the State. This essay clearly links issues of the female victims' sexuality and their roles within the military apparatus.

Mariclaire Acosta, a Mexican human rights activist, studies the Comadres of El Salvador. Through the voice of a Salvadoran woman, we witness her personal and political struggles in one of the poorest and most repressive countries in Latin America. Acosta's essay begins with a historical introduction to the political situation in El Salvador and then, through the voice of one victim, the reader observes the transformative process suffered by one of the women and her participation in the human rights movement in the country.

The essays in this section, written by social scientists, reveal the patterns of opposition and political mobilization in the areas most affected by repression during the 1970s and 1980s: Chile, Argentina, Guatemala, and El Salvador. They also reveal how the politicization of women emerged as a response to the violation of their relatives' human rights. From the personal tragedies of these women emerged a political and ethical movement. In this sense, the personal indeed became political, and the struggle for human rights proved to be an important impetus to the movement for women's rights in the continent. Also, through these essays we observe that the western concept of human rights in Latin American countries has been embraced by the women themselves, and this is one of their greatest accomplishments.

Children and Human Rights

The section on children is intrinsically related to women's human rights because, like women, children have been the hidden objects of human rights violations and state terror. The statistics dealing with children in Latin America are frightening. In El Salvador alone, 58% of the children suffer from malnutrition; a recent study by a U.S. medical delegation found an infant mortality rate of 48% in the area of San José las Flores, mainly due to the army's violence. According to the United Nations Children's Fund (UNICEF), in twenty-one Latin American countries, an average of 77 of every 1000 children die before the age of five and 40,000 children below the age of five die each day in the developing world—that is 14 million a year—due to the effects of war and poverty. Thus, the issue of human rights must be expanded to include these most vulnerable victims of repression who are always linked to their mothers' economic and political circumstances.

The essays in this section deal with the violation of human rights faced by children for political reasons. In Latin America, children have been tortured alongside their parents, have been forced to watch their parents being tortured, have been orphaned and, particularly in Argentina, have been abducted and adopted by military officers or placed in orphanages. Infants were deliberately given false birth dates and false identities, making tracing them even more difficult.

Historically, children's human rights have been neglected by international law. Only on November 20, 1989, did the General Assembly of the United Nations adopt the first pact to set standards for adoption, child labor, child abuse, and other issues not covered by existing human rights laws. This treaty, called the Convention on the Rights of the Child, was the result of ten years of negotiations. It is encouraging to point out that world leaders are serious about changing the trends in children's rights. At the world summit for children at the United Nations in September of 1990, more than seventy world leaders signed a declaration stating goals for this decade. Among these are the reduction of the infant mortality rate by half, universal access to clean water and sanitary means of waste disposal, universal access to education, and improved protection of children in especially difficult circumstances. The latter refers to homeless children, refugees, and children of war. Sixty countries have now ratified the UN Declaration of the Rights of the Child, making its provisions binding in these countries.

Readers of this anthology will notice that many of the essays in this sections are written by health care professionals. Because of political repression in Latin America throughout the 1970s and 1980s, medical professionals throughout the world have taken a courageous stance against human rights violations and have devoted their energy to working in defense of these rights. Groups such as Physicians for Human Rights and the American Association for the Advancement of Science (AAAS) have set up special divisions on scientific freedom and responsibility, establishing fact-finding missions throughout the world. The AAAS sponsored a symposium in Washington, D.C., on medical ethics and torture in January 1981.[13]

While some health care professionals have taken vigorous measures against the violation of human rights, others have actively participated in the torture and murder of political prisoners under Latin American dictatorships. This exploitation of medical technology has been widely denounced.

The first essay in this section, by Elena Nightingale, a pediatrician and special advisor to the president of the Carnegie Corporation in New York, provides an overview of the general situation of children and human rights in Latin America. Nightingale also outlines the development of the protection of children by UN statutes, and explores the psychological effects on children of the disappearance of one or more of their parents. This type of emotional trauma is often accompanied by material losses and physical displacement. In an atmosphere of psychological stress, economic difficulties, and often lack of support from the community, children are traumatized by their losses and by witnessing violent arrests and abductions. Nightingale addresses the situation of Latin America globally, with a vision toward the future of these children, pointing out its precarious uncertainty as well as the challenges we face in enforcing their rights.

Brinton Lykes, a child psychologist and human rights activist, has written her essay, "Children in the Storm," on the psychosocial trauma in Latin America. This essay, which explores the ways in which mental health workers have begun to document the effects of State-sponsored violence on children and to develop strategies to work with them, explores the situation in Argentina and Guatemala and is written from the point of view of a health practitioner.

Jennifer Schirmer's essay, "Chile: The Loss of Childhood," focuses on a rehabilitation center in Santiago, Chile, dedicated to healing children who have lost their childhood to political violence and complements Brinton Lykes' "Children of the Storm. "

Among the central issues Latin American countries face as they move toward re-democratization are the ethical and moral dilemmas that arise from the relationship of the previous military regime with the civilian population, especially with the families of the disappeared, who demand justice and acknowledgement of the fate suffered by their loved ones. The Grandmothers of Plaza de Mayo in Argentina have been searching for not only their children but for their grandchildren, who were abducted from their homes or born in clandestine prisons.

The essay by Rita Arditti and Brinton Lykes, "The Disappeared Children of Argentina," explores the formation and the work of the Grandmothers and the way in which modern genetics has been used to trace grandpaternity through blood tests. In this essay, we observe how science has worked for the preservation of ethics and justice.

The essays in this section are unified by the common thread of the effect of state terrorism on children. The section concludes with the voice of a child describing his daily plight while living in El Salvador. As we can see through these essays, the violation of human rights in Latin America and throughout the world is an undeniable fact that requires individuals to take moral and ethical stands because these abuses will have far-reaching consequences, in not only the present but in future generations. These stands have already been taken by civilians since their war-torn governments have been unable to do so.

This section also reveals the permanent damage these children from South and Central American regions suffer: they are underfed, and forced into child labor and the armed forces. All these factors cannot be considered separate from the governments that have inflicted such misery upon them.

This anthology has been a rewarding—and painful—experience. Working with such a diverse group of professionals has been a tremendous challenge and a source of inspiration. It has been painful because of the subhuman conditions still experienced by so many women and children in Latin America and throughout the world. Despite the return to democracy in most of the countries mentioned, there is still no answer concerning the fate of the almost 90,000 disappeared in Latin America, and their families still experience the anguish of uncertainty. Others have discovered the grim reality of finding their loved ones' remains in clandestine cemeteries and unmarked graves. Yet, not one of the generals responsible for the disappearances and tortures is in prison.

Human rights is a way of life, a calling that must be of extreme importance for all citizens of free democracies. Renée Eppelbaum, one of the founding members of the Mothers of Plaza de Mayo, has said we must all be militants for human rights.[14] This anthology demonstrates how, in the most difficult circumstances, ordinary Latin American women have shown the exemplary qualities of the human spirit in their struggle for justice, freedom and life.

It is also remarkable that the victims of State-sponsored terrorism have been the agents of political change in their silenced societies. Bravely, they began as Mothers, searching for their missing ones and built, through their own efforts, communities of women where social dissent became a path for the truth and justice present in the democratic governments of Latin America. These women's groups, formed in the '70s, continue to initiate actions that will bring about social and political change and have now began to behave as subjects of their own history.

It is impressive to observe the efforts made by the scholars, health professionals, and human rights activists who, while not direct victims of repression, have devoted their work to denouncing the violations of human rights by repressive governments and rehabilitating their victims.

The visions that have inspired the writers of these essays, as well as the visions of the women who have inspired them, spring from the concept that under totalitarian rule an entire society must be healed. These essays aim to contribute to this process of rehabilitation with the hope that readers will hear the voices of women screaming alone in the chambers of horrors and the voices of the mothers who continue to ask where their children are.

The decade of the '70s was characterized throughout Latin America as an epoch of political terror. The end of the '80s signaled the transition to democracies in the entire region of South and Central America.

The aftermath of political violence and the traumatic legacy of state terrorism upon the individuals is one of the many legacies faced by these new democracies. How to deal with the perpetrators and the traumatic lives of those who were victimized by the regimes remains a constant struggle between the new democratic government and the victims of former state terror.

Most of the new democracies remain fragile and unsettled since the oppressive aparatus formed by the armed forces during the previous dictatorshops remains intact. Torturers are free and able to incorporate their lives into a normal and almost uneventful existence. This is not the case with the former victims and their families, who still search for their missing loved ones and, especially, for their bodies.

Despite the fact that these democracies have created commissions to investigate the human rights violations in their respective countries, the whereabouts of the victims remains unknown and the guilty ones that issued the orders to torture and kill have not been tried for murder.

In Argentina in 1989, President Raúl Alfonsin authorized the first trial in Latin America against the military junta, condemning and jailing nine military officials. Two years later, an amnesty was declared, giving freedom to the high military authorities and those who obeyed their orders.

The particular situation of women and human rights remains a very bleak and unsettling landscape. There is evidence that torture still takes place in many countries. From a legal point of view, the widows of missing husbands are still unable to collect their pensions since the status of a missing husband remains to be clarified by law. Former human rights organizations, such as the Vicarite of Solidarity in Chile, an organization affiliated with the Catholic church and a leader in the field of human rights advocacy, has closed its doors, and its human rights program now consists of the sponsorship of soup kitchens and craft workshops.

Democracy has brought greate indifference and solitude to the families of the missing. There seems to be a conspiracy of secrecy and amnesia. As Judith Lewis points out in her ground-breaking work *Trauma and Recovery* (New York: Basic Books, 1992), "The ordinary response to atrocities is to banish them from consciousness; certain violations of the social compact are too terrible to utter aloud. This is the meaning of the word unspeakable."

Women and the human rights movement in Latin America occupy the same position now as they did in the decade of the '70s: they carry the banners of justice and memory. As in past decades, they demand truth and answers to questions about the missing. In the '90s, they lobby for memory, acknowledgement, and a public truth—a truth that will involve the collective legacy of a people.

The present agenda of women and the human rights movement is to restore among themselves and their countries a sense of growth, a sense of connections between their individual selves and the collective trauma that their countries suffered. They also believe that a public crime must not be covered in secrecy. They continue to speak on behalf of an entire missing generation so that the struggle for a better society will not be forgotten. They continue to speak the unspeakable. This is their major victory.

—Marjorie Agosin

Translated by Janice Malloy.

Women's Political Mobilization Around Human Rights

"Those Who Die for Life Cannot be Called Dead"[1] *Women and Human Rights Protest in Latin America*

Jennifer G. Schirmer

But suddenly, as though taken by the wind, they disappeared. They were pulled from their houses, from work, from the university, or they waited to detain them in the silenced and solitary streets. Since then, they have ceased to exist, the slate was wiped clean as though they had never existed. We don't know how quickly they were silenced; there appeared [though] to be one more order: to convert the disappeared into inhabitants of the silence and of the forgotten. They didn't want to give our relatives any human destiny, neither to live nor to die. But [to be] forever in doubt.[2]

I want to know where my son is, if he is alive or dead. I want them to finally tell me the truth about what happened, and if they killed him, I want to know where, when, why and who did it. Only the day they have responded to all those questions will I stop fighting.[3]

It is ironic that in violating human rights, repressive states may sow seeds of new forms of resistance. Groups of relatives of the disappeared of Latin America who confront their governments as mothers seeking their missing children and as wives seeking their missing husbands are an important example of such resistance.

By examining the evolution of human rights resistance taken by three groups of relatives of the disappeared—the Plaza de Mayo Mothers ("Madres") in Argentina, the Mutual Support Group ("GAM") in Guatemala, and the Group of Relatives of the Detained-Disappeared (*Agrupación*)[4] in Chile[5]—one can understand why such movements have evolved in the ways they have, why they are led by women, why they have taken particular actions, and how these groups have managed to endure. More specifically, the experiences of these groups reveal the ironic circumstances created by the repressive state. On the one hand, the state valorizes motherhood and the family; on the other hand it simultaneously undertakes systematic repression through the use of forced disappearance. As a result, the repressive state has found itself confronting new forms of resistance based precisely on motherhood and the family. Using the language of sacrifice and the traditional values associated with motherhood as both political protection and political tools, these women have been willing to take public action during the worst years of repression in Argentina, Guatemala and Chile. Their persistence raises the following question: what is it about this method of repression—forced disappearance—that creates such mobilization of, for the most part, previously apolitical women? Moreover, given the importance of religion in these societies, how has the religious language of obedience and submission been transformed into these women's form of political expression?

While these "motherist" groups are only part of the larger human rights movement in Latin America, they reveal how protest is shaped by a particular type of repression and how repression can be transformed into possibilities for change and hope. Through dramatic acts of civil disobedience—launching street demonstrations with flowers, candles and photos of their missing relatives; staging hunger strikes; chaining themselves to government buildings; blocking traffic—the women in these movements counter the cults of "everyday death"[6] with celebrations of daily life. By presenting writs of habeas corpus to the supreme courts in their respective countries (often without the help of lawyers, who fear for their lives), while at the same time remaining skeptical of the legal process, these women demonstrate both the potential and limitations of law within their societies. Perhaps what is most striking about these groups is that they are led primarily by women "who would never in their lives before have considered demonstrating in the street against government on any issue whatsoever."[7] As in past resistance movements, these women use the image of the weak and powerless female to their advantage as a protective means for mobilization, resistance and survival.[8] As in the bread riots of the past centuries,[9] these women represent the defiant transformation of the powerless victim into the political actor.

These "mothers" test the limits of permissible political action by demanding the right to know what happened to their missing relatives and the right to reclaim justice from the state. Not mobilized by ideology but by the sheer weight of social and political circumstances that accompany the loss of a relative and the destruction of the family, these women, as disobedient female subjects of the state, dramatize powerlessness and help to demystify the powerful.

> These protagonists are not the traditional political actors from parties or unions, [but] in the majority of cases, are simple mothers of families who are not militants and do not belong to any part of the opposition. [They are] women who, by their condition as mothers, wives, sisters or daughters of the victims, have been intensely, *culturally* mobilized by the repression [in a manner] without precedent in Latin American history.[10]

In an attempt to censor the collective memory of society, the state has used forced disappearances and amnesty laws. Yet, because it was not absolutely certain that those who were abducted were actually dead, there remained hope, and the absence of bodies created a presence of protest.

"Forced disappearance" may include abduction, torture, secret imprisonment and murder. It became the primary instrument of the governments of Guatemala, beginning in 1966; Chile beginning in late 1973; and Argentina since March 1976.[11] While it is difficult to chronicle the exact number of victims, one source estimates that over 90,000 people have disappeared in Latin America.[12] The United Nations believes that forced disappearances constitute the most negative of human rights violations.[13]

While the victims—individuals and entire families—come from diverse backgrounds, they are often members of the political opposition, members of particular ethnic groups (as in Guatemala), or live in a zone targeted for security operations. These are significant features for the organization of and the membership in these resistance groups. Victims of this technique of political repression are kidnapped and "disappear:" their friends and relatives cannot find out whether they are being held (and perhaps tortured) or have been killed. Only rarely has a disappeared person later been found in custody or reappeared alive, yet it is difficult to verify that a disappeared person has died. Mutilated corpses found by the sides of roads or dumped in public places to terrorize potential opposition, or bodies from unmarked graves in a state of decomposition or burned beyond recognition,[14] are impossible to identify.[15] While more visible public violations of human rights produce negative reactions in world opinion, secret and anonymous disappearances give no evidence and provide no identification of either the victim or the perpetrator. It is the perfect crime, as the crime itself is invisible, except to those who are victims or relatives. Both are meant to suffer silently, individually, and alone. The victim is denied martyrdom; those left behind are prohibited the final ritual of bereavement. Disappearance then is a form of censorship of memory by the state, best exemplified by the Argentine junta's "Presumption of Death Because of Disappearance" law, which gave relatives an expedited procedure by which to declare certain of the disappeared legally dead.[16]

Paradoxically, however, the military in these societies preach traditional family values and valorize motherhood in an attempt to strengthen patriarchal rule in the home.[17] This insistence upon the woman's sacrifice for and obedience to the family and to her children has backfired on the military as women have demanded to know what has happened to their sons and daughters. The clandestine nature of forced disappearance has unintentionally politicized the family because of the state's refusal to acknowledge either death or life. As a result, these women have launched actions of civil disobedience and placed themselves at risk at a time when there has been virtually no other visible protest against the regimes.[18] This contradictory doctrine of at once valorizing and destroying the family has made their resistance possible: they have had to behave *as mothers* in order to survive. This contradiction must underlie any understanding of these "motherist" groups in terms of their actions, identity and motivations.

This essay is divided into sections: Section I gives a brief descriptive history of each group; Section II deals with the political practices and language common to all three groups, and the groups' claiming of "political space;" Section III examines the paradoxes generated by the repressive state and the groups' use of Catholic political symbolism of motherhood and sacrifice.

The groups of resistance: The Argentine Plaza de Mayo Mothers (Madres), the Guatemalan Mutual Support Group (GAM) and the Chilean Group of Relatives of the Detained-Disappeared (Agrupación)

Mothers of the Plaza de Mayo (Madres): Argentina

Fourteen mothers of the disappeared in Argentina first marched on April 13, 1977 in the Plaza de Mayo in the center of Buenos Aires, just one hundred meters from the Junta's offices.[19] While making the rounds of morgues, cemeteries, offices and chaplaincies of the armed forces, receiving derisive replies to their incessant question about missing relatives—"your son has run off with someone," or "your daughter's been killed by terrorist colleagues"—Azucena DeVicenti, well into her sixties at the time, announced to the thirteen others: "It's not *here* we ought to be—it's the Plaza de Mayo. And when there are enough of us, we'll go to the Casa Rosada and see the President about our children who are missing."[20]

It was at the Plaza de Mayo, the most closely guarded spot in Buenos Aires, that the fourteen Madres began to appear every Thursday at three-thirty in the afternoon, when bank employees left work. They would circle the Pyramid, two by two, wearing white headscarves.[21]

The second meeting drew twenty mothers; by December 1977, there were some 300 mothers, grandmothers, sisters and daughters of diverse backgrounds.[22] The two women who later became president and vice president of the group represent the unusual kind of cross-class alliance that the circumstances created. Hebe Bonafini is the wife of a factory worker who disappeared with her two sons. The sons were both active trade unionists and university graduates. Adela Antokoletz, wife of a diplomat, is the mother of a lawyer who disappeared after defending political prisoners.[23]

After three months of demonstrating in the plaza, meeting with foreign journalists and congressmen and officials from the United States, as well as presenting 159 writs of habeas corpus to the courts, in June, 1977,[24] these women became known as "crazy women"[25] by government officials. The government's stance toward the women is indicated by the Press and Public Information Official's question to a foreign journalist covering the protests: "Really, don't you have better things to do than to cover *'las locas'* [the crazy women]?"[26] "What disappeared? There are no more than in most countries."[27]

On October 15, 1977, some 300 Madres were dispersed from the Presidential Palace by tear gas and arrested by the federal police after gathering to present a petition, with 24,000 signatures, calling for investigations into the disappearances.[28] They were interrogated and later released.[29] With their growing numbers and the interest they were arousing, the Madres' immunity had come to an end, and they, too, like their relatives, became subject to the state's definition of subversion.

On December 8, 1977, after working on a full-page advertisement calling for "A Christmas in Peace," which was to be printed in *La Nación* to mark International Human Rights Day, nine members of the group, including a French nun, were kidnapped by Navy operatives from the door of the Church of Santa Cruz.[30] In a related operation two days later, Azucena DeVicenti, the sixty-year-old leader of the Madres, disappeared after being arrested, together with a young artist, near her home in a Buenos Aires suburb. Another French nun was arrested at the same time.[31] The abducted women were never seen again.[32] These disappearances, not only of middle-class mothers demanding their children but also of nuns, shattered the illusion that the mothers were somehow protected by their status and moral stance. With the list of contributors for the advertisement in the kidnappers' hands, none of the mothers could feel entirely safe, and some women asked that their names be withheld from the next advertisement.[33]

Despite call for prudence and moderation by human rights organizations, the Madres held a press conference in December 1977, expressing their anger and pain:

> They kidnapped these women to muzzle us, but they didn't succeed. They fear us, they fear the bad image which we give to Argentina. They are uneasy about their World Cup. But we make fun of their cup; we want our sons, husbands, fathers. We ask nothing more than the truth, and to say that is a

crime.[34]

In reaction to the kidnapping of the French nuns, France boycotted the World Cup in Buenos Aires on June 1, 1978[35]. On this day, one of jingoistic fervor for the regime (which used the World Cup to express a "common bond" between the Junta and the masses),[36] the Madres took the opportunity to march around the plaza in front of foreign television cameras with signs that read: "We do not have news of our children, our grandchildren, or our parents."[37] The government was furious, issuing a statement that blamed the twelve disappearances on "nihilistic subversion."[38] The day after the World Cup, lawyers defending the Commission of Relatives were themselves kidnapped.[39]

After another march on the Presidential Palace and the presentation of another petition in December 1978,[40] the government barred such public meetings[41] and the women began to meet illegally in churches of a few sympathetic priests who, out of fear, asked them to sit without lights and without talking, passing notes from pew to pew.[42] The women soon decided to organize themselves into a more formal, legally-registered organization, to hold elections and, with overseas financial support, to open an office.[43]

In the face of mounting pressure in the fall 1979, the military government passed two laws in order to "transfer emphasis of the relatives from one of investigating the disappearances to one of deciding patrimony and property rights."[44] The "Presumption of Death Because of Disappearance" law (Law 22.068), issued on September 12, 1979, declared dead those who had been reported missing during the previous five years. This law was strongly condemned by the Organization of American States ("OAS") for failing to address the question of whether people were alive or dead, and virtually no relatives made use of it. Nonetheless, it was one of the first attempts by the military to annul the effects of its "disappearances" through legislation.[45]

The second law, called "Social Security Benefits in the Case of the Absence of the Person" (Law 22.062), was actually an amendment to Law 14.394, which pertained to claims to property of people who were missing.[46] This law gave anyone with legal right under the pension laws, for example someone with matrimonial ties, claim to such benefits upon presentation of evidence that such person had been absent from his domicile, without any news of his whereabouts, for one year. After a year there was a presumption of death. The law basically shortened the period of waiting before a claim could be made.[47]

Interior Minister General Harguindeguy announced that "in order to end the fountain of uneasiness for numerous Argentine homes,"[48] the government had prepared these two laws to regulate the situation of persons "presumably dead" regarding pensions and retirement of their debts.[49] The implication was that the disappeared were no more than unregistered deaths. Similarly, on May 29, 1979, General Viola had referred to the disappeared as *"ausentes para siempre"*" (absent forever), with an emphasis upon the future benefits for families:[50]

> One cannot honestly prohibit women who find themselves alone, some for several years, from founding a new home as they wish, not permit them any longer from assuming without some small help the burden of the education of their children. If some of the persons are even still living clandestinely or have left the country, it is certain that others have died as a consequence of their actions and it is thus suitable to regularize the legal situation which penetrates their prolonged absence.[51]

By legally burying the dead, without producing the bodies, the military government wanted to make the *"locas"* just go away. One of the Madres responded, "[t]his law is scandalous ... Do they really think they can buy the silence of a mother? ... I already have a husband and I don't want their dirty money."[52] The government's attempt to deflect criticism was less than successful. In November 1979, approximately 700 relatives of the disappeared presented a petition to a Civil and Commercial Court judge declaring the "total unconstitutionality" of Law 22.068.[53]

By August 1980, the Madres began to gather more and more public support[54] and by mid-month over 2,000 Madres were again in the plaza with another petition. After such an impressive showing, the police refrained from dispersing the group.[55] General Videla felt obliged to respond publicly: "The dead and the disappeared in Argentina are the price which had to be paid so that Argentines could live in peace, dignity and liberty. We are proud to have destroyed the forces of evil."[56]

Political Turmoil and the Malvinas War

Up until March 1982, the Madres had developed growing support at home and abroad with their incessant demands for justice and truth.[57] Once the war started, however, nationalism became the acceptable form of political release within the state, and the Madres once again became branded as parents of "reprobates" who had died or disappeared for offending the guardians of the nation; they were harassed by nationalist sentiments feeding on the Junta's war. "Politically and socially, the [Madres] would stand alone on the side of the 'traitors.' The 'war against subversion' would be sanctified as the necessary prelude to the war for the Malvinas."[58]

Demonstrations by different groups of women based on traditional roles, including the Madres, multiplied during the Malvinas War.[59] Women publicly challenged the status quo by responding to the government's pro-draft slogan, "Papa, what will your son do in the war?" with, "Mama, what is your son doing in peace?" or "The Malvinas are Argentine, and so are the missing."[60] The Madres intensified their actions—leafletting, petitioning, traveling abroad, presenting writs of habeas corpus to the courts—which culminated in a series of large marches by the Madres and other human rights groups.[61]

It was clear that human rights organizations had gained new political recognition and voice, and the protests on behalf of the *desaparecidos* became a prime source of the regime's discomfort. As a result, there were more kidnappings, assassinations and acts of torture during the military's demise. Some twelve judges were threatened and physically attacked; the Madres were also assaulted.[62]

The Madres and Re-democratization

On October 29, 1983, the state of siege was suspended and free elections took place. On December 10, 1983, the civilian government of President Raul Alfonsín was sworn in. The assumption of civilian governance, however, did not end the impact of the military regime on the tens of thousands of relatives of the disappeared, and the Plaza de Mayo Madres continued to press for "the truth" regarding those responsible for the disappearance of their relatives. Among other protests, at a National Meeting of Madres on June 24, 1985, they accused the District Attorney of accepting the military's distinction between innocent and guilty victims. They were angry that certain of the disappeared had been declared "terrorists" or "subversives," because this implied that the victims themselves were on trial rather than the former government. The Madres vowed to continue to protest against these false characterizations which unfairly "dirt[ied]" the images of the victims.[63]

With the advent of the new government, the Madres—together with human rights organizations in Argentina—have had to learn to deal with "post-repressive" situations in which domestic public opinion may no longer want to be reminded of "*El Proceso.*"[64] According to a 1985 survey conducted in Argentina, fifty-nine percent of the population disapproved of the activities of the Madres.[65]

In December 1986, President Alfonsín called a special session of congress to pass a law providing that further prosecutions of members of the armed forces, police or prison services accused of crimes committed between 1976 and 1983 be initiated within sixty days or not initiated at all. It was, for all intents and purposes, an amnesty law.[66] As a group of the Madres explained in an interview in Buenos Aires in January 1987:

> We Madres have always been suspicious of the Alfonsín government's intentions, with the modification of the Military Justice Code, with trying all cases within the jurisdiction of the Supreme Military Council, and with accepting the majority of sentences handed down by the military court... But now, with [this] *Punto Final*, we interpret this as a total moral and ethical abomination of justice. To place limits on the time there may be investigations is never to know what happened to all those disappeared.[67]

Mutual Support Group for the Reappearance of Our Sons, Fathers, Husbands and Brothers ("GAM"): Guatemala

GAM arises from a thirty-year history of government violence in a country with the highest number of disappearances in Latin America. It is estimated that 38,000 people have disappeared over the past two decades.[68] It is one of the only countries without an internal human rights monitoring group, although a few citizens groups have organized in protest to the government's policies.[69] One of the first such citizens committees, the Committee of Relatives of Disappeared Persons, was formed in 1967 after the abduction of twenty-eight Communist Party and union leaders in 1966—an abduction which established the method and usage of *desaparecido* for much of Latin America.[70] GAM, however, is one of the last of the groups of resistance to organize in Latin America in the 1970s and 1980s and is the first human rights group able to survive in Guatemala.[71] This history reflects the intense, systematic repression of the successive military regimes.

The mobilization of the resistance groups was triggered by a fortuitous event. In 1976 an earthquake struck Guatemala, causing extensive destruction. Trade unionists and community activists went into the countryside to help communities rebuild. For many, this was an introduction to the poverty of the countryside. As a result, the previously separate indigenous-ladino (*mestizo*) demands for better working and living conditions became aligned and mobilized through an umbrella labor organization called *Comité Nacional de Unidad Sindical* ("CNUS") which linked unions and peasant leagues.[72]

The reaction of the government was swift and harsh. A "Reign of Official Terror" began in 1978 under General Lucas García. After government-sponsored death squads had targeted key unions, peasant and political leaders, they began to take actions against anyone suspected of "dangerous" opinions: 311 peasant activists were killed during 1980 alone, and 400 students and faculty members of the university of San Carlos were murdered over a period of four-months.[73] The killing by government-sponsored death squads was becoming "positively unproductive, driving whole sections of the urban middle class against the regime."[74]

Additionally, the 1982 coup by General Ríos Montt resulted in massacres of between 50,000 and 75,000 indigenous peasants and the destruction of 440 hamlets, forcing 50,000 to 75,000 to relocate to "model villages."[75] The forced recruitment of 900,000 peasant men into the Civil Patrols left between 100,000 to 200,000 orphans and widows behind in the highlands.[76] The 1983 coup by General Oscar Humberto Mejía Víctores did not change the state's policies. Violence continued to be used as a form of social and political control against the urban and rural sectors of society.[77] In 1986, there was hope that all of this would change when President Cerezo, the first democratically-elected civilian president in twenty years, took office. Although President Cerezo has said he is committed to changing the human rights situation in Guatemala, the killings continue.[78]

Given the absence of an internal human rights monitoring group, and the danger involved in collecting such information, it is not surprising that GAM began to organize slowly and carefully. On June 5, 1984, three women formed the Mutual Support Group in Guatemala. Like the women in the other groups, they continually met one another at the morgues, cemeteries, police stations, hospitals, or at the Peace Commissions of the university rectory in their search for their relatives.[79] They began meeting once a week in the local headquarters of Peace Brigades International,[80] where they heard a tape recording made by mothers of missing Salvadorans (the "CoMadres"), and decided they needed to organize such a group.[81]

By August 1984, there were 130 members and within one year, there were nearly, 1,000.[82] At least two-thirds of the GAM members are poor, indigenous women (without any previous political experience),[83] reflecting the magnitude of the violence in the highlands and the nascent indigenous-ladino alliances made in the 1970s.[84] Many of the original members of GAM are relatives of the nineteen students and professors at the university who were kidnapped in early 1984 over a four-month period.[85]

At first, GAM was careful not to accuse the government of being responsible for the disappearances. In 1984, the group requested interviews with the National Police Chief and Foreign Minister without success.[86] GAM also began to document the cases of disappearances presented to them by their membership. At this time, GAM had reports of 416 persons who had disappeared between 1980 and 1985, most of whom were men between twenty and forty years of age, some women (several pregnant), and children between six and sixteen years of age.[87] GAM also began public demonstrations.[88]

After many requests, President Mejía Víctores agreed to meet the women. On August 1, 1984, he told them the disappeared had run off to join the guerrillas or had left the country, but he promised to investigate the incidents.[89] Despite assurances to establish a Tri-Partite Commission to investigate the "disappearances," GAM noted his disinterest in the problem as demonstrated by the President's references to the disappeared as "the supposed kidnapped" and "those incorporated with the guerrillas."[90]

GAM continued its public protests.[91] All political parties were reluctant to give their support, with some openly calling GAM "subversive."[92]

Because of the lack of institutional support and lack of alternatives, GAM became more forthright. They publicly charged divisions of the security forces with direct responsibility for the capture and subsequent disappearance of their family members. "At first we didn't blame the government, because we thought that if we didn't blame them the disappeared would appear," said one of the women. "But there comes a time when you have to tell the truth."[93]

They continued to press the government. On January 9, 1985, GAM began petitioning the Tri-Partite Commission to allow them to present their own testimonies on the disappearances.[94] Every Friday the women would protest at the Public Ministry, blocking traffic, playing flutes and whistles and beating drums. They demanded the results of the investigation that "they say they are conducting."[95] They also occupied the National Constituent Assembly, requesting that a category of political prisoners be created in the new Constitution "to diminish the inhumane practice of kidnappings."[96]

The Mejía Víctores government, unaccustomed to any form of opposition, and especially public denunciations of its authority, sought to discredit and terrorize GAM. Three days after GAM's fourth and increasingly combative meeting with the Chief of State in November 1984, two of those listed by GAM as "disappeared" (a journalism student and university professor) were found dead with signs of torture.[97]

In March 1985, the departmental governor of Guatemala City called in four GAM members, telling them to sign a certificate which said that "provoking public disorder was a subversive act."[98] Likewise, President Mejía Víctores announced:

> We have accepted their petitions and nonetheless they are still pressuring. They pressure the National Constituent Assembly, they take out paid ads—I don't know where that money comes from. I imagine the [Mutual Support] Group is being manipulated and directed by the subversion ... making problems for the peaceful Guatemalan population.[99]

The GAM responded with a public statement refuting these charges. However, the government didn't stop at public condemnation. On March 31, 1985, Héctor Gómez, one of the few men on the GAM directorate, was kidnapped and his body was eventually found with signs of torture.[100] On April 1, 1985, 400 people attended Gómez's funeral, at which María

Rosario Godoy de Cuevas, wife of a disappeared student leader, read a statement by GAM that his death would not be forgotten. On April 4, 1985, she was kidnapped from a shopping center with her younger brother and infant son. The three were later found dead.[101]

What is clear is that the Guatemalan repressive state will not allow either the disappeared or those who seek them out to become martyrs around whom others might mobilize. It is also clear that the "appearance" of these tortured bodies was meant to terrorize GAM into silence.

The Minister of Government, Gustavo López Sandoval, claimed that "the police can't control the wave of violence due to the excessive number of inhabitants in the city ... We understand the activity of these persons because it is logical and natural that they express their pain and feelings for the disappearance of their relatives."[102] The implication is that these women may grieve for their lost relatives, and the state will tolerate such expressions, provided they do so individually and privately, not through public demonstrations.

By January 1986, following the inauguration of President Cerezo, the issues of peace and disappearance had become such a central and autonomous force in Guatemalan politics that Cerezo was forced to repeat that "I am ready to comply with all my responsibilities. I never promised to prosecute anyone. That is for the courts ... I cannot be responsible for what past governments did."[103] Not only did Cerezo "orally agree" to the amnesty law (Decree Law 8-86) that was put into effect a few days before his inauguration, but he subsequently said he would respect it.[104] After much vacillation, he eventually agreed to establish an independent investigatory commission.[105]

In May 1986, the new Supreme Court assigned the 2,337 habeas corpus writs (which represent 1,367 cases of the disappeared) that it had received from GAM to a single criminal court.[106] However, after working a year on the investigation, visiting military bases, police stations and detention centers, the judge in charge of the investigation produced meagre results.[107] He claimed that 105 cases had common explanations; in most cases, he declared them dead, but the exact causes remained obscure.[108] He also claimed that nineteen persons reported to be "disappeared" were issued passports by the Immigration Office.[109] None of the findings have held any security forces or military officials responsible, contradicting the testimony by GAM, witnesses, and other human rights organizations.[110]

In late June, members of the Christian Democratic Party met with a presidential assistant to discuss the Law of Social Service with the widows and orphans of the disappeared. Fewer than a dozen GAM members have accepted President Cerezo's financial aid offer, and GAM has adopted the policy of expelling members who accept the aid.[111] GAM responded to this aid much as the Mothers in Argentina had: "We don't want money stained with blood, money taken from the same people through their exploitation, condemned to live in misery."[112]

On August 4, 1987, GAM met for the first time in eleven months with President Cerezo to demand the establishment of an impartial investigatory commission that included "conscientious" members from the Catholic Church, Supreme Court, and International Red Cross.[113] In September 1987, GAM members were again forcibly ejected from the National Palace, and the demonstrations continue.

The Group of Relatives of the Detained-Disappeared (Agrupación): Chile

The Group of Relatives of the Detained-Disappeared began in late 1974 with twenty members. Until that time, they had been individuals seeking their disappeared relatives with the support of the ecumenical Committee of Cooperation for Peace in Chile (known as Comité Pro-Paz or "COPACH"), which was formed three weeks after the coup, on October 6, 1973.[114] By March 1975, the *Agrupación* numbered seventy-five, by June 270, and by the end of 1975, there were 323 members. This figure represented "a high proportion of those affected, given that the estimated number of disappearances at the time in Santiago was about one thousand, and some women had lost more than one relative."[115]

Between September 1973 and the end of 1977, as many as 2,000 Chileans disappeared following their arrest by agents of the security police.[116] After the massive arrests and executions between 1973 and 1976, the government changed its policy, selectively eliminating potential political activists and establishing an illusion of normalcy.[117] There was a final suspension of disappearance by the military regime as a method of elimination at the end of 1977, which was replaced by other forms of repression.[118]

The membership of the Chilean *Agrupación* differs ideologically from the other two groups. Because of the high degree of politicalization by the left in Chile during the time of Allende (1970-1973) and the specific elimination of the Marxist left in Chile between 1973 and 1976, the *Agrupación* membership reflects these ideological tendencies of the left. Yet, despite the fact that many of the original members of the *Agrupación* had children in the *Movimiento Izquierdo Revolucionario* ("MIR")—a leftist group advocating violent change—these women had no previous political experience.[119] This changed in late 1975 when the DINA (the Chilean secret police) launched a second operation of repression against the Communist Party and *Movimiento de Acción Popular Unitario* ("MAPU")—a socialist political group.[120] This wave of anti-communist repression brought new members into the *Agrupación*, causing a qualitative change in its activities. As Vidal explains:

> The militant communist [woman] has political experience forged with decisive, disciplined and conscious standards which generally embrace the whole family. For [her] the possibility of prison, torture and death is an act inherent in revolutionary action; it is foreseen and discussed within the family ... It is likely that the psychic energy of suffering would be channelled towards social activity which goes beyond the restricted radius of individual mourning that characterizes the suffering of the mothers of the MIR and Socialist Party members ... From here on, the most intense corporal sacrifices incurred in favor of the disappeared began to be understood as celebrations of life ...[121]

Vidal emphasizes, however, that these ideological demarcations did not create internal divisions within the group; the traumatic experience of having a disappeared relative overpowered any class or political distinctions. Leadership positions of all the different committees, for example, rotate to all members without limitation, and the women talk about a common thought and action created by the experience of pain and suffering.[122]

Despite the particular political background of the *Agrupación's* membership, however, their political practice and language resemble that of the other "motherist" groups. Throughout 1977, they carried photos of their missing children; launched street protests; staged a hunger strike; and traveled to the United Nations, OAS, the International Court of Justice, and several European countries to break through what they called "the circle of silence" surrounding their missing relatives.[123]

In April 1978, a law was passed granting amnesty to all those who "as principles or accessories, committed criminal offenses" under the state of siege between September 11, 1973 and March 10, 1978. It applied to the perpetrators of violence as well as to their victims, attempting to close the book on cases filed by the relatives.[124] In response, the *Agrupación* organized the Long Hunger Strike (*La Huelga de Hambre Larga*) supported by a broad cross-section of Chilean society. The 100 hunger strikers proclaimed "Our Life for Life" ("Nuestra Vida por la Vida").[125] The government eventually agreed to an investigation of the 619 cases of disappeared persons within three months; the *Agrupación* demanded instead an investigation in thirty days.[126] A government official attributed the disappearances to the "civil war," but added that "whatever the specific truth in each situation, the government will explore any serious information that may be presented to it regarding any particular case."[127]

Thus, national mobilization and international pressure had obliged the government to respond directly to the *Agrupación* for the first time, abandoning its position that "the disappeared are in hiding," or that "they are persons who have no legal existence."[128] The issue of the disappeared thus became legitimized by the military government through the use of the government-controlled mass media. Yet the *Agrupación's* skepticism about the "semi-promise" by a repressive state to investigate itself proved valid. The government stonewalled and blamed the Supreme Court for delays.[129]

The Law of Presumed Dead (*Ley de Muerte Presunta*), passed in June 1978, which is similar to the Argentine and Guatemalan laws, was an attempt to buy the conscience of the relatives by making and offering indemnities to the survivors after establishing patrimony.[130] The enactment of the law had an effect opposite to that intended by the military regime: it mobilized the members of *Agrupación*, who filed a criminal complaint against the DINA chief, Manuel Contreras. They presented a letter of denunciation to the Interior Minister and on November 6, 1978, chained themselves to a building in protest.[131] Several members also traveled to Spain, Venezuela, Colombia and the United States to create international pressure.[132]

After the discovery in 1978 of the clandestine graves at Lonquen[133] and of those at Yumbel in 1979,[134] there were long marches to the graves and masses held at the sites.[135] In April 1979, the women chained themselves to the fence of the National Congress in protest against the amnesty law and the loss of democracy in Chile.[136] The police erred in treating the women disrespectfully and sometimes violently. This aroused the crowd that had formed and it "reacted against the rough treatment of maternity and femininity invested in the patriotic mantle by the National Anthem of Chile."[137]

The women had consciously emphasized the fact they were both mothers and women as a protective measure during their demonstration. But they were unexpectedly detained by the Chilean secret police (the DINA were now referred to as the "CNI") and subjected to lengthy and cruel interrogation.[138] The CNI treated the chaining as a subversive plan of the Vicariate.[139] Lawyers of the Vicariate submitted a writ of habeas corpus on behalf of the women, which was rejected. After spending five nights in the Women's Prison, they were released.[140] For these women, their challenge to the military government included a challenge against the judicial power, against law itself.[141]

In 1984, the *Agrupación* entered the Supreme Court building and unfurled long banners from the balcony, which asked "General Contreras [of the DINA], General Pinochet, where are they?" and stated "For life, for peace, for justice, for freedom, we will find them [the Disappeared]."[142] They were quickly routed out by the police.[143]

In 1985, the unusual triple abduction (in front of several witnesses) and murder of three members of the Communist Party led to an investigation which turned up more evidence about past disappearances and linked them to the government. In a surprising move, the CNI cooperated with the investigation being carried out by the government-appointed special investigative judge, José Cánovas Robles.[144] Judge Cánovas also received testimony from a member of the DINA regarding the disappearance of eleven Communist Party members in 1976.[145] This gave the group some hope that the case of the *desaparecidos* and other disappearances would be cleared up.[146] In an open letter to Air Force General Matthei, the *Agrupación* requested an interview "to expose, case by case, in detail and with proof, grave violations of human rights in which personnel of your institution are involved."[147] Although indictments were eventually brought against thirty-eight military and police officers and two civilians,[148] the Santiago Appeals Court voided the indictments, citing the 1978 Amnesty Law, and the Supreme Court affirmed this decision.[149] The women of the *Agrupación* continue their acts of civil disobedience, despite their disappointment and growing cynicism with the legal apparatus.[150]

Women's Actions Compared

Using symbols of the Catholic Church and of motherhood, all these groups have sought to present themselves as apolitical and nonviolent. Most of these women wear their relatives' photos on their breasts or carry them on large placards at marches and demonstrations. These photos reassert the presence of the disappeared in the mind of the public, thus negating, to a certain extent, the chronicle of announced death which appears daily in the newspapers of some of these countries. By countering the state's effort to obliterate the memory of the disappeared, these photos function (as does public protest) to substantiate these women's political message and purpose.

All of these movements have refused to be silenced either by brutality or by re-democratization, as in Argentina or Guatemala. If anything, they have become more defiant and scornful that their civilian governments have not gone far enough in ridding their countries of repression. This defiance is illustrated by headlines such as "We Will Neither Negotiate Nor Halt Our Activities"[151] on the Madres' newspaper.

These women of the disappeared simply refuse to accept the state's definition of their children as "subversives" or "deviants," or of themselves as "bad mothers:"[152]

> When I tell [the authorities] that my two sons disappeared four months ago, they respond that I should have been more concerned with them before. If they have been taken, they say, it is undoubtedly because they were part of a subversive movement. That I should have paid more attention to their friends and their homework, and I should be satisfied that they don't call me to account for not being capable of educating them properly. They are monsters ... .[153]

Nor do these women accept the state's claim that a human being has never existed: "They will never, ever be able to make honorable men vanish into thin air, as if they were nothing."[154]

Their frustration and growing defiance stems from dealing with authorities who refuse to recognize not only the capture, disappearance, death or even *existence* of their relatives, but authorities who also refuse to recognize these mothers' demands as no more than individual domestic, and thus nonpolitical, dramas.[155]

The loss of relatives has changed these women's view of society: everything becomes for them expressive of the same pain and determination, and for those with little previous political participation, it has evoked a schism of realities "before" and "after" the disappearance. This is especially true for the middle class housewife who often accepted without question the rules of society: "I had lived until that day as just another Chilean from a respectable family, useful persons to society in their work and rectitude who could depend upon the police and justice if something happened . . . ."[156]

These women's lives have changed not only in terms of increased political consciousness. For some women who have lost a breadwinner, just being able to pay bus fare to demonstrations has become difficult. The Plaza de Mayo Madres noted how demonstrations in the first two or three weeks of the month were always better attended than those at the end when funds became short or nonexistent.[157] As several *Agrupación* women state:

> [O]ur lives are changed because of our loss: I had to move back in with my parents [when my husband disappeared] ... The land and house deeds are in our husbands' names, so we often lose the right to the property. We must work eight hours a day and there is child prostitution now in the *poblaciones* so women can feed their families. There are different ways to repress: with fear, lack of shoes for the children, lack of work—and state terror...We are saying "*¡Ya, basta!*" [Enough!][158]

None of these groups would hear of a feminist interpretation of their actions: "We are *mothers*, not women," one *Agrupación* member explained, "[w]e are looking for our children. Our fight is for our families not to be forgotten and to reclaim justice from the state."[159] All three groups say they are fighting the "disintegration" and daily dismemberment of families of today and of tomorrow: "The family [is] the basis of society: as wives and mothers we are grieving the insecurity and future of our children and grandchildren."[160]

All of these groups have used the conservative image of women without husbands to care for them, together with photos of children, to appeal to a "natural order" of family and motherhood. When policemen began attacking Plaza de Mayo Madres in the square, they responded indignantly, "Aren't you embarrassed to attack defenseless mothers? ... Don't you have children? Wouldn't you do what we are doing if you had a disappeared child?"[161]

As a protective strategy, it has also been a conscious decision by some of these groups not to allow men to participate. Among the Plaza de Mayo Madres, for example, the men were asked to leave (a decision which has not been made by GAM):

> We [Madres of the Plaza de Mayo] estimated, when we were organizing, that young people and men should not be allowed to protest for reasons of security. To be young and male in Argentina carries a presumption of guilt; they are *a priori* suspect of subversive ideas, of belonging to a revolutionary movement. We decided we would be the standard-bearers, we women of mature age, *madres de familia*, with all that that represents in the Argentine tradition.[162]

These decisions and public actions moved women quickly away from their individual, immediate search for relatives toward a longer-term, broad-based protest on behalf of everyone who had disappeared in the country. Several *Agrupación* members in Chile, for example, explained that even if they did not find their own husband or son alive, "we will find another *compañera's* relative. The struggle to find them has validity for us all. And it is a struggle we will all win."[163] The "Family" then takes on a more public and massive presence—and begins to lose its intimate apolitical character.

Although dismissed as mad and apolitical by both the repressive state and other human rights groups, these women have turned this image into a positive force: "[This 'mad image'] was appropriate enough. We *must* have been crazy to challenge such a regime. But our craziness came from our feelings of pain and grief."[164]

While dismissed by the state as "crazy," these women have sometimes been labeled subversive and subjected to the same methods of elimination as had their disappeared relatives. All of these groups have suffered. Over twelve members of the Plaza de Mayo Madres disappeared, two of the GAM leaders have been tortured and assassinated and many more exiled, and members of the *Agrupación* were arrested and physically abused. Leaders of these groups, such as Renée Epelbaum of the Plaza de Mayo Madres and Nineth de García of GAM, believe they are still alive only because of international support.[165]

While the groups of women in Argentina and Chile were harassed, both groups had some semblance of physical immunity. Their offices were never entered by the police or the security organization.[166] GAM, on the other hand, has had until recently an unofficial office at the Peace Brigades, with its leaders having to move from their homes and constantly be escorted by Peace Brigades members. However, given the long history and more widespread forms of violence used in Guatemala, the women of GAM believed less in the "protectiveness of motherhood" than did the women of Argentina and Chile. It is a cruel lesson of Guatemalan history, as one exiled GAM leader explained, that "the government doesn't distinguish among men, women, children, catechists, priests, professors, workers; it kills them all."[167] This may explain why GAM is the least segregated of the groups by gender.

Claiming Political "Space": Street Protests

The women of these groups initially kept meeting one another at the public institutions of death: hospitals, police stations, army garrisons, morgues and cemeteries. Once these women decided to take public action the traditional political fora were not open to them. They thus took to the streets, carving out both political power and a sense of political purpose. "We decided to take to the streets, and it was the streets that taught us. That was what gave us our political strength."[168]

Indeed, in the case of the Plaza de Mayo Madres, it was the state which caused them to move around the Plaza in a great circle, because to stand around would have been tantamount to holding a meeting, and that was against the law.[169] The Interior Ministry provided office space to receive inquiries about the hundreds of cases of disappearances, and this was their original meeting place.[170] As they began their weekly vigils, state officials named them in relation to that space—"The Mad Women of the Plaza"—a name which the women partially adopted.

All these groups have their specific public meeting place and time, which provide them coherence and continuity. These public demonstrations represent more than the capture of political space and a statement of political purpose: they also represent a temporary suspension of any kind of institutional control.[171] Within a repressive state, which brutally eliminates all political opposition and defines as subversive all public displays and ceremonies which are not directed or controlled by the state itself, these protests in public squares and at public building are displays of a defiantly different social order. Indeed, the "public" takes and occupies national buildings, supreme courts, cathedrals, plazas, and streets to symbolically regain the rule of law and justice, while the government represents the institutionalization of death.

The public squares, rather than being instruments for the forces of order, are charged with collectivity and "transformed ... into a temporary stage on which they dramatize the power they still lack."[172] All these groups have been stunned first by their ability to confront the police and then by the brutalities they are dealt. For these regimes, "keeping women in their place" has meant keeping them off the streets and under control.

Ironies Revisited: Forced and Involuntary Disappearances as a Method of Repression

While these repressive states have invaded the sanctity of the family, destroying the very symbol of life, they still expect women to remain in their traditional roles as reproducers of life and guardians of death.[173] Women are expected to be passive, individual "witnesses to war," as though repression has no effect on cultural traditions of life. The tactic of disappearance of their relatives, however, denies these women this traditional role of bereaver such that their "sorrow is unspent, their grief unexpiated" and they live in "an encapsulated, never-ending past which deprives the present and the future of meaning."[174]

Nonetheless, because any form of opposition is suspect within the repressive states, even in making this seemingly private, familial plea, these women challenge the state and cross its artificial boundary from private mourning to public politics. While men in these societies are by definition political beings, women must first make the decision to be active (and this may be the "simple" act of resistance to their husband's or son's or daughter's arrest, or going to police stations or military garrisons in search of their missing relative). These women then become subject to the same kind of treatment as were their disappeared relatives. Perceived not only as "subversives" but also as vulnerable sexual beings, these women are often dealt with in particularly brutal ways through repeated rape, prolonged torture, genital mutilation, and slow death.[175] Thus, while torture turns the body into a faceless, nameless object, it also specifies its techniques in terms of the body itself, making women more vulnerable to sexual abuse.[176]

Yet the repressive state has made some major miscalculations. In addition to the failure of repression as a form of long-term control, these groups demonstrate that parents who may not share their children's political opinions may become politicized by the repression directed at their children. Similarly, women who were not as active as their husbands or children may have reacted strongly and publicly when their relative was kidnapped for having—or being suspected of having—"subversive" opinions. Contrary to the state's calculation, relatives of victims from different classes and political or religious persuasions have indeed supported one another in an active and political manner. Furthermore, even if the state had anticipated some resistance, it did not anticipate that in the process of searching and learning from each other these women would become legally aware and politically vocal.

Moreover, the tactic of disappearance has its irony. Because it is not absolutely certain that the people who have been arrested or kidnapped are dead, there remains hope, with many relatives translating this vague limbo of uncertainty into a positive force of protest. These women present themselves publicly as survivors, as chronic mourners who refuse to allow themselves and their relatives to be forgotten. Contrary to the final assurance of death, the very absence of bodies has created a *presence* of protest for ongoing life: "If they'd tell me that he died and allow me to bury him, then at least I'd know he no longer exists."[177]

The Political Symbolism of Motherhood in Catholic Societies

While the symbolism of the Church has been central to their movements, the Madres, the GAM and the *Agrupación* have all had ambiguous relationships with the Catholic Church.[178] It is precisely this tension between the competing ideologies of the repressive state and the Catholic Church which has provided the political space and language to these "motherist" movements in Latin America. This state's political use of Catholic images is not without precedent. Indeed, it has not been uncommon for past fascist regimes in Italy and Spain to borrow heavily from religious symbolism and discourse, and to recognize how useful submissive, sacrificial women could be to their movement.[179]

The contradiction of viewing women as non-political and yet still punishable for the political acts of others partly rests on the traditional Catholic view of women as naturally culpable for men's transgressions. That is, while a mother herself may be apolitical, she is held responsible for her son's, brother's or husband's behavior and politics—a kind of "privileged female guilt."[180] An example is that of the Argentine military officer, previously quoted, who blamed a Plaza de Mayo mother for not "taking proper care of [her] son, making sure he did his schoolwork, knowing who his 'friends' were ..."[181] Within this conservative Catholic schema, women are assumed to be custodians of their children and husbands, sacrificing their own identities for the family and blamed for their children's and husband's "transgressions."

Another part of this schema rests on the image of the Virgin Mary, with "*marianismo,*" a counterweight to "*machismo.*" The Virgin Mary represents purity, emotion and ethereal goodness that remains untainted by corrupt politics.[182] Once a woman is perceived as "political" she becomes "tainted," soiled and, by definition, sexually aggressive and active—she becomes a whore.[183] She is then punished (as she was during the witch trials of another century) through disappearance, sexual brutality, and often death.

The tradition of the Catholic Church and the repression of the state rebound upon and reinforce each other. For example, they both recognize the family as the only proper sphere for women's conduct.[184] If women act outside this traditional sphere they are punished. Women are to be kept and "put in their place," as one Guatemalan official warned the GAM women in 1985.[185] The repressive state borrows heavily from Catholic ideology of familialism and in particular the image of the woman as mother. It is this very appropriation that allows the Catholic Church's own adulation of the Virgin Mary and the Holy Family to be subverted within the cult of death.[186]

What is curious about these movements of women in Latin America, however, is how they have remained faithful to the Catholic symbolism—particularly the Catholic image of mother—while at the same time politicizing these traditions against the repressive state. These movements use the Catholic image of Woman as mother both as a form of protection (calling upon the state to fulfill its own theoretical claims of defending motherhood) and as a form of identity as *madre de familia* (mother of the family). These women are not protesting as women, i.e., feminists, but as "mothers looking for our children." It also helps explain why previously apolitical women are more vocal than ever before while their demands are not particularly new or radical. While these women remain supplicant to Church doctrine and use the language of sacrifice and obedience, they politicize these meanings beyond what the Church hierarchy usually desires by adding the language of rights and dissent.[187]

Conclusion

The women of the Plaza de Mayo, of the Group for Mutual Support, and of the *Agrupación* illustrate a series of ironies. For one, these women have taken the church and state at their word. In trying to hold their families together, they have turned against the state the very symbols which the state claims to uphold and protect: motherhood and family. Ironically, the clandestine tactic of forced disappearance, which is meant to silence opposition, creates new protest, by its very uncertainty and refusal to acknowledge life.

The Church, moreover, with its centuries-long tradition of female obedience to and sacrifice to the family—to the point of death—has provided a basis for women's ability to challenge repressive regimes and exercise their new-found public power. GAM's use of the children in ads seeking the whereabouts of their fathers—"¿Dónde estás, papito?"[188]—is the height of this use of Christian familialism. Yet it is because of this contradictory doctrine that these women's resistance is possible: these mothers had to behave as *mothers* in search of their sons in order to survive.

In transfiguring their intimacy of pain and domesticity of silence into social protest, these women dramatize the contradictions of the repressive state in its feigned valorization and real destruction of family. By openly and defiantly questioning the state, these women help to demystify its force and methods of control. By staging demonstrations with flowers, candles, photos of their relatives, and songs, they counter the cult of death with a celebration for life. Thus, their protests signify political defiance against a purposeful ignorance on several levels and break ground for later mass mobilizations in all these countries.

By claiming public space in order to demand the right to know where their sons and daughters are, these women reverse the optic of governance: their momentary appearance in the streets and in the plazas represents justice and order, while the national palaces and ministries come to represent monuments of death. The image of these women, who are not motivated by ideology but by sheer weight of circumstance, circling the plazas and marching in the streets, contrasts sharply with the statements of the repressive state denying that disappearances are even a political issue. At the same time, these women, in confronting the repressive state and forcing the issue onto the "silenced and solitary"[189] streets and into the emptied plazas can no longer be viewed as the symbolic weeping woman, the symbolic female witness to repressive acts. They have become political actors helping to gain political recognition for the now decimated political sectors of their terrorized societies.

Such politics for the preservation of life and the reestablishment of justice by these women illustrate yet another irony: while the state seeks new and more brutal forms of repression, it miscalculates how politics are generated in society and creates its own dynamic of dissent. Human rights resistance by these groups of women that arises in reaction to the brutal dismembering of the family reflects the repressive state's underestimation of both the autonomy of culture and the new, emergent forms of cultural resistance in Latin America.

The final irony may be that once these groups are successful in helping to change the repressive terrain by claiming important political space, they may be eclipsed by the dominant political forces. In challenging the institutions of society—the Church, the courts, the political parties, the military authorities—these women are charged with interfering with the "democratic processes" (by the radicals and opinion polls in Argentina and the Christian Democrats in Guatemala), and are, to this day, granted little institutional hearing. That is, in the act of re-democratization, these women are once again marginalized politically, and the traditional gender roles which had been transformed by the immediacy of repression fall back into place. Yet, these women are determined not to have their individual tragedies dismissed as personal dramas and their relatives forgotten. They believe that if a society censors its memory and continues to deny the past to its children and grandchildren, then there can be no hope for a just social order of any kind.

Women of Valor: An Interview with Mothers of Plaza de Mayo

César A. Chelala

"Repression against us is carried out many different ways, from threatening and insulting us to evicting us from the plaza at bayonnet point. Many times the policemen drag us, holding us by our dresses and tearing our clothes while they push us into vehicles to take us away. When we get to the police station, sometimes they put us all together, and sometimes they lock us in cells that are dirty with urine and full of lice and fleas where we have to spend the night. It also happened that a group of forty mothers was obliged to share a cell with a dead young man. On seeing him the pain came back ... we didn't know if he was one of our own sons. That young man had died in a car accident, but they [the police] do these kinds of things to put pressure on us, to make us suffer, to show us how powerful, how regrettably powerful they are."

The woman speaking is Hebe Pastor de Bonafini, President of the group Las Madres de Plaza de Mayo (The Mothers of Plaza de Mayo). She is talking about the repressive measures carried out by the military against her group, which, since its formal organization in May 1979, has become one of the most vocal human rights groups confronting the last military government in Argentina. They are demanding to know the fate of their disappeared sons and daughters, many of whom are innocent victims in the struggle between that government and its opponents.

I talked with Señora Bonafini and Señora María Adela Gard de Antokoletz in July of 1981 in New York, where they had gone prior to their return to Buenos Aires from Houston, Texas. They were in Houston to receive the Rothko Chapel award, one of the many prizes the group received. The 1980 Nobel Peace Prize awarded to the Argentine sculptor and peace activist Adolfo Pérez Esquivel is considered by many as a prize to the mothers as well, since they have been working closely with him on the human rights situation in Argentina.

I asked the mothers about the origins of their movement. I wanted to know how it had been possible for these women, whose lives are so closely tied to their homes and to the lives of their families, to take such a bold and dangerous step. María Adela is a small, elegantly dressed woman, with carefully-styled, silver-white hair. She was then 71 years old. Her only son, a lawyer, disappeared on November 10, 1976.

"At the beginning," she said, "each mother is so overwhelmed by a situation she does not understand, that she goes out in search of her *own* son. But then she changes, and she searches not only for her son but for all other children. We work for all of them.

"When ours sons disappeared," she continued, "we tried to exhaust all possible legal channels that could shed some light on their fate. When we saw that nothing was effective, we decided to follow the advice of one of the mothers, who suggested that we meet and demonstrate at the plaza, and then cross the street and try to talk to the President at the Presidential Palace."

The first time they met at the plaza, in April 1977, they could not get in to talk to the President. They decided, however, to continue meeting there every Thursday and to stage silent demonstrations against the government for its refusal to account for their missing children. Although only a few at the beginning, the number of mothers grew with every meeting, and the group has now more than 2500 members and has spread all over the country.

Since its formation, the group has constantly been harassed by the police. A meeting of mothers and relatives of the disappeared that was taking place in a church in December 1977 was interrupted by a gang of heavily-armed men. Nine women (one of them a French nun) and two men were abducted and never heard from again. Another French nun, sister Leonie Duquet, was abducted two days later. All of them, including the two French nuns, are now presumed to be dead.

I asked what happened after the abduction of that group. Hebe, a short, dark haired, vibrant woman, then in her middle fifties, whose two sons have disappeared said, "Following their [the group's] disappearance there came chaos, anguish and fear of returning to the plaza. But we believed that we must return; otherwise, it would be a way of retreating. So we decided to go back, although we were only a few in number, and this gave strength to the other mothers who were afraid to go back. And the group grew in such a way that we got to be 2000 mothers at the plaza."

However, harassment against the mothers continued. There were more arrests, and the mothers decided to cancel their demonstrations at the plaza. I asked Hebe what tactics they had developed to deal with this new wave of repression.

"One of the mothers suggested that we should meet in churches, so as not to lose strength and cohesion. So we started going every Thursday to the same church to explain to the other mothers how we worked and what we did. In the middle of the rosary, María Adela used to stand up and say, 'Well, ladies, now we are going to do such and such ...,' and then we continued to pray. In that way, we kept abreast of events, with great caution, because [police] repression was very strong. When we protested at the plaza, our demonstrations were very short so that the police would not be able to seize us. As we were afraid that the group would disperse, in May 1979 we organized ourselves as a formal group, the association of Mothers of Plaza de Mayo."

For a while, the Mothers concentrated on developing their organization. They gained new members and set up a headquarters in Buenos Aires.

"When we regained our strength," Hebe went on, "we decided to reoccupy the plaza. On January 29, 1981, we returned to Plaza de Mayo. From that moment we have never left it."

I wanted to know why fathers had not marched together with the Mothers at the plaza, why they had not participated openly in their struggle. I also wanted to learn what had been the fathers' reaction to the participation of mothers in this conflict. María Adela explained that the fathers did not march together with them at the mothers' request. She said that they wanted to be women alone because they were moving in a very turbulent period and they thought that the fathers would be the first victims, that they would be imprisoned and would surely disappear.

To this Hebe added, "Our husbands play a very important role, perhaps the most important one. It is the silent role of going to work with their heads down in order to earn sometimes a miserable salary to support the households, of waiting for their wives to come back from marching in the plaza, of enduring the anguish when one is late or is arrested. Most of our husbands take care of our other children. I have a 15-year-old daughter, and when I am away, my husband plays the role of mother and father, and he does it splendidly, because he is an exceptional being. I have ... I *had* a wonderful family that has been maimed by the absence of our sons. And my father and mother also help me a lot, and many mothers have their own mothers who help them. The grandmothers of the disappeared sometimes suffer more than we do because of their helplessness. We channel our suffering through action, but our husbands and parents suffer even more because they cannot act. The role of the fathers is silent, but as with all silent and quiet things, they are sometimes the most significant. To return home and find some hot food, a smiling face waiting for us without recriminations—sometimes a smiling but anguished face, worrying about our delays but thinking that what we do is important—that is what makes it worthwhile, is it not?"

When this interview took place, the government in Argentina was a military junta. When the armed forces took power from the ineffectual President, "Isabel" Perón, in March 1976, they were quietly supported by a great number of Argentines, who hoped for an end to the incompetence and corruption of the regime and to the terrorism disrupting the country.

To put down the guerrillas which had arisen in opposition to the government, the military authorized its own terrorism. People suspected of any sympathy or connection with the insurgents or who might possibly be tainted with their "godless" ideology, were kidnapped from their homes, abducted from their places of work, and made to "disappear." Thousands were never heard from again. (Conservative estimates place the number of disappeared at 15,000). Even then, when guerrilla activity was no more, the government pretended to know nothing concerning the fate of the disappeared—neither where they were being held (if they were alive), nor whether they had been killed and if so under what circumstances.

Disappearances did not follow a regular pattern, the Mothers told me. In a few cases, persons who disappeared were later transferred to ordinary prisons where their relatives could sometimes visit them.

As Hebe explained, "There are some mothers whose sons disappeared and, because of strange circumstances, reappeared later in prisons. On the first visiting day, the mother would be in front of a stranger, somebody she could not recognize, a thin, withdrawn person. In many cases, I know at least four of them, they were brought to their mothers in a pitiful state. [The guards] would not allow the prisoners to go to the bathroom for two or three days, so that they had to relieve themselves on their clothes. When the mothers saw them, their sons were dirty, foul smelling. One was confronted with a being who was not one's own son. This is a terrible thing, done just to make one suffer and to ... I do not know. This is something one cannot find an explanation for; one cannot understand how these things can happen. People who go to visit their imprisoned sons are very badly treated. They humiliate the mothers; they search them exhaustively. When mothers take children to the prisons, the children do not want to go back because they, too, are humiliated."

The children of the disappeared have become one of the most important issues for the Mothers of Plaza de Mayo. As Hebe explained, "The main and only goal that had united us [at first] was the search for our 'disappeared' children, to find them alive. But during our search, the Mothers became aware of the needs of the children of our sons and daughters."

The needs of such children are especially acute in cases where both parents have disappeared, and relatives, often grandparents in modest circumstances, must take over the care of the children.

"Sometimes," Hebe continued, "a mother comes and says, 'On such and such a street there is a family, a grandmother who lives with her grandchildren and who needs your help.' The group visits the grandmother, evaluates the real needs, and we try to help her in a dignified way. This help is very limited because we have very little money, but we hope to have a foundation through which we will be able to help these children grow and develop as if their parents were here ... as they would have wanted it."

An even more urgent issue is that of young children and babies who have disappeared along with their parents. A serious charge against the Argentine military government is that some of these disappeared children have been found in neighboring countries or have been adopted by childless military couples. When I asked Hebe what she knew about the disappearance of children she said, "There are various ways in which children and babies disappear. We know of a great number of disappearances, from three-month-old babies to twelve-year-old children. There are children who disappear together with their parents; there are children who are taken away because their parents cannot be found; there are children whose parents are killed and the children are taken away; and there are children born inside concentration camps."

When asked to describe a specific case, Hebe continued, "There is the Jotar case, two Argentine girls who disappeared with their parents. Last year, thanks to a search conducted by their grandmothers, they were finally found. They had been adopted by an Argentine couple not connected to the military. They [the girls] had been offered to them for adoption without this couple knowing that the children came from disappeared parents. The adopted parents knew nothing about the case, and now that they know, they are frightened by the way they were entrapped, because this is like a trap.

"Many people say that some military have [adopted] children of disappeared parents ... Sometimes one finds out [about them] through a clandestine letter or piece of paper. One day, during mass, a woman ran up and gave me a piece of paper with information about a girl who had been adopted by a couple, a son and a daughter of the military, and where she was ... We know this is the way it is with crimes; there is never a perfect crime; there is always something that is left; there is always something that remains. I believe that little by little we will be able to find those children. We hope to recover the children of our children."

Cases as poignant as those of missing children are those of women who were pregnant at the time of their disappearance and whose children have been born in prisons or in concentration camps. A group called Grandmothers of Plaza de Mayo has a thoroughly documented list of over 83 children, as well as of a number of pregnant women, whose fate is still unknown. A group at the United Nations is working on the cases of disappeared children and pregnant women.

I asked Hebe if she knew of any woman who had given birth to her child in prison. She said, "A young woman I know gave birth to her son in a concentration camp. She told me that when she was ready for delivery she and her husband were taken to an isolated place in the countryside, her husband was tied to a tree, and she was left alone in the car to have her baby. They took her there in the morning; the baby was born at noon. Her husband could not help her because he was tied up. She was desperate because she was badly placed in the car. When she thought the time had come to do it, she cut the umbilical cord and thought that she and the baby were going to die. But God did not want them to die, and at four in the afternoon, when the guards came back, they wrapped her up, untied her husband, and took them back to the concentration camp."

Hebe paused for a moment, as if unable to find words adequate to express her feelings, and then went on. "This horror that is the disappearance of children and babies in Argentina I believe to be the greatest violation of human rights, because one cannot say … there is no … it has no justification …"

The missing children are the most innocent of all the disappeared in Argentina. But over and over again, María Adela and Hebe expressed their consternation at the number of adults, either disappeared or killed, who were also completely innocent victims. Hebe described the case of Alicia, a woman who lived on her block. One day when Alicia went to answer the door of her home, she was machine-gunned on the spot by armed men. They left her on her doorstep for everyone to see. Her husband was also killed. Yet neither she nor he had been involved in any kind of terrorist activity. And, what makes this case even more appalling, Alicia was pregnant.

People had been arrested and made to disappear for the most casual of reasons, sometimes only because their names were in the address book of a suspected person. The fear created by such tactics eventually spreads and is bound to affect the lives of everyone. A rationale used by the military government to justify the methods used against the guerrillas is that the guerrillas started a "dirty war." The government calls it that because conventional war rules do not apply, and, therefore, it is necessary to fight according to different rules, those of a "dirty war." I asked the mothers their opinion on this argument.

"The 'dirty war' is a hoax," María Adela replied. "There is no dirty war. My son, for example, who was a lawyer, did want a change, quite clearly, quite definitely. His work as a lawyer, for the six years before his disappearance, was geared to the defense of the political prisoners. But he did not hide his address or his phone number. He did not have an office because some lawyer's offices had been blown up by bombs, so his legal office was in the courthouse. How can anyone say that he carried out a dirty war when he acted in broad daylight, without arms, doing the work that he had sworn to do without caring who it was that needed his help? For him it was only someone who needed legal defense. What kind of a dirty war is that? … In Argentina there are almost 300 lawyers who have been assassinated, imprisoned, made to disappear, or who have had to leave the country so as not to have the same sad fates that I have described. And this is the case for many people, not only for lawyers."

María Adela, despite her seventy years, had been conducting an open and determined search for her son since his disappearance in 1976, but she believes that many families have not yet even reported their disappeared relatives.

"Even now," she said, "after [over] five years of this process, some people are still coming forward to report that a person in their family disappeared two, three, or four years ago."

María Adela believes that several factors account for this, including the size of the country and ignorance as to how or to whom to report a disappearance. And she believes there is an even more important factor:

"There is also fear," she said. "There are people who are still very threatened, who do not dare act because they know that they, their husbands, or [others] of the family could be victims of reprisals."

María Adela lives in Buenos Aires with her two sisters, one of whom is a volunteer worker at a children's hospital. This sister has brought home from the hospital a severely handicapped, orphaned child. María Adela told me proudly how well the child is growing up and how she and her sisters feel a tremendous sense of fulfillment in providing the child with a secure, happy home environment. Perhaps because of the experience with this child, the memory of María Claudia Grunberg still haunts María Adela.

"This young woman, who was horribly handicapped, was 24 years old when they took her away. She had suffered from an unrelenting rheumatism from eight to twelve years of age that had affected her physically. To walk, she needed an orthopedic apparatus, somebody had to feed her, and she needed help for most of her activities. However, her great capacity and her zeal for overcoming obstacles led her to fight for a law by which the government would reserve 4% of federal posts for handicapped people. In order to have this law approved, María Claudia Grunberg, overcoming her physical handicaps, talked on the radio, appeared on television, made an effort completely out of proportion to her strength, thinking only of people in her own situation, wanting to provide them with work opportunities within the country. She was able to get this law passed and went on with her life. One day, as she was going to the rehabilitation center where she usually went, she was arrested. They made her leave the orthopedic apparatus that allowed her to move; they took her away, and until this day she has not reappeared. I do not believe that she is still alive. She had to be fed; she had to be helped with everything. Who would have taken care of her? How can something like this be explained? ... And her poor mother is almost insane ... It can't be any other way. It can't be any other way ..."

Because cases such as María Claudia Grunberg's are becoming well known, the two Mothers believe that support for the anti-military movement is growing, both within Argentina and in other countries as well. One example was the attitude of the Argentinian writer, Jorge Luis Borges.

"At the beginning," María Adela explained, "our beloved Borges thought that military action was essential, but when he realized what military action had become, he repudiated it ... He says that he is sorry to have seen clearly so late, when so much harm has already been done."

Also encouraging is the help that the Mothers of Plaza de Mayo have received from within the Catholic Church. "In all countries that we have gone to," Hebe said, "we have been listened to and understood. We have the invaluable support of the Scandinavian countries, of France, Italy and Spain. In the United States, we have been well received by senators, congressmen, and by officers at the State Department. In addition, a group called 'Friends of the Mothers of Plaza de Mayo' has been formed in this country, organized by an influential group of people under the coordination of Ms. Patricia Derian."

Both Hebe and María Adela emphasized that their group has no ties to any political party.

"The movement of Mothers of Plaza de Mayo is completely nonpartisan," Hebe said. "We are very much aware that what we do is essentially political, but we are totally nonpartisan. When a mother comes to our headquarters and says, 'My son has disappeared,' that is the only thing we care about. We never ask what her political ideas or religion are, who her son was or what he did. She is simply another mother who needs to find her son."

Although I knew it would be painful for her to do it, I asked Hebe to tell me the circumstances of her sons' disappearances.

"My son Jorge was abducted from his house in La Plata [Buenos Aires Province] on February 8, 1977. That same day, in La Plata, they took six hundred people. In my inquiries and searches, I learned that my son had been taken along with a young woman who studied with him at the university and who lived in General Lamadrid [Buenos Aires Province]. I went to that city. I inquired in each and every house asking for a young woman who had disappeared under such and such circumstances, until I finally found her. I begged her to tell me what she knew about my son. At the beginning, she did not want to tell me, but because I persisted and she realized I knew how they were treated, she told me that my son had gone through a very rough period, that he had been cruelly tortured for ten days. After they tortured him, they threw him into a bathroom full of excrement, and then they tortured him again. While he was in that bathroom, he had communicated with her by means of soft knocks on the wall. When everybody thought he was going to die because of the torture—the things that human beings are able to overcome—he slowly recuperated, and friends helped him and fed him. When the young woman was set free after 21 days, my son was already standing up, was feeling better, and had been able to talk to her. That was one of the times I heard something about my son."

Hebe paused for a few seconds and then went on. "Four months later I had some more news. A man who had been arrested for stealing a watch, who is my same age, had been put in the same cell with seventy young people, in subhuman conditions. There was a hole in the middle of the cell used as a toilet for all of them. The knob to flush water that would wash away the excrement was outside the cell, and the guard pressed it whenever he wanted. If he felt the prisoners misbehaved, he would let three days go by without flushing the water. Those seventy people were in that place, almost unable to breathe, completely undernourished, to the point that when the guards threw them a piece of bread, they would fight over it. The man arrested for stealing the watch was with my son, and my son would talk about me, and through an incredible coincidence, this man had been with me in elementary school. He promised my son that if he ever got out of there, he would look for me and give me news about him. Because such things happen, once in a while somebody comes out."

Hebe, who up to now had spoken in a slow, calm way, became visibly shaken by her recollections, twisting a handkerchief she had been holding in her hands. "My other son, Raúl, was kidnapped from his house together with a young woman on December 6, 1977. My son was very interested in the labor movement; he was a student and a worker. He had been talking with this woman about a strike that was taking place in Alpargatas, a footwear factory. This young woman was set free six months afterwards, and during all that time she had been with my son. That is why I know how he was treated, to what extent the prisoners were tortured, what they ate, and in what condition they were. Everybody says that there are very cruel guards. This young woman told me that there was a guard who had a whip that she used to smack against her boots. The guards played Nazi military marches, with which they deafened the prisoners. Every time the guards were near them, they hit them fiercely, only to show them how much power they have when the other person is weak and handcuffed. My son was handcuffed with other people to a cot on the floor. He is a very happy young man, and I was told that whenever he could, he sang. That gives me a lot of strength because in spite of what he was going through, he showed those vicious people that he had done something that meant a lot to him."

A woman of humble origins, Hebe never had the opportunity of continuing her education after elementary school. She told me that she is very proud of having learned many things from her sons, and that her concern for others partially came as a result of her conversations with them.

After the military junta took power, Hebe used to question Jorge and Raúl about their political activities. She asked them why they struggled and told them how afraid she was for them. But they explained to her that they were struggling for their disappeared friends and that they could not stop.

"And now," Hebe said, "I really understand them, because I am doing the same as they did. And I cannot stop."

By passing a law by which all disappeared persons are declared dead if nothing is known about them after a certain period, the Argentine military government had tried to quell the groups that demanded information on the fate of the disappeared. Indirectly, the Argentine government had received support from officials in the U.S. government, who insisted that the situation in Argentina had improved and that people were no longer disappearing. I asked the two Mothers if this was a correct evaluation of the situation.

"No, it is not," María Adela replied. "How could the situation have improved if none of our disappeared have reappeared, if violations continue, if disappearances—although fewer—still occur? No, the situation has not improved."

"I believe," Hebe added, "that the Reagan administration has to realize that silent diplomacy does not work, that silent diplomacy was employed by some Argentine Catholic bishops and that with it we have not saved even one life, we have not recovered a single disappeared. What should be done is to speak out very clearly so that the world will know what happened in Argentina and what is still happening. I believe that even one disappearance justifies a denunciation by the American government—if they truly fight for human rights. Otherwise, we will have to say that the rights they respect are political, not human rights."

I then asked the Mothers if they did not think that the use of terrorist tactics against the government by their sons or other disappeared persons did not justify the harsh repression exerted by the government.

"We, who have lived in Argentina through its worst period, know that there were young people who used tactics that were clear violations of human rights," Hebe responded. "But we also know that in our country there are laws, there are judges. We believe that these young men should be judged according to our Constitution, and as it is guaranteed there we should be allowed to see them and help them, as happens in every civilized country. Our sons were political dissidents, or lawyers of political prisoners, or else they were fighting against an unpopular and anti-democratic government. We are not asking for the unconditional release of our children; we are asking for a return to the rule of the law. We ask the Argentine government to tell us what happened to our children. We want them alive because they were taken alive; they did not die on a battlefield."

Hebe, who had been speaking passionately, paused. She looked at María Adela and then went on, her voice gentle but determined. "We are well aware that without truth, there will be no freedom. And without justice, there will be no peace."

We were seated in a mutual friend's apartment, a sunny, bright place with an impressive view of downtown Manhattan. In this comfortable, peaceful setting, I couldn't help but think how these two women's lives would change on their return to Argentina. I asked them if they were not afraid to carry out this unequal confrontation against the Argentine military government.

"Ever since they took my sons away I have never thought about myself," Hebe said. "I never think what could happen to me. Every morning when I wake up I only think about them and about what I can do to rescue them from where they are. It is as if lions grew inside of me, and I am not afraid. I am determined to carry out this confrontation, and if my life serves that purpose, then so much the better. It means that I was chosen by God. I am doing all this work to recover all our children. I do not know if I can still recover mine, but I know that there are many others who expect a lot from us."

On their return to Argentina, the two Mothers were detained by Air Force officers, and the Rothko Chapel award, which they had received for their commitment to "Truth and Freedom," was confiscated by the Argentine police. Nonetheless, in late December, nine Mothers of the Mothers of Plaza de Mayo's group staged a limited fast as a continuing protest for the government's refusal to account for the disappeared. They were joined in the fast by Father Antonio Puigjané, whose own father is one of the disappeared persons, and later on by another group of mothers.

During the Falklands' war against the British, the Mothers continued with their demonstrations in the plaza, in spite of counterdemonstrations against them staged by groups who supported the government and who considered the Mothers' protests as unpatriotic acts in a time of crisis. During these demonstrations, the mothers showed their determination marching with banners reading: "The Malvinas are Argentine ... so are the Disappeared."

After the defeat by the British, a new wave of activity was directed against the Mothers. At the end of August, posters accusing them of being puppets of the guerrilla movement were placed in many building all over Buenos Aires. Groups of people identifying themselves as belonging to the Federal Police came into the buildings where the leaders of the movement lived and placed those same posters in them. Additionally, death threats continued on the telephone.

This new wave of harassment against the Mothers and against other human rights groups in Argentina was interpreted by some observers as an effort by the military government to discredit those groups as a prelude to a general amnesty that would absolve the military officers involved in torture and repression in the country. By discrediting and intimidating those groups, there would be considerably less resistance to such a measure.

The Mothers' fears were later confirmed when measures taken by Presidents Raúl R. Alfonsín then Carlos S. Menem (both democratically-elected civilian governments that followed the military regime) led to the release of all military officers condemned for human rights violations.

Undeterred however, up to this day, the Mothers of Plaza de Mayo continue with their demonstrations. On learning about this, I think again of María Adela's answer to my last question.

"Yes, I am afraid, but I will continue with this activity until I die. I want to know where my son is and how he is and where and how are all our other sons, and I won't rest until I know."

A Tragedy and a Miracle: Leonor Alonso and the Human Cost of State Terrorism in Argentina

Marifran Carlson

On September 16, 1976, Leonor Alonso was abducted from her home by members of the Argentine security forces. She and her daughter, María Abinet, were tortured at the Navy Mechanics School in the city of Buenos Aires. This happened six months after a military junta headed by General Jorge Videla overthrew the troubled government of Isabel Perón. María was seven months pregnant at the time, and it is believed that she was killed after she gave birth to a daughter. There was a special section of the Navy Mechanics School for pregnant detainees. Doctors kept a list of married couples who could not have children of their own and were prepared to adopt a child born to one of the pregnant prisoners. Leonor was freed after enduring three days of cruel and dehumanizing physical and psychological torture. Leonor's granddaughter, Elena Gallinari, was the first child born in captivity to be located by the Grandmothers of Plaza de Mayo, with the assistance of a team of North American and Argentine forensic scientists. Elena had been illegally adopted by a police officer and his wife, but she was returned to her birth family in 1987.

On a damp and gloomy morning in July of 1990, I waited for Leonor Alonso to arrive at my apartment in downtown Buenos Aires. Several days earlier, when I first met her at the offices of the Grandmothers of Plaza de Mayo on Corrientes Street, she had promised me an interview, but she was almost an hour late. I was worried that she would not come. She had told me that she had grave reservations about telling her story to any more journalists or researchers. She was tired of having her ordeal exploited for sensationalist purposes. The Argentine tabloid press[1] had already used her experiences, and those of other survivors of the "dirty war," to titillate the public's morbid curiosity about the perverse conduct of the security forces in the clandestine detention centers and concentration camps between 1976 and 1983.

Leonor does not trust most North Americans. She believes that the Reagan administration helped to prolong the misery imposed on the Argentine people by the military government. The United States government continued to support the junta economically and morally long after massive human rights violations had been proven beyond any doubt. Even though Leonor knew that I was opposed to my government's human rights policies, I understood her reluctance to see me. Her nervousness made me feel that she had other, unstated reasons for not wanting to be interviewed.

Since her granddaughter, Elena, was returned in 1987, life has been good for Leonor. Her family life is warm and loving, and she is involved with satisfying work as an anthropologist at the University of La Rioja. Her work with the Grandmothers, although sometimes discouraging, is mostly fulfilling. The group has managed to locate 50 of the more than 196[2] children who disappeared with their parents or were born in captivity. Daily life has a purpose and is peaceful.

I asked myself why she should expose her emotional vulnerability to a complete stranger. Why talk to me about the tragic past and stir up all the old memories of persecution, humiliation, and loss? I was feeling more and more embarrassed and guilty about my tenacious attitude, but I was determined to learn about the lives of the victims of this violent persecution. I explained that beyond collecting testimonies, my ultimate goal is to give English-speaking readers the opportunity to learn about the human cost of state terrorism. Leonor's testimony is particularly important because she is one of only 100 survivors of the Navy Mechanics School prison. Close to 5,000 people perished there. I felt awkward standing there trying to describe my purpose to a woman who had already been through so much, but I persisted.

Leonor was silent for several minutes. Finally, she relented. She took my hand and patted it. She had apparently decided to trust me. Her eyes filled with tears, but her face brightened when she showed me a photo of her thirteen-year-old granddaughter. "This is truly a miracle," she said. I really wanted to get to know her.

• • •

While I waited for Leonor that gloomy Saturday my mood was becoming as dark as the day. Had she changed her mind? And could I blame her if she did? I had about given up on the interview when the doorbell rang. Within a few moments Leonor's cheerful and energetic presence filled my tiny apartment. She apologized for her tardiness, explaining that she had been travelling by bus for more than two hours from her family home in Bella Vista, in the province of Buenos Aires. As she peeled off the many layers of clothing all *porteños* (people of the port areas) wear to protect themselves from the damp, penetrating cold, I offered her a cup of coffee. She was visibly pleased to find that I had made coffee for her. Having been in Buenos Aires for only a week, I hadn't yet learned that the average middle-class salary is between two hundred and five hundred dollars a month, leaving no allowance for the much-adored bitter black liquid the Argentines call coffee.

For Leonor Alonso the decision to do more than just to survive was made long ago. She is 66 years old, very pretty and youthful looking, with thick and lustrous grey hair, bright blue eyes and a shiny pink complexion. She dresses simply and elegantly, like most middle-class women in Argentina. Her pristine appearance seems a denial of all that has happened to her.

While I was setting up my equipment, she took a large cosmetics bag out of her purse and began applying make-up. "But I'm not going to use a video camera, just a tape recorder," I said. "It doesn't matter," she replied. "I put on make-up every morning. I know that vanity is not supposed to be a virtue, but I can't help it."

We agreed that a healthy dose of vanity is probably psychologically healthy—at least we found various dictums in Freudian narcissistic theory to justify our application of cosmetic masks. Ironically, the next few hours represented the complete unmasking of an extraordinary individual with a unique, terrifying, and fascinating history.

• • •

Leonor was born into a politically active Italian immigrant family, Her father was an anarchist and her mother was a socialist. Although her parents were life-long companions, they never married because they did not believe in the institution of marriage, either civil or religious. Leonor told me that while in secondary school she won an award for her art work, but she described herself as a rebellious adolescent who didn't apply herself to her studies.

While still in her teens she married and became a practicing Roman Catholic. She did these things despite the protestations of her parents—a testament to the fact that Leonor's parents raised her to think for herself, and so she did. Before she was thirty years old she gave birth to six children. Unfortunately, her marriage was not a happy one. She was physically abused by her husband, and she desperately sought counsel from her parish priest. Her husband's violent behavior was so notorious in the community that even the priest advised Leonor to leave him, despite the Catholic church's anti-divorce doctrine.

After her separation, Leonor studied philosophy, psychology and anthropology at the University of Buenos Aires, and after graduation she began an academic career. During this period she met the man who would be her companion until his death in 1977 and with whom she had her seventh child. She adored him, but also told me that in the beginning she was suspicious of his career as an accountant. Alberto Morales was a man with traditional, conservative values but he was open to change. Because of this flexibility, he had no objection to Leonor's membership in the Communist Party or to the increasing political militancy of Leonor's daughters, María and Marián.

María was associated with the left-wing of Peronism. She was involved with the Montoneros (named after the gaucho fighters during the War of Independence), as was her companion, Miguel Gallinari. All Leonor's children had political commitments with varying degrees of militancy. In the 1960s and 1970s, Argentine young people were highly politicized and all the radical political groups looked to students and workers to be the vanguards of mass mobilization for socialist revolution.

As Leonor says, she respected María and Miguel's social and political commitment to the underprivileged poor and working classes. She, too, wanted something to be done about the gross inequalities of Argentine society. But she disagreed with the violent, incendiary tactics of the Peronist left. Her party, the Communist Party, was anti-Peronist and advocated the peaceful road to socialism. Leonor believed that the alliance of the upper-class and the military would not be easily broken and that the militant Peronist leaders were dangerously naive because the majority of the Argentine people were not interested in making a socialist revolution. Leonor's convictions are best explained in her own words:

"Evita [Perón] died young but she was a genuine revolutionary who truly cared about the people. Juan Perón always had fascist leanings and Isabel [Perón] was a true fascist ... The Montonero leaders, particularly Mario Firmenich, took advantage of the youthful idealism of their followers by using them to perform suicidal, terrorist missions. This led to the useless death of thousands of young people ... Firmenich preached a kind of revolutionary narcissism. He romanticized the cult of death. These were values inherited directly from the right-wing Catholic youth movement. But these ideas were not consistent with the humanistic vision of the socialists and communists ..."

At family conferences around the dinner table, Leonor and her husband tried to convince María and Miguel not to take the nihilistic path of the Montoneros. They were sure that no group could challenge the military.

"I am not completely certain about Miguel's activities. He was an active trade unionist with the metallurgical union. But I was afraid that María would be persecuted if there was a military coup because of her general involvement with Peronism. If you were politically active, the military labelled you as a 'subversive.' I was afraid for all young people, but especially for María and Miguel."

Leonor's evaluation of the political situation turned out to be painfully correct, and her worry for María and Miguel was well-founded. After the March, 1976 coup, her worst fears were realized. On June 23, Miguel was kidnapped—to this day nothing is known about what happened to him. Miguel's kidnapping was the first in a series of tragedies in the Alonso and Gallinari families. In the early morning hours of September

16, Leonor and María's bizarre tragedy began.

"Men from the provincial police came very late that night. They immediately put a hood over my head. I only had a camisole and a nightgown on, and I was shivering. One of them said, 'Señora, take your bedspread and cover yourself with it.' I guess he knew how cold I was, but he didn't permit me to dress. One of them grabbed my son's scarf and told me to take it with me. When I was released, I still had the scarf but they robbed me of my bedspread ...

" 'This is not an assault,' one of them said to me in a soft voice, 'This is like the inquisition. If you didn't do anything, nothing will happen to you, and if you did something, you will be judged and you will pay. Who will be condemned is determined by us.'

"They put me into a car and even though I couldn't see because of the hood, I was sure they had taken me to the Naval Mechanics School. [Escuela Superior de Mecánica de la Armada]. The 'ESMA' was famous by then. I was separated from the other prisoners. They kept me on the first floor where the offices were located and where the staff had their meals and snacks. I could hear screaming coming from other areas of the building, and it was then that I truly became terrified ...

"A guard took me to the bathroom near the dining hall, and the men laughed as I passed by. They shouted obscenities at me at the same time they were ordering their coffee and whiskey.

"I was there less than an hour when they took me to the torture chamber. They took off my nightgown and camisole, so I was completely nude. It was terribly humiliating. Then they started hitting me, and they threw me down on the *parrilla* [a grill used for barbecuing meat.] Nobody ever actually sees the equipment ... They dampened my body with wet rags and then began applying the electric prod to all the orifices of my body. The most terrible pain was on my toes and the roof of my mouth.

"The effects of the electric torture are still with me because my vision is impaired and my kidneys still don't function normally. I have repeated infections, and I urinate too frequently. I was tortured twenty to thirty times in three days. I lost count ... I suppose I was one of the lucky ones, because they took me to the toilet when I asked. I've heard from other ex-prisoners that they had to urinate and defecate on the floor. Perhaps this was one indignity they didn't want to inflict on an old woman, or perhaps they would have found it repulsive to clean up after me. I don't know. They also didn't rape me like they did most of the younger women like my daughter ...

"At the end of one session, I had a cardiac arrest. The doctor who was present at all the torture sessions told them to stop several times. They only stopped when he told them that I would die if they didn't."

I asked Leonor if the officials at the "ESMA" asked her to give them specific information about her family, and if they wanted to know about her political activity.

"My torturers asked me for information about guerrilla operations but I am certain they knew I didn't know anything. Shortly after I arrived they told me that María was there. They were giving her [what one guard called] 'serious torture' but they just wanted to torment me. I couldn't tell if the screams I was hearing were those of my daughter, so they succeeded in their goal.

"I believe that the officials of the prison knew all along that they were going to let me go. It was a sadistic, vicious game they were playing. It amused them to taunt me. One time they covered me with what I thought was a blanket and paraded me up and down the halls. One of the guards later told me that they had used an old, ragged Argentine flag to cover me, and this was the cause of the hysterical laughter of the personnel when they saw me. I guess I must have been a pretty funny sight to them—an old woman with contusions on my feet, limping and pitiful, draped in our great national symbol...

"When not in the torture chamber, I was in a cell by myself with my arms and feet tied up and there was another rope that tied me to the wall. One guard said, 'We have to tie you up like this because you are a very dangerous prisoner.' Then he laughed. The guards were always laughing. Perhaps it was because they were drinking whiskey and most were from poor families. I guess they used the alcohol to dull their senses. Some of the guards were young, eighteen or so. Their constant laughing is one aspect of my imprisonment that I will never forget ..."

Then I asked Leonor about María.

"Yes, I finally saw María, but they had to torment me more. They took off my hood, put me in a chair, took out their pistols, and one of them pulled the trigger. For an instant, I thought I was dead, but it was a simulated execution. Then they put my hood back on and brought me a glass of liquid which they said was poison. 'You must drink it,' one of them said. 'But before you drink the poison, we want you to say your prayers because you told us that you are a very devout Catholic.' They handed me a cross on a heavy chain, which they said was a rosary, but of course I knew that it was not a rosary, and I told them so. It was then that I realized that this was my daughter's necklace, the one she always wore. I cried and accused them of killing María. They said nothing … but the poison was another one of their sadistic jokes. They never asked me to drink it again … They left me alone for a few minutes. I was completely filled with despair and I was sure I would never see my daughter again. Then the guards returned with some plates of food, including a steak sandwich. They told me to eat and enjoy myself. Then they brought my daughter to me …

"I could tell that María was very bad off even though I couldn't see her. They told us to eat because it would make us feel better. María was pregnant and badly in need of nourishment, so we ate the food. We were sobbing and the men tore us out of each other's arms and took her away. One of the guards was ashamed because he kept trying to soften the behavior of the others. He even gave me a portable heater for my cell. He warned me not to provoke the wrath of the cruelest ones. I begged him to protect my daughter. He said he would, and I believe he was sincere even though other victims have told me that they always had one guard who played the kindly role …

"After my daughter was taken from me a naval official who was well-educated and soft-spoken entered the room. His demeanor was completely different than that of the ill-mannered and rough-talking men who did all the dirty work. He explained to me that I was going to be released. But my daughter would have to remain because she had been found guilty of distributing anti-government pamphlets. He promised that they would let her go in a few days because of her advanced pregnancy but they needed to interrogate her further. This man, the boss torturer, said they made a mistake in arresting me. He said, 'We realize that we have made an error in your case, but I hope you will always remember *what we are capable of.* You must return to your work at the University or none of your family will be able to rest comfortably.' Then he flattered me and threatened me at the same time. 'You are a great person,' he said, 'and an excellent professor. You and your two daughters must stop all your political activity. If you say anything, we will murder your two children, María and Marián, and your grandchildren.' To be sure that I understood his demands, he played a cassette with my son and his children's voices on it. Then he warned me to be cautious so that I would return home safely. I began to cry and the boss said, 'I'm sure you want to see your beautiful little blonde grandchildren very soon. Be sure that we will kill them if you talk …'

"I was taken from the prison soon after. They put me in the back seat of a car and tossed me out a few blocks from my home. They had used my son's scarf to blindfold me. I was wearing only a camisole and a blanket. I couldn't stand up straight because my body was swollen and twisted from the beatings and electric torture. I felt dead with fear and I wanted to hide ...

"I am still not sure why they released me. I know for sure they had a system. Bruno Bettelheim wrote about the psychological sadism of torturers in *The Informed Heart.* I now have what Bettelheim called 'symbolic wounds' from the psychological torture. I am sure of that. I also have [persisting] physical problems as a result of the beatings and the electric shocks. They let me go with all that fear so that I would fill others with fear also. This was their system."

Leonor paused for a moment and apologized for talking so much. She said that she hadn't started to talk about her feelings until 1983—seven years of speaking in monosyllables had led her to the opposite extreme. She thinks she babbles incessantly now because she had to repress her feelings for so long. I told her that what I had just heard did not sound like babbling. It sounded like the heart-breaking testimony of an intelligent and courageous person.

Later I asked her if she had returned to her art work. For years she felt deprived of material for her painting because she no longer cared about nature. The seasons would pass and she was indifferent to the color of the sky or the placement of the sun. It was just in the last few months that her interest in art returned, and she is painting now.

Shortly after her release from the "ESMA," Leonor went to a private hospital. The doctors diagnosed a serious case of pneumonia, but also questioned her about the lacerations, bruises and swelling all over her body. She claimed to have fallen down the stairs. Although the doctors doubted her story, they asked no further questions. The Argentine physicians were afraid they'd be arrested if they reported cases like Leonor's to the authorities.

Leonor remained in the hospital for ten days and then spent three months at home attempting to recover from her physical problems. It took that long for her eyesight to be partially restored and for her lung and kidney infections to be cured. She attempted to return to work but her broken ribs were still not completely healed. Her pain was excruciating.

For the next two years her family was constantly harassed by the police. Her son was arrested and beaten up after he purchased a broom from a local hardware. He was finally released after being accused of buying the broom to use as a weapon.

In addition to the harassment, there were two more terrible tragedies. Leonor's husband died a painful death from cancer. And, soon after, her daughter, Marián, the child who was closest to the disappeared María, met a terrible death.

Marián had repeatedly told the family that she believed that María was dead, but that she had given birth to her baby in prison. She wanted the family to try to find the child. One night she made a phone call to her mother in which she restated her belief about María's baby, and asked her mother to come to see her. Leonor went to Marián's apartment to comfort her. She found that her daughter had been thrown out the window and had died instantly. The police called it suicide and refused to investigate. Leonor believes that Marián's death was the result of fear on the part of the police because she and Marián had been making inquiries about María and her infant. "I tried to file a writ of habeas corpus and was refused, as were all the others. I also registered María's disappearance with several human rights organizations in Buenos Aires."

In 1978, Leonor decided to leave Argentina because she knew her life was in danger and she thought there was a good chance that her family would be left alone if she went into exile. She went first to Bolivia where she spent several weeks in church dormitories for exiles. Then she went to Cuzco, Perú where she found permanent shelter and work at a research center run by a French Jesuit priest. She lived among the poor doing social work and anthropological research. "It was one of the most valuable experiences of my life," she said, "because I was able to reaffirm my commitment to social justice in Latin America. I also felt less alone in my suffering because of the camaraderie I shared with other exiles from Argentina, Chile, Paraguay and Brazil."

Later in 1980, Leonor returned to Argentina. International pressure on the military government had caused state terrorism to lessen, and she wanted to search for her daughter and her grandchild. She was still afraid to apply for work at a university because many exiles were arrested when they applied for jobs. After the election of Raúl Alfonsín in 1983, Leonor joined the Mothers and the Grandmothers of the Plaza de Mayo, and in 1984 she obtained an appointment in the anthropology department at the University of La Rioja. She is now one of the most important human rights leaders in that city, as well as a supporter of feminist causes, including the pro-choice abortion rights movement. Leonor also teaches sex education to young women. Her courage and emotional stamina were to be tested again when she found out that there was a good chance that María's child was alive.

"On one of my trips to see my family in Buenos Aires, I decided to give a blood sample to the newly-formed blood bank. The forensic doctors were cooperating with the Grandmothers of Plaza de Mayo with the goal of identifying the close to 200 children who were kidnapped with their parents or who were born in captivity. I was having dreams about my grandchild and felt sure that the child would be found.

"The return of my granddaughter, Elena Gallinari, to our family was the direct result of the testimony of neighbors of the family that illegally adopted her. Her adoptive father was a police officer in the city of La Plata. Perhaps because of his arrogant personality, he did not bother to cover his tracks sufficiently enough to hide the sinister way he obtained Elena.

"The couple, whose surname is Madrid, were accused of being involved in a business in which they sold the stolen personal belongings of disappeared people to families in the neighborhood. Because of their alleged corrupt business dealings, the Madrid family's personal life was gossiped about in the neighborhood. It was noticed that they had a new infant in 1977 ... when the wife had never been pregnant.

"The Grandmothers began an investigation of the Madrid family. They found that the infant was named Viviana Nancy, that Madrid's wife was unable to bear children, and that the child was born in the home of Madrid's father, not in a hospital. With this evidence in hand, a federal judge ruled that their adopted infant was the child of a disappeared couple. All the dates coincided. Madrid was informed by the authorities that he had to present the child for a blood analysis. He complied without protest, but we were afraid of what he might do.

"It took eight months to prove the Madrid family's guilt. Because several couples with illegally adopted children fled the country, we watched the family closely. It is possible that Madrid and his wife didn't want to try to start over in another country or that they didn't have the economic means to escape. Without their now illegal business they had to live on a policeman's salary.

"On the appointed day, Judge Borrás and other government officials came to deliver Elena and arrest the Madrid couple. When Madrid saw the authorities, he pulled out a gun and started threatening Elena's teacher, the person who, along with a court-appointed psychiatrist, was entrusted with the job of telling Elena the truth. Madrid was taken away. He was crazy. Imagine the life Elena had with him?

"Doctor Raquel Berisso, a judge in the Minor's Court, explained to Elena that her parents had been kidnapped. Elena did not cry, but she asked two questions. First, she wanted to know if the people she called Mamá and Papá knew where she came from, and second, what really happened to her parents. The judge and the psychiatrist told her that all that was known for certain was that her parents were among the disappeared. Then I was introduced to Elena as her grandmother .

"There was so much confusion and I was so filled with emotion, I told Elena that we had spent years looking for her and that we would do our best to answer any questions she had. The psychological team from the Grandmothers of Plaza de Mayo were present to observe Elena's reaction to all the shocking revelations. They said that she did not seem to be severely traumatized. Perhaps they thought this because she was the first, and they didn't have other cases to compare hers with ... Elena says she always knew that she didn't really belong with the Madrids, perhaps because they told her she was adopted when she was already five of six years old.

"Within one hour she was writing her new school notebooks ... I think she was trying to get organized, to establish some control over her life ... In the meantime, there was a family conference going on. We were trying to decide where Elena should live. For a while she lived with her paternal aunt Silvia because she and her husband have a daughter who is about Elena's age. Now she lives with María's brother and his wife, but this is not working out very well.

"I have to admit that I really wanted Elena to live with me, and I was jealous of whoever was taking care of her. After a few months of therapy I came to accept that I am only the grandmother, not the mother. I spend a lot of time with her but she needs to be around young people.

"When Elena asks me about the tortures her parents endured, I respond as best as I can. One night she asked me whether or not I had been tortured. I told her the truth. Yes. She looked at me for a moment and turned out the light and went to sleep. I believe that it is best to tell her the truth ... She is always asking me about her mother—about what she was like as a young girl. I tell her that María worked with people in a poor neighborhood and that she wanted all children to live in a comfortable home and attend good schools.

"At first Elena said that she wanted to be a social worker like her mother. Now she wants to be a biochemist. I think it's because she wants to continue the search for the children of the disappeared. She is always asking to look at the book published by the Grandmothers which contains pictures of the children with disappeared parents. She says she wants to see if she can identify anyone."

• • •

On the seventh of December, 1988, the policeman, Domingo Madrid, brother of Elena's adoptive father, and four other men from the security forces presented themselves to Elena in a courtroom in the city of La Plata. A judge was in the process of finalizing some documents relating to Elena's legal situation. Madrid tried to harass Elena and she became very angry and asked him, "What are you doing here? Why are you bothering me?" The police intervened and arrested four of the five attackers. Domingo Madrid was allowed to go free even though he threatened members of the Gallinari family. This is just one of the many incidents Elena's family has had to endure. Elena has a psychologically sophisticated and supportive family, but she is not an untroubled child.

• • •

Leonor and I had a lengthy conversation about the research being conducted by a team of psychologists at the clinic located at the offices of the Grandmothers' organization. She supports the clinical work they do with the children of the disappeared, but she is frustrated because so little is known about the effects of the traumas Elena and so many others have endured.

Dardo Tumas, head of the team of psychologists and social workers, shares Leonor's frustration. Tumas conducts family therapy sessions and treats children individually and in groups. When I later interviewed him, he explained that their clinical work is highly experimental because they lack precedents to set up a theoretical framework in which to work. The therapists are just beginning to understand how to treat the children of "the disappeared." They are currently collecting clinical case studies with the goal of developing theoretical conceptual frameworks.

The problems for the therapists are overwhelmingly complex. Most of the children will never receive therapy because of the fear or ignorance of the families. Some children do not want counseling, so the therapists try to make an evaluation based on a simple diagnostic interview. A few of the children they counseled were doing fairly well, but the social stigma of being children of the disappeared people is very difficult for adolescents to tolerate. Some of them wonder if their parents were guerrilla terrorists and if they would be disloyal for not wanting to follow in their parents' footsteps.

In technical terms, Dardo says, the "psychic apparatus" of children ends between the ages of 18 and 20, although it is never closed definitively. He is concerned about what will happen to the adolescents as they grow into maturity. He cited the cases of two famous survivors of the Nazi concentration camps, Bruno Bettelheim and Primo Levi. Both of them committed suicide more than forty years after their personal traumas. Dardo believes that there is no way to know what the emotional health of the descendants of "the disappeared" will be decades from now.

Elena Gallinari suffers from one of the typical symptoms of children in her situation. The fact of not knowing the fate of her parents has become an obsession. She recently told Leonor, "I want to know where my parents are. If they have died, I want to put flowers on their graves, even though it will be just a tiny spot in the cemetery." It is impossible for Elena to mourn the death of her parents because there is no grave, no actual proof of their death.

In the past few years, a team of forensic scientists has exhumed hundreds of bodies from the common grave sites the military used to dispose of their victims. Some families are relieved to find even the partial remains of their relatives. The formality of burial initiates the grieving process and helps them to go on with their lives.

Leonor does not believe in the present government's exhumation policy because she feels it closes doors for the military that should remain open. "I don't want bones, I want my daughter back alive." She has accepted the fact that her daughter is dead, but she insists that her position is the only morally defensible attitude to take. But for Elena's sake, she signed the legal documents that would allow the identification if María or Miguel's remains are discovered. She has set aside a principle that is very important to her in the hope that Elena will have some peace of mind.

Leonor believes the human cost of state terrorism has been a very high one, and the long-term effects of thousands of family tragedies are just beginning to unfold.

While Leonor and I were having dinner in a local restaurant, I commented that people don't want to talk about what happened between 1976 and 1983, that the 1985 criminal conviction of the officers who led the three juntas seemed like a faint and distant memory. I told Leonor that I was going to name Argentina "the society of forgetting." I also wondered if she was ashamed because her fellow Argentines don't give her and the other survivors the respect they deserve. I asked her what sustains her in an atmosphere that is so unhealthy for human rights work.

"It is the job of the Mothers and Grandmothers to keep the memory of 'the disappeared' alive. Last year three of us went to Europe to campaign against the pardon President Carlos Menem promised to give the generals who were convicted of crimes against humanity. We want European leaders to put pressure on Menem to change his mind ... Argentina has no moral credibility because of the pardon. We are trying to stop it! ... A generation of idealists was murdered in Argentina. I'm sure that without memory it will happen again."

Subversive Mothers: The Women's Opposition to the Military Regime in Chile[1]

Patricia M. Chuchryk

The 1973 military overthrow of the democratically-elected government of Salvador Allende ushered in a period of intense political repression and economic crisis. Legal institutional channels of political expression were systematically dismantled, including Chile's bicameral parliamentary system, trade unions, political parties, and to some extent the universities, especially areas that had a humanistic focus. Fortified by the Doctrine of National Security and the notion of "internal threat," as well as by the experience and expertise of their Brazilian colleagues (Lernoux, 1982:142), the Chilean military declared war on the Chilean people.

The first "transitional" phase,[2] from September 1973 to June 1974, was a violent, chaotic, and bloody reign of terror, with no one appearing to be accountable to anyone for anything (Arancibia, et al., 1984: 32). As the world watched in horror, thousands were exiled, executed, imprisoned and tortured. Many disappeared. Although it is difficult to accurately estimate the actual number of victims, even the most conservative estimates are devastating. A U.S. Embassy's unofficial report suggested that 5,000 persons were executed during the first months after the coup (Dinges,

1983: 110). A report from the Inter-Church Committee on Human Rights estimated that as many as 30,000 were killed (Arancibia et al., 1984: 36). An Amnesty International Report (1974) cites church sources that estimated that by the end of September 1973, there were 45,000-50,000 political prisoners—7,000 in the National Stadium alone (Arancibia, et al., 1984: 31).

With the creation in June, 1974 of the DINA (Dirección de Inteligencia Nacional), Pinochet's private secret police force, disappearances began to be carried out in a much more efficient and systematic manner. It is estimated that up until its dissolution in August, 1977 (and subsequent replacement by the Central Nacional de Inteligencia—CNI), the DINA was responsible for well over 2,000 disappearances. Unofficial estimates are much higher, and to this day, the military junta does not acknowledge them. (Barnes, 1983:111)[3]

During this reign of terror and its political, as well as economic, consequences, it is not surprising that women, as the mothers, wives, sisters, daughters and grandmothers of the victims of repression, were the first to mobilize in opposition to the dictatorship. Men were the victims of abuse more often than women. Women during the socialist regime of Salvador Allende tended to play what were considered marginal or secondary roles in the targeted organizations, principally political parties and trade unions. It was precisely women's traditional public invisibility which allowed them to become politically visible during a time when it was extremely dangerous for anyone to do so.

Two organizations that emerged as a direct response to this repression, the Association of Democratic Women (Mujeres Democráticas) and the Association of the Relatives of the Detained and Disappeared (Agrupación de los Familiares de Detenidos-Desaparecidos)[4], are especially worthy of notice.[5] In these two groups we see an outstanding example of how traditional roles provided women with the impetus and initial motivation to organize against the military regime. Indeed, women of the Agrupación were the first to demonstrate publicly against the junta ("La Mujer Chilena,"1979:18). To this date, after the emergence of democracy in Chile, these associations continue to be active political agents, especially in demanding trials for the military junta.

Association of Democratic Women

Less than three weeks after the coup, on October 1, 1973, the

Association of Democratic Women was formed to do solidarity work with political prisoners and their families. At first, there were only five members; later their numbers swelled to 120, but to date, this movement has continued to grow and consists of approximately 300 members.[6] Their activities included helping to provide basic food stuffs for prisoners and their families, strike support work, and taking food to soup kitchens in poor neighborhoods. Especially during the early years, much of their work had to be done clandestinely, and this is the reason they gave for their organization being comprised of women. They suggested that it was easier for women than for men to work in the underground, partly because the military tended to ignore women.

In the beginning, while their numbers were still small, they met as one group, knowing each other on a first name basis only, and using traditional female activities to facilitate meetings. That is, the women organized tea parties and group knitting sessions, and indeed, their meetings actually took this form. In many cases, their families had no knowledge of their activities and believed that they were only going to tea and/or knitting parties. As the organization grew, this structure was transformed for reasons of security and necessity. Women now meet in small groups of ten or twenty. Each group elects a representative (*cabeza del grupo*). The *cabezas de grupo* meet from time to time to coordinate the activities of the group[7].

Over the course of its existence, this group has expanded not only its sphere of activities but also its self-definition—although its principle task has always and continues to be defined as solidarity work with the victims of political repression. They situate their group, now as in the beginning, within the political framework of the struggle for the return of democracy. They see themselves as a flexible organization which changes in accordance with the circumstances and demands of the moment. What is interesting is that now they also see themselves as having a political role *after* the return to democracy in Chile. This role consists of encouraging and participating in the political education of women so that women can begin to participate in traditional political organizations on an equal footing with men. During the group interview, several women pointed out that women have held few leadership positions in other political organizations during the Allende years, in part due to women's familial responsibilities, and in part due to *machismo.* They also emphasized that while theirs is a women's organization and not a feminist group, they have no argument with the feminists and find some of the issues raised by the feminists "extraordinarily interesting." Many members of this group have often participated in dialogues with the feminist coalition (especially since 1986). The Association of Democratic Women is also a member of MEMCH 83, an umbrella group which was formed in 1983 to coordinate women's opposition to the military junta.[8]

Most of the women involved in this group are older, middle class, housewives, and professionals (Silva, 1986: 146). Many had never before engaged in political activity. During the interview several of the older women pointed out that one of the reasons they initially became involved in the group was because there was no "space" for older women; they didn't seem to fit in anywhere else, and younger women could organize in the university. It was emphasized that this group is political but non-partisan.[9] While some individual members may be active in a political party, the group itself has no links to any political party.

While in some sense, perhaps much of the work of this group could be seen as a kind of "Ladies Auxiliary"—providing baskets of food and clothing to poor, needy families, visiting political prisoners and their families, and working with children,[10] it is the context itself which makes this work political—politically necessary as well as politically dangerous. During the first months after the coup, many of these women acted as liaisons among political leaders who had gone underground. They played an important role in taking the first tentative steps toward rebuilding destroyed political networks. Many women, especially wives and sisters of political leaders who were dead, imprisoned, or disappeared, were forced by circumstances to take on leadership roles for the first time. Some of these women were also involved in the formation of the Agrupación.

Association of the Relatives of the Detained and Disappeared

Groups seeking the whereabouts of detained and disappeared family members have emerged in a variety of Latin American countries, although perhaps the most internationally well-known of these is the Mothers of Plaza de Mayo formed in 1977 in Argentina. The first such group appeared in Guatemala in 1967 following the escalation of repression and massive disappearances in that country in 1966. In 1980, the Latin American Federation of Associations of Relatives of the Detained-Disappeared (FEDEFAM) was organized. At its first congress, held in 1981 in Costa Rica, it was estimated that during the previous twenty years, there have been over 90,000 disappearances in Latin America (del Olmo,

1986:42). FEDEFAM continues to meet almost every year and to gather representatives from different Latin American regions affected by the situation of the missing.

The Chilean Agrupación was formed in 1974. It emerged in response to the same conditions and circumstances which produced similar organizations—the implementation of military strategies consistent with the Doctrine of National Security and designed to eliminate the internal enemy—and as such is part of a continent-wide phenomenon. Nevertheless, the Agrupación is at the same time uniquely Chilean, born as it was within the Chilean historical context.

As was the case in other countries, in Chile, women besieged by political violence kept running into each other outside of prisons, in hospitals, and in government offices, all seeking information about the whereabouts of their loved ones. After a time, these women tentatively began to trust each other. With the help of the Committee for Peace headed by Archbishop Raúl Silva Henríquez, an Inter-Church organization formed shortly after the coup to help the victims of repression and their families, they formed a group, thinking they could do more and get more answers if they worked together. The Committee for Peace was eventually forced by the government to discontinue its activities. It was replaced by the vicariate of Solidarity, a Roman Catholic organization directly under the authority and protection of the Archbishop of Santiago and, to this date, one of the most active human rights organizations in Chile. It was about this same time that the list of 119 detained-disappeared appeared. These 119 are the only detained-disappeared who have been recognized by the military regime, only because they were found and declared dead in Argentina. The appearance of this list had the effect of consolidating the efforts of the Agrupación which, since that time, has worked closely with and has been supported by the Vicariate of Solidarity. The Agrupación continues working and is still under the auspice of the Vicariate and continues to provide legal assistance to the families of the disappeared.

There are now roughly 150 members of the Agrupación, of whom between 45 and 50 could be considered active members. Only two of the present members are men. The rest are primarily middle-and working-class housewives and mothers, some of whom are also professionals. They range in age from 15 to 70 years old (Silva, 1986: 154; "¿Dónde Están?", 1982: 19). All are missing a loved one, often a husband or son, sometimes a brother, sister or daughter. As a result of their participation in the Agrupación, many have been arrested, some as many as ten times.

From the beginning, the objectives of these women were clear and have not changed. They want to know where their family members are. They want the truth about these disappearances to be known. They demand justice and that those responsible be punished. At first, their efforts focused on the traditional mechanisms of the criminal justice system, for example, habeas corpus, and court depositions. When these strategies proved useless and futile, they began to use more unconventional methods such as hunger strikes and chaining themselves to the gates of the government palace and the Supreme Court. As indicated earlier, these women were the first to take to the streets to protest against the military regime.

What is interesting is how their objectives and activities have evolved within a political framework. Many, if not most, of the women initially involved had never been politically active and sought the emotional support of the group, seeing themselves as individual accidental victims of history. The problem of the detained and disappeared was not, at first, conceived as a political issue. After the central committee of the Chilean Communist Party fell in 1976, however, many Communist Party members became integrated into the Agrupación, engendering a tension which culminated in an internal crisis during 1982-83. Those already politicized sought to educate those who were not. The consequences of this tension and its subsequent resolution are several.

While maintaining its "absolute autonomy" from any particular political party, members of the Agrupación are no longer as reluctant to identify themselves (to each other) as political party members. The issue of the detained and disappeared is defined as a political one. The objectives of the Agrupación now include the need to politicize the issue both nationally and internationally. It is a member of the Latin American Federation of Associations of Relatives of the Detained-Disappeared (FEDEFAM). The Agrupación also participates in the general struggle for the return to democracy and includes such demands as rights for workers and the return of exiles ("La Mujer Chilena," 1979:19).

Their political activities are both internally and externally directed. In 1978, fourteen members formed a folk group designed not only to articulate protest in a different and new way but also to provide a therapeutic function for its members. Other make *arpilleras,* burlap tapestries depicting the political and economic conditions of their lives. There are workshops in political education, public relations, and leadership training for the membership. A youth group has been formed, which is comprised of the children, grandchildren, nieces and nephews of the members.

Externally-oriented political action is directed at raising public awareness, politicizing the issue within Chile itself, and mobilizing international support[11] and using the criminal justice system to exert pressure on the Pinochet regime.

Participation in either or both of these groups, the Association of Democratic Women and the Agrupación has had important personal consequences for the participants. The following discussion situates the emergence of these two organizations and the consequences of participation in them, within both an ideological and historical context.

Subversive Mothers: An Exception to the Rule?

The traditional interpretation of women's roles is often used to excuse or explain women's assumed or real political conservatism. The literature on this subject generally locates women's resistance to social change in an analysis of relative social powerlessness (Elliot, 1977: 5), isolation in the home and lack of personal identity given that women are almost exclusively defined in terms of motherhood and housewifery (Círculo, 1980: 6-8).[12] Women are often considered incapable of organizing themselves politically[13] in part because women's roles lie outside the realm of that which traditionally has been considered political.

In Chile, as well as in other Latin American countries, there are several examples of how the ideology of motherhood has been used to mobilize (some suggest manipulate) women politically. This is nowhere as clear as in the case of El Poder Femenino (EPF), a primarily middle- and upper-class women's organization that emerged in 1971 in opposition to the government of the Unidad Popular. The leaders of this profoundly conservative (and anti-feminist) organization involved images of the family under attack by the specter of communism. As of EPF leader said, "Women felt their fundamental values of family and motherhood threatened at the onset of Marxism; it touched the insides of women's being ..." (Crummett, 1977:110)

By preying upon values associated with women's domestic role, EPF attempted to unite women in political action against the Allende government. One of the contradictions here is that the use of the "preservation of the family" was a politically-motivated strategy which attempted, at the same time, to maintain the status of the family as "above" politics.

Another is that the EPF manipulated values which traditionally justify women's place in the home, and thus encourage women to take public political action to defend their roles as homemakers. Ironically, Pinochet had no doubt as to the political nature of EPF when, much to the dismay of many of the participants (Crummett, 1977:112), he ordered it to disband after the coup.[14]

Since the Junta took power in 1973, the military has made conscious and deliberate use of the traditional ideology of motherhood and the family. Pinochet has assigned to women, as mothers, the sacred duty of defending the integrity of the Chilean family and saving the Fatherland from subversive communism. Through their self-sacrifice and abnegation, their suffering, their dedication to the family, and their unwavering loyalty to the Patria, women—in Pinochet's plan—will ensure that Chile's sons and daughters grow up to be patriotic citizens.

The two key institutions used by the military to promote this image are the Mothers' Centers (Centros de Madres) and the National Secretariat for Women (SNM). The latter was created in October, 1973 with Pinochet's wife, Lucía Hiriart de Pinochet, as its director. These Mothers' Centers (CEMAs), originally created by the Christian Democratic government of Eduardo Frei, were substantially reorganized and converted into an ideological tool to promulgate the image of the self-sacrificing patriotic housewife. CEMA-Chile is also directed by Mrs. Pinochet.

It is extremely important not to underestimate the role played by Pinochet's control of these two organizations. In 1983 it was estimated that throughout Chile there were approximately 10,000 CEMAs, with 230,000 members and 6,000 volunteers (Lechner and Levy, 1984:2). CEMAs are directed primarily at lower-class women whose activities are controlled and directed by middle- and upper-class women volunteers, many of whom are military wives. The National Secretariat for Women (SNM) is an organization directed primarily at middle- and upper-class women in their capacity as volunteers. Its principle objective is an ideological one: the dissemination of family and patriotic values.

Through the vehicles of their respective publications (*Revista Amiga* and *Revista CEMA-Chile*) both of these organizations promote the same image of women—an image defined exclusively in terms of women's reproductive function. Women are conceived of as pillars of the society who defend and transmit spiritual values. Sacrifice, abnegation, service, honesty, diligence, and responsibility are women's chief characteristics, according to the official discourse.[15]

It is important to underline that the Pinochet government did not create the image of the suffering, self-sacrificing, patriotic mother who is the Chilean women. It is only using and manipulating the image to serve its own purposes.[16] By focusing on motherhood and the family, Pinochet is, in effect, attempting to depoliticize women and situate them outside of the realms of that which is traditionally considered political.

The groups of mothers that search for their disappeared in Latin America represent a radical departure from the way in which the ideology of motherhood has traditionally been manipulated and exploited by conservative forces. Yet, at the same time, it is motherhood (or women's traditional roles in a more general sense) which justifies the entry of women into the public political sphere.[17]

> [As women we participate in the Agrupación because] ... we are the women and mothers of this land, of the workers, of the professionals, of the students, and of future generation. ("¿Dónde Están?," 1982:20)

Many of the women interviewed pointed out that they had always been outside of politics; their husbands, fathers, and sons were the ones who carried out the political roles. When the men were imprisoned, detained and disappeared, what enabled women to overcome their terror was their sense of obligation as wives, mothers, sisters and daughters.

When asked why these organizations are comprised primarily of women, the women considered the question to be irrelevant. Men were those more affected by repression. The fact that the Agrupación is comprised of women, they argue, is merely a consequence of the particular circumstances, that is, a situation of extreme urgency—to search for a missing son or husband. Upon reflection, some suggested that, above all, men are the heads of families and therefore could not and cannot get involved for fear of losing their jobs. It was also suggested that the men who had participated during the beginning probably felt isolated whereas the women felt companionship with other women. Furthermore, they felt that they, as women, have more time than men to devote to such activity. In any case, all of the suggestions were based on some notion of women's traditional roles.

This discussion underlines the potential flexibility of the traditional ideology of women's roles. What is especially interesting is the extensive impact that participation in those groups has had on the women themselves. All the women I spoke with, indicated, to a greater or lesser extent, that their experience in these groups has had tremendous personal consequences. Presently, many of the women from Mujeres Democráticas and the Agrupación continue to participate in the politics and in the transition towards democracy. Although it is not necessarily a self-conscious process, many of the women had acquired a new sense of themselves as political beings. They see themselves as occupying a public political space that they had not occupied previously. For them, their participation has involved the process of becoming politically educated.

Although not conceptualized in these terms, their activity has involved both a confirmation and contradiction of their traditional roles as women. This includes a notion of their activity as an extension of women's role[18]—a role that has involved, nevertheless, considerable personal sacrifice. In some cases this has meant marriage breakdown and dissolution[19] Women whose husbands do not want them to be involved are often forced to choose between their activity in the group and their marriages. One woman who previously had never been involved politically became politicized as a result of her husband's imprisonment. When he was eventually released from prison, he demanded that she become "uninvolved." She refused and eventually left her husband. Some women also felt considerable guilt because they felt that, to some extent, they were not giving their children the attention required and hence they were not being "good" mothers. However, this was not enough to prevent their participation.

One of the early demands of the Agrupación was the right to "reconstruct their families," which were destroyed by disappearances. Many women suggested that the Agrupación had become, for them, a second family, a means of personal integration. More importantly, many also suggested that their participation also signified a form of personal liberation.[20]

> Many times I have cursed these four walls of my house, that in spite of having contained so much joy, have also isolated me from the world, from other people, from the problems we all share, and from those whom I love and whom I no longer have at my side. ("¿Dónde Están?," 1982:19)
>
> As a person, I have changed a great deal. Before I was shy, I never spoke up ... I've grown as a woman, now, I am much more aware ... (Interview)

> At the beginning, my husband and I participated together, but later he decided that we shouldn't continue ... but I insisted and that was my liberation ... (Interview)

Without exception, these women talked about their personal growth as a result of being involved in political activity with other women, and herein lies the contradiction. There is no consciousness of this process itself as a political process. Rather, it is conceived as an individualized consequence of their individual participation and becomes stronger by the collective efforts in the search for their relatives. Nor has it been conceived, in any way, as a contradiction of their traditionally defined roles as women. Nevertheless, it is possible to place this process within the context of the growing women's opposition to the military regime.

Since the mid-1970s, there has been a remarkable growth of non-governmental women's organizations in Chile. As one feminist activist put it, "Like mushrooms after a rain, organized pockets of women are springing up in union, in shantytowns, and in neighborhoods all over the country." (Santa Cruz, 1983:34) Among these groups are the Women's Department of the National Trade Union Coordinator, The Women's Committee of the Chilean Human Rights Commission, MOMUPO (Movimiento de Mujeres Populares de la Zona Norte), Women of Chile, Movement of Socialist Women, the Women's Liberation Front, the Feminist Movement, Women for Life, and the Committed for the Defense of Women's Rights, to name only a few.[21]

Some of these groups are organized around what we could call traditionally defined political goals (among these we can place both the Agrupación and the Association of Democratic Women). These focus primarily on politically educating women and encouraging them to participate in the general struggle for the return to democracy. Other groups focus on integrating women's specific concerns into that struggle and in the process, they attempt to reconceptualize that which is traditionally defined as political.

For a variety of reasons, most of these groups reject the label "feminist." But I have found in my work with many of these groups that the right to be a person is becoming increasingly articulated not only as a consequence of political activity but also as a political demand. In the process of developing political platforms and strategies and building autonomous (i.e., non-partisan) women's organizations, all of these groups, to a greater or lesser extent, have begun to incorporate demands related to the nature of women's position in society. In the Agrupación, many women have come to experience themselves, for the first time, as public political activists with the right to "occupy" political "space" as well as having the capacity to occupy leadership roles. In their meetings, the Democratic Women now talk about *machismo* as one of the barriers to women taking on political roles. In all of these organizations, women are beginning to define and demand their right to exist as a person.

Whether these groups define themselves as feminist or not, whether the groups consist of *pobladoras* or of middle-class women, they cannot alter the important consequences women's renewed political activity has had on Chilean politics in general. Women are beginning to view themselves as equal partners in the political process. A concern with women's rights is becoming increasingly more legitimate as a political issue. Public awareness is also beginning to motivate the opposition to Pinochet to re-examine its own values—values often consistent with Pinochet's own political project for women.

The Chilean situation offers a moving example of how intense repression can foster resistance and strength. The political mobilization of women in Chile has confronted an ideology which seeks to deprive women of their right to be persons. Regardless of the nature of their political focus and strategy, women in Chile are struggling for this right. In doing so, they are carving out a new chapter in their collective history.

Two of the women's organizations in Chile, the Association of Democratic Women and the Agrupación, are, to some extent, based on traditional notions of women's roles. Had the military not declared war on the Chilean people on September 11, 1973, these two groups would not exist. They are direct responses to the repression and, as such, direct consequences of the imposition of a bloody and inhumane regime. While they affirm traditional female roles, at the same time, they represent an important departure and challenge to these same roles. They are also part of a more generalized political awakening where women are beginning to more actively define their own roles in the political process.[22]

Surviving Beyond Fear: Women and Torture in Latin America

Ximena Bunster

Military regimes in Latin America have developed patterns of punishments specifically designed for women who are perceived as actively fighting against or in any way resisting the oppression and exploitation visited upon their peoples by dictatorial governments. The attempts to dominate and coerce women through terrorism and torture have become organized and systematic—administered by the military state. The more generalized and diffused female sexual enslavement through the patriarchal state has been crystallized and physically literalized through the military state as torturer.

Punitive sexual enslavement of female political prisoners is found throughout Latin America. However, the armed, organized terrorizing of women may best be understood in the context of political, economic, and social forces present in a given historical-national situation. We, therefore, see a somewhat different profile in the victimization of women taking place in Nicaragua, Salvador, Guatemala, and Honduras than that which has become characteristic of the countries of the Southern Cone: Argentina, Chile, Uruguay, Paraguay, and Bolivia.

In the first cluster of countries—those forming part of Central America—political torture reaches women as daily terror. Women are most often injured or killed in contexts of generalized violence: in massacres, attacks on churches during mass, and the burning of villages. This generalized violence affects different segments of the population who happen to be present during the attacks—men, older people, children, and even domestic animals. By contrast, in the countries of the Southern Cone, where a military government or succession of military governments have been entrenched for decades, women are *systematically identified*—with names, address, and family composition—as "enemies" of the government. They are methodically tracked down and incarcerated. There are institutions within the military government dedicated specifically and exclusively to this task.

For the purposes of this essay, I have concentrated on an analysis of sexual torture of female political prisoners who are or have been citizens of Argentina, Chile and Uruguay. The Argentine state has been militarized on and off since 1930 and the Chilean and the Uruguayan states since 1973. I have selected these three countries for the following reasons:

1. Each at one time was a flourishing democratic government, later aborted by military takeover.
2. These nations have had years of military dictatorship during which torture as a method of "security" has become institutionalized. These institutions incorporate scientifically-trained torture specialists, physicians, modern hardware, and "refined" methods in the systematic torturing of political prisoners.
3. Each of these countries had a highly organized, politically-conscious urban proletariat from whose ranks prominent female union and community leaders emerged.

In her work *Female Sexual Slavery*, Kathleen Barry says:

> Female sexual slavery is present in ALL situations where women or girls cannot change the immediate conditions of their existence; where regardless of how they got into those conditions they cannot get out; and where they are subject to sexual violence and exploitation. (1979:40)

My analysis of the nature of the torture endured by Latin American female political prisoners stems from Barry's groundbreaking work. I believe, and have tried to document in the pages that follow, that once one has listened to firsthand and eyewitness accounts and has read and analyzed the written testimonies of how pain and suffering are inflicted on women prisoners, a distinctive pattern of torture emerges.

In the state torturers' efforts to force confessions, elicit information, or to punish, a pattern in structure and in content is clearly discernible. These common elements experienced by female political prisoners in violent sexual attacks upon her body and psyche are consciously designed to violate her sense of herself, her female human dignity. The combination of culturally-defined moral debasement and physical battering is the demented scenario whereby the prisoner is to undergo a rapid metamorphosis from madonna (respectable woman and/or mother) to whore. To women, through processes of socialization, this violent sexual treatment administered by the state becomes most cruelly doubly disorienting; it exacerbates and magnifies the woman's already subservient, prescribed passive, secondary position in Latin American society and culture.

In order to better understand—while maintaining an awareness of the pitfalls that cultural generalization entails—how societal archetypes and stereotypes are manipulated by the torturers, it is important to look briefly at the delicate balance and complementarity of the male and female roles and the culturally assigned gender differences in Latin American society.

Many authors have discussed the bipolar conception of *machismo/Marianismo* underlying the socialization of men and women in Latin America. *Machismo*, or the cult of virility, has been described as embracing an "exaggerated aggressiveness and intransigence in male-to-male interpersonal relationships and arrogance and sexual aggression in male-to-female relationships"; *Marianismo*, as "the cult of feminine spiritual superiority which teaches that women are semi-divine, morally superior to and spiritually stronger than men." (Stevens, 1973:91) *Machismo* and *Marianismo* are New World variations of Old World themes.

Machismo is obviously a Latin American manifestation of global patriarchy, whereby males enjoy special privileges within the society and within the family and are considered superior to women. *Marianismo, Mariology,* or the cult of the Virgin Mother—she who embodies simultaneously the ideal of nurturing/motherhood and chastity—permeates the world view of Latin America and all aspects of its culture and institutions. Latin American women are supposed to pattern their role as women after this perfect model inspired through pervasive Catholicism. The patriarchal madonna/whore schema, too, is global.[1] Its particular manifestation in Latin America through the cult of the Virgin shows the extent to which Catholic ideology and the sexual stereotypes it introduced have been assimilated. Latin America has clearly absorbed the Spanish culture introduced by the conquistadores, itself marked by seven centuries of Arab-Muslim domination. The manipulation of these images proved useful to later waves of exploitation through capitalism.

Perhaps one example at this point will serve to bring home the fact of the double brutalization involved in socializing women in particular modes and then using that very socialization as a method of torture. One of the secret detention camps in Argentina, called Olimpo, was opened in the Western zone of Buenos Aires in August 1980. Testimony provided by Argentineans who were detained there describe how the torture of detainees involved icons of the Virgin Mary:

> In the very corridor leading to the torture rooms, along which new inmates had passed naked and in which they were beaten when they were first kidnapped, a small chapel was installed. It is a strange kind of Christianity these people have, enjoying punishing and beating until the victim loses consciousness—in front of the image of the Virgin Mary. (Amnesty International, USA, 1980:10)[2]

Two important characteristics, then, of Latin American culture are crucial to an understanding of the specific nature of female sexual torture in these countries. First, women are basically recognized and valued only as mothers, after the Blessed Virgin Mother. Second, women have adopted and internalized these patterns under the historical weight of Hispanic-Arab and Christian heritage and are now faced and overburdened by contemporary underdevelopment—a situation that must be felt and understood in its dailiness. Latin America has undergone conquest and colonization, and with these has seen Western values imposed over those autochthonous belief systems represented through high Indian civilizations at the time of the conquest. It is in this context that we hear the resonance of the Latin American/Caribbean Women's Collective in exile in Europe today: "domination in Latin America has been a prolongation of the history of man's exploitation of man and of men's domination of women." (Latin American and Caribbean Women's Collective, 1980:8)

In view of this cultural heritage and the ways in which the cultural baggage affects patterned gender differences, it is important to ask whether it matters that the state as torturer is a military state. It seems clear, from the countries examined and the systematic, ordered processes of torture of female political prisoners that are evident, that it does, indeed, matter. The fact that these states where torture has become institutionalized are military states should be kept in mind. It seems that military regimes exhibit the impulse of the state to secure and defend the patriarchal structure and the privileged status of "masculinity" more blatantly than do other authoritarian states. The military state understands itself to be run for the perpetuation and extension of the values of the military, masculinity, power, and public authority to a greater extent than do other patriarchal states. It is founded on the assumption that women and notions of the "feminine" are tools to be used by men; simultaneously, militarism as an ideology purports that women are fearsome threats to public order, to the hierarchy defined and controlled by men. It is important to stress the fact that although other patriarchal states also torture women, militaristic states rely more than civilian states on the use of coercion to strengthen and perpetuate their public authority. (Enloe, 1983)

The military elites of Argentina, Chile and Uruguay have brought internal police forces under their control and have strengthened and further entrenched the institutionalized torture machine through formal coordination of internal security bureaucracies and military bureaucracies. Thus, not only have the internal police come within the cloak of the military regimes but the military has also taken an active role in internal security matters. In Argentina, for example, one of the most infamous torture and detention centers is not run by the police, but by the navy. In Chile, separate torture centers are run by the air force, the navy, and the army. In attempts to unify and tighten their bureaucratic torture machines, the military regimes in both Argentina and Chile have brought in the internal intelligence agencies and "publicly employed" physicians, who supervise torture directly under their control.

The woman who is abducted is made to understand that she is under the control and at the mercy of a military state in every aspect of her life, her socioeconomic future, her family life, her sexuality, her internal feelings and sense of herself. Torture is the chosen method to convince her of these "truths."

Arrest, Intimidation and Brutalization as Punishment

It seems viable to use, as a point of orientation, the definition of torture—the "standard" definition—as adopted by the Inter-American Commission on Human Rights:

> Torture is understood to be the practice or instigation, by means of which physical or mental pain or suffering is intentionally inflicted upon a person, having taken into consideration the age, sex or condition or the person, for the purpose of intimidation, or in order to obtain a confession or information from the person or in order to punish the person for an act committed or which it is suspected that the person committed. (1982:91)

Although I have used this definition simply for the sake of clarity, and for consistency when using data gathered through various human rights agencies, it is important for us to realize this definition is itself limited and limiting when it comes to an understanding of the special nature of female sexual slavery and torture.

There is a distinctive pattern of torture when female political prisoners are involved. We must recognize and have recognized the fact than when the issue of torture of political prisoners is raised as a human rights issue it never deals with women. We must recognize that the physical and psychic torture of *women as women*—female sexual slavery in patriarchal societies reaching its "logical" extension and quintessential crystallization in the military state—is made invisible. As the military state so often tortures women as a mode of punishing their "man," so even to many human rights advocates the "desecration" of the female is processed as torture of the male.

To delineate specific phases and stages of the brutalization and attempted extinction of women as human beings, I have used both composites derived from the large number of recorded violations in Argentina, Chile and Uruguay, and examples from personal interviews, conversations, and correspondence with women who have witnessed and survived the torture.

Due to common elements in their recent histories, a relatively large body of literature exists dealing with human rights violations in Argentina, Chile and Uruguay. Free public primary, secondary, and university education has provided thousands of women with occupational and professional degrees. From the ranks of the working class and enlarged middle class, female members of the house of representatives (*diputadas*) and senators for the national congress (*senadoras*) emerged. Women committed to change and the abolishment of social injustice have been particularly active in these countries. Human rights organizations such as Amnesty

International and the Inter-American Commission have, therefore, been able to amass evidence of the extent of institutionalized torture. These publications document organized phases of terror in the sexual enslavement and torture of female political prisoners.

I must at this point speak to the bravery of those women who have survived what is in fact unspeakable physical and psychological torment and have then come forth to bear witness. We know the psychic pain involved for each of us as we work with these issues; the survivors of these horrors relive their experiences in the telling—their courage and commitment to the rights of human beings must remain for us, here, the inspiration to continue. The bulk of the cases utilized in this study cover the period 1973-81, when the experiences of these women took place. I have been in touch with women who have survived torture since 1973; the most recent conversations and interviews have taken place in 1982-83.

It was not deemed necessary to identify the country in each of the cases that follow as my analysis is directed toward an understanding of the nature of the commonality of pattern of sexual slavery in torture—a pattern that typifies the experiences of all women political prisoners in the Southern Cone of Latin America.

The aim of the first phase in the psychological and physical maltreatment of female political prisoners staged by military, navy, air force or police torturers is to intimidate and create a sense of anxiety in their victims. Two categories of women are targeted for attention.

Captors representing the state as torturer direct their established institutions of violence at the many Latin American women whose political consciousness has spurred them into political activism on behalf of the establishment of a more just social order within their own countries. This has been the case of Chilean women who worked within the Allende government toward the construction of a more egalitarian socioeconomic order. This has also been the case of Argentinean, Uruguayan, and, following the coup, Chilean women who became active in the struggle to liberate their countries and peoples from repressive dictatorships and the complicity of those regimes with foreign interests exploiting the human and natural resources of their nations. This group of women, many with public roles—as union leaders, lawyers, doctors, professors—are targeted because of their commitment to a people's struggle.

Institutionalized violence, torture, is also aimed at a second category of women—women, who do not have a publicly recognized identity of their own, but, from the perspective of the state, derive their identity from their relationship to a male. These women are targeted because of the activism of a husband, lover, son, father, or brother. The "super-macho" military system brutalizes these women as an extension of the ego and as a possession of the male whom they consider the "enemy" in an "internal war" and are then savagely tortured to get even with their men—the enemies of the military regime in power. The sexual enslavement of women belonging to this category is used to intimidate, emasculate, bring forth confessions from, and, in many cases, destroy the men to whom they are legally or emotionally attached.

Intimidation begins with the process of arrest. In the majority of cases, these women have been arrested at home or at their place of work. There are, however, a significant number of seizures in the streets, where women are taken on their way home from a day's work at a factory, office, hospital, school, store—a variety of work sites. A consistent modus operandi is used when making an arrest in the street. The woman's way is blocked by three to five men dressed in civilian clothing; only in a very rare instance do these men identify themselves in any way. The woman is grasped violently by the arm by one of the kidnappers while others flank her on each side with their bodies. She is then pushed into a waiting vehicle, handcuffed, and her eyes taped. Sunglasses are usually placed over the Scotch or adhesive tape. She sits with eyes lowered and her body tensed with fear. The agents of the government try to use caution lest the fact of their taking a hostage be noted by onlookers. If there is a passer-by in a highly congested city area or an oncoming car with passengers, the woman is rapidly thrown to the floor of the vehicle and slapped or beaten with the butt of a revolver.

Probably the most terrorizing arrest is that which takes place when the woman is at home with her family. This violent military operation, envisioned only for the most dangerous criminals in countries with stable democracies, is carried out by an *allanamiento*, a large group of soldiers who come in two or three vehicles and surround the house or building where the apartment of the woman is situated. They carry machine guns and an assortment of other weapons. If any resistance is offered, there is an official housebreaking and search of the home, accompanied by the destruction of furniture, the ripping of mattresses, and the armed intimidation of all the people who are in the house at the moment. This inhumane and cowardly action takes place at night—all reports place such action between midnight and 3:00 a.m..

Arresting a woman in the home, in front of her children, is doubly painful to the Latin American woman. The family is traditionally run by the mother. The main agent of socialization of children, she has the culturally-prescribed role of guardian of the moral values of the society; it is she who must ensure that the guidelines for the social and sexually accepted behavior of family members are adopted and absorbed. She represents the popularly accepted stereotype of the ideal woman exemplified in the Virgin Mother. This cultural pattern permeates all social classes and all adult women, be they mothers or childless. The women are to be morally superior and spiritually stronger than men, sexually pure as opposed to promiscuous, submissive and understanding of the frailties and patriarchal whims of their fathers, husbands, and sons, yet strong beneath that submissiveness. The identity of the Latin American woman is derived from her position in the family and especially from her "sacred" mothering role, where she is overprotective in her nurturing, absolutely devoted to her children, and willing to sacrifice her own desires to please her family—especially the male members. Her love is sacrifice and selflessness personified. It is crucial to understand the extent to which the conceptions are internalized; these attributes provide the foundation on which the edifice of the Latin American woman's self-perception and self-respect is built. These attributes also reflect upon the male members of her family, whose sense of personal honor and dignity is conceived as directly related to and dependent on the sense of moral propriety of the women in their family.

Given all these cultural antecedents, when a woman is taken in her home, the protection and refuge of the home that she represents is shattered, and the control and coherence she maintained in the intimate sphere of the household is destroyed as well.

This assault on a woman's sense of self and the manipulation of her traditional role as wife and mother is used by the torturers to break, punish, and ultimately destroy her. During this violation of her human dignity, torture as intimidation and torture as punishment blend into the same criminal act. This is the stage in an enslaved woman's torment when *family torture* is enacted by her captors. The following cases exemplify this strategy of the state tortures:

> N.N., a forty-six-year-old widow, was taken in her proletarian home and punished for not releasing names of left-wing workers. She was beaten in front of her fourteen-year-old son. As she kept repeating that she was ignorant of the facts, the

torturer beat her fourteen-year-old son in her presence, fracturing his jaw, breaking part of his rib cage, and inflicting pain on both arms.

V.L., a young married mother of three children, was assaulted at one o'clock in the morning. She and her children were at home when three men in civilian clothing—members of a military torturing squad—broke in. They raped her repeatedly at gunpoint in front of her children, aged five, four, and two, while threatening to shoot her if she cried for help. This heinous act was repeated on six other occasions over a two-month period, creating a constant state of terror for V.L. and her children. Her husband had previously been detained by the authorities; she was subjected to this repeated sexual torment in the state's effort to lower her defenses and obtain information concerning the husband's political activities.

V.P.R.'s apartment was broken into and the building surrounded by soldiers armed with machine guns. Everyone was dragged from bed at gunpoint. She, her husband, their twelve-year-old son, and their maid were immobilized, guns aimed at their heads. The smaller children, a girl, aged seven and a boy, aged eight, awoke and, entering the living room, were confronted with the spectacle of their mother at gunpoint. Terrorized, the two children started shaking with violent convulsions and crying out loudly. The captors cut off the electricity to the apartment and walked out with the mother, father, brother and maid, leaving the two children huddled together in anguish and complete darkness within their own home. The father subsequently was executed, his skull broken with brutal beatings. The mother was subjected to further torture through beatings, multiple rape, and electricity applied to her genital area.

A.C. de R., a nineteen-year old woman, was sleeping with her husband. They were living at her parents' home at the time of the police operation. The household included A.C. de R.'s mother and two sisters, aged thirteen and fifteen; her father, a commercial pilot, was away. During the 3:30 a.m. arrest, the young husband was gunned down in the bedroom in his wife's presence; he died instantly. The young widow, her mother, and two sisters were blindfolded, hooded, and taken as hostages for interrogation. The mother and two younger sisters were eventually released; but A.C. de R. is one of the many persons "missing" in the Southern Cone of Latin America today.

After the terror or arrest, the hostage woman is forced to face a series of phases of torture through which her state torturers hope to destroy her psychically as well as physically. Again, it is to obtain a confession or information, or as authorized punishment that these "security" methods are applied.

Both male and female detainees are tortured; some methods are applied equally to both sexes: incommunicado detention, wall-standing, the electric prod, the electric grid, the submarine, the dry submarine, the *pau de arara*, and inventive variations on the theme of beating. (see Endnotes)

The overall terrorizing environment of the detention centers should be understood as the backdrop for the torments particularly designed for women. From the institutional perspective, these are orderly affairs. The state's bureaucratic torturing system has incorporated doctors. Physicians are in charge of supervising the physical and psychological torment of prisoners—their scientific knowledge allows them to indicate when a given method of torture should be suspended if the death of the hostage is not desired.

Carefully designed mental torment is applied in counterpoint with the physical torture of detainees in a premeditated effort to increase the total feeling of powerlessness and pain. Simulated executions are staged in the middle of the night; captors threaten that a loved one will "disappear" or that a spouse, an aging parent, or small child will be tortured if cooperation and information are not forthcoming. Prisoners are forced to witness the torture and death of other detainees or are placed in rooms or cells where they must listen to the moaning of other hostages being beaten with the butts of machine guns, rifles, and revolvers. Often, standing naked and blindfolded, survivors report having to listen to the screams and "almost animal howls of pain" of prisoners being tortured in the same room or an adjacent one. Blindfolds are removed, however, when the detainee is forced through buildings to encounter a flow of fellow prisoners who can hardly walk or talk following torture sessions.

This is a climate, a world, of mounting and disorienting fear. For the prisoner, this is a totally unstructured situation—with "reality" defined and composed by the torturers. Prisoners have no moment-to-moment, daily control of their lives; they survive in a dim present with very little hope for the future.

Torture Designed for Female Political Prisoners

Female and male prisoners, then, are subjected to many of the same torturing practices, whose aim is to inflict physical pain, mental distress, and general suffering. However, the torture of men, while horrible, has as its object something less than the extinction of their sexual, gender identity. The primary form of sexual torture of men is directed toward their sexual confidence; their humanity is debased by placing them in powerless situations, where they cannot defend a female political prisoner—usually a wife, daughter, mother, lover, or friend—from brutal sexual torture performed in their presence.

Women's torment is comparatively much worse than men's because it is painfully magnified a thousand times by the most inhuman, cruel and degrading methods of torture consciously and systematically directed at her female sexual identity and female anatomy. The processes of imprisonment and torture of women political prisoners is female sexual slavery in its most hideous and blatantly obvious forms. It represents "macho" patriarchal contempt and misogyny crystallized and implemented through military-police structures of organized violence. These are not simple males "out of control with permission"; with a demonic irony, the sexual torture of women is named "control" and is authorized state "security." This fact should not surprise us; the military is, by definition, the most sexist and patriarchal institution of the many institutions that reinforce ideological subordination of women in the family and society at large. (Chapkis, 1981)

The sexual violence unleashed against women political prisoners is seen as the key in controlling them, through punishment and interrogations. Gang rape becomes the standard torture mechanism for the social control of the imprisoned women. Politically committed, active women who have dared to take control of their own lives by struggling against an oppressive regime demand sexual torture—as do the women who have stood by their men in an organized political effort to liberate their country and themselves from a coercive military regime. One of the essential ideas behind the sexual slavery of a woman in torture is to teach her that she must retreat into the home and fulfill the traditional role of wife and mother. It is this role only that provides her with respect in a society where she is ideologically defined as inferior to the men from whom she derives her secondary identity—she is some male's mother, sister, wife, and *compañera.* With a too usual contradiction and reversal, the method of the "lesson" forcing a return to the *marianismo* ideal simultaneously violates that possibility. There seems to be not only a willingness to violate cultural notions of what the "natural" social order is, but, in fact, to direct torment with excruciating precision just to those areas of societal definition. We can only describe these patterns of state torture; we cannot make them rational.

Behind the sequence of brutal sexual acts committed on a woman's body and mind while she is in captivity lurks the criminal attempt to humiliate, degrade, and morally and physically destroy her through and within the social, cultural, and political environment that is familiar to her. It is, in an important sense, too distancing to speak of culturally accepted and defined gender distinctions. The ideological conceptions, the myths, and the realities of the paradigmatic vision of Woman are much of the ground from which springs a woman's sense of herself and from which she derives the emotional needs and the gratifications that give meaning to her life—the love and respect of her family and the esteem and caring of her co-workers.

A woman's self-respect, sense of dignity, and physical integrity are shattered when at the hands of her captors she unwillingly becomes the participant-observer of the planned and enforced destruction of her culturally defined womanhood. In every sense of the word, in every level of her being, the torturer's invasion involves radical disorientation.

The sequence of types and examples of torture that follows is from cases of women in Argentina, Chile, and Uruguay. There is always a danger when cases of the torture of people are summarized and then classified: As painful as it is, we must not allow ourselves to forget, even for a moment, that we are speaking of pain and torment inflicted upon individuals. Even in the notions of selection of "evidence" of what is held to be a viable methodology we neutralize the FACT of the agony for these women, woman by woman.

The woman prisoner is brought blindfolded and hooded to one of the many *casas de tortura* (torture houses) administered by the security forces of these countries. They are most often established in regiments, police quarters, naval and air force bases, and academies, and in houses rented and equipped for purposes of torturing. The woman has already undergone the trauma of arrest and the geographical disorientation of being taken blindfolded to the torture house. She has been cut off from her family, or, if her arrest went unobserved by relatives, neighbors or passer-by, she has "disappeared"—she knows that no one knows where to look for her. Some victims captured on the streets start shouting their own names aloud so that the family will know they were dragged away.

While she presumes that she is at the information desk or in the "reception room" of the detention center—"presumes" because survivors report that it takes a while to look from under the blindfold without being discovered and beaten—her name and address are taken and entered into files with a number. While she is giving the information demanded, her body—especially her breasts and buttocks and entire genital area—is fingered and pawed by countless male hands. Her body is squeezed and explored, producing in her a sense of outrage, sometimes physical pain, shame, and despair.

She is then taken to another room, where a group of men undress her, literally tear her clothing, and start slapping and beating her continuously. No sooner has she been able to get on her feet when she is again thrown to the floor or against a wall. Her nose starts bleeding, and she aches all over. During the course of this brutal battering, she is given orders to sit down. There is never a chair, so she falls to the floor. She is then given contradictory orders to march in a given direction, and, obeying, hits herself against a wall. Then she is told to kneel and squat because she has to go under a table. In the meantime, she is the target of crude verbal abuse and vile ridicule of her naked body. She becomes the pathetic jester who amuses the torturers by aimless movements directed to make her fall, roll on the floor, crawl on all fours, and jump over obstacles that are nonexistent. Fun is made of the shape of the woman's breasts, her birthmarks, or the scars left on her abdomen after a Cesarean birth. This stage of torture is marked by the captors sadistic objectification of the women at their mercy.

Questions are interjected during the process of physical and verbal abuse. Depending on her presumed "profile," the woman is interrogated concerning the whereabouts of her husband, or a key male political figure who is in hiding, or about whether or not she is active in a specific political party. If the woman political prisoner claims ignorance or refuses to cooperate, the sexual violence of the torture escalates. She is thrown to the floor, splashed with cold water all over her body, and the electric prod is applied to her eyelids, gums, nipples and genital area.

As interrogations continue, sexual torture is increased. Cigarettes are extinguished on the woman's breasts and nipples; her breasts are slashed with sharpened instruments; blades, hot irons and electrical surgical "pens" are used to brand different parts of her body.

> R.B. was detained because she had been the secretary of a prominent woman senator belonging to a leftist party. She was undressed, punched in the stomach with brass knuckles, and given systematic electric shocks. But her most excruciating pain was produced when the torturers tied her nipples with a cord and started pulling them with sadistic violence first forwardly and then in all directions as if intending to uproot them from body. As a result of the prolonged sexual torture, she had a miscarriage and a stroke that paralyzed the left side of her body.

> M.A.G.C. was a professor of mathematics at the time of her arrest. She was accused of collaborating with "international Marxist forces"; she was considered a threat to the military state. M.A.G.C. was methodically immersed head down in the swimming pool of the Naval Academy in Valparaiso, Chile, until she was on the verge of asphyxiation. This violence was alternated with beatings and regular squeezing and biting of her breasts by her torturers.

> V.L.M., a homemaker married to a politically active husband who was in hiding, had the Communist party symbol of the hammer and sickle branded with electricity—she describes it as "an electrical pen used on the flesh"—on her thigh. This was done, she was told, so that "she would stop being a Marxist."

Many women have had the words "Marxist" or "Mirista" (MIR is a political party that the military junta in Chile calls the revolutionary leftist movement: its members have been systematically murdered), "extremist," and/or "dangerous" tattooed across their breasts. These words are often also imprinted on their foreheads. It must be understood that this organized political torture is not applied only to women thought to be Marxists. It is applied to women from a variety of political parties, to women who are active in center political parties, and to women who are not involved in politics at all. Women are branded if their captors believe them to be against the military government.

There is a male-bonding in the violence of massive criminal rape, performed in succession, by three to twenty-seven men in some cases, against women political prisoners. Rape is part of almost every torture sequence endured by a woman, especially women from twelve to forty-nine years of age. Power and domination are exerted on the victims of sexual slavery in a torture situation where women cannot leave nor fight back. Testimonies of older women political prisoners who have survived correspond in their hair-raising accounts of massive rapes perpetrated on the younger women upon arrival at the "houses of torture." Following these vile sessions of rape and other forms of sexual abuse, many women suffered severe hemorrhaging for days with no medical attention.

The use of animals to physically and psychically torture women is yet another phase in this unutterable process. Women's mental stability and physical health have been seriously threatened, sometimes destroyed, by the introduction of mice into their vaginas. Foreign objects, such as sticks and dull instruments, have also been introduced into the vagina and anus; but it is difficult to compare even such abuse with the psychological and physical suffering brought about by a scratching, biting, disoriented mouse forced into a female's genital region. Women, now in exile, who survived this torture, explain that they have not, nor do not believe they ever can, really recover from the trauma of this experience. Many of them developed ulcers within their vaginal walls as a result of the rodent's action inside them.

Many female political prisoners in Chile have been raped by trained dogs—usually boxers. (Denuncia y Testimonio, 1975:99) This is evidently one of the most brutalizing and traumatic experiences suffered by women prisoners. The survivors of this torment find it very difficult to report their exposure to this extreme sexual debasement. With sickening canniness, the torturers traumatize their victims into feeling shame for their own bodies. The women who are able to do so are willing to recall these events in an effort to make known these atrocities, although they suffer anew by speaking of them.

The military state—the patriarchal state in distillation—with its dependence on coercion to mold human beings to the ideology that will sustain its authority, uses the paradigm of female sexual enslavement, rape, in as many forms as it can imagine. Patriarchy under stress tends to reveal itself with contradictory zeal. The notion of Madonna/Whore in the context of male linearity of thinking (Barry 1979:262) as it melds with rape systematically applied to exert absolute control is illustrated through the case of A.N.M.R. This courageous young widow, whose husband had been assassinated during a "military" operation, was seized by the police and mercilessly tortured for long periods. As she refused to talk, she was given electric shocks, sent to her cell for a short while, and then dragged out again by the officer in charge of the supervision of her sexual torture. Officers would shout to groups of soldiers inviting them to rape her with the following order: "Come and have a good time with this whore because she needs it." They did rape her. She sums it up in her own words, "Thus I was debased and raped countless times." As if continual rape were not enough "control," her uterus was later ruptured by a high-voltage shock with an electric prod.

Rape is used during sessions of "family torture," usually to extract information from a noncooperative male prisoner. It is for this reason, for leverage in interrogations, that women in the family are kidnapped along with the male "subversive." Numerous wives and daughters of male prisoners have been sexually debased and massively raped in front of their husbands, lovers, or fathers. If a man is wanted and in hiding, his wife and female children are incarcerated in a manipulative attempt to extract information concerning his activities and hiding place. If the wife does not cooperate with her captors, she is raped. If this does not produce the desired information, she is threatened with the rape of her daughters. In addition to physical suffering, the psychic strain of having to deal with such a confrontation of loyalties and the consequences of any so-called "decision" are devastating. Unfortunately, many threats are made good by the torturers, and mothers are forced to witness in shock and powerless pain violent sexual acts committed upon their innocent female youngsters.

The case of L. de las N.A.M., single, is, unfortunately, a typical example of a most vile form of "family torture." At the time of the arrest she was twenty-three years old. She was imprisoned together with her father and fifteen-year-old brother. To extract information from the father and the daughter, the torturers first applied electricity to the father in front of her, she in turn was administered electricity in front of her father so that he would talk. Her fifteen-year-old brother was savagely tortured in her presence. Watching this suffering was the only time in her prolonged torture when her blindfold was removed. In order to psychologically and physically weaken her further, L. de las N.A.M. was battered and bruised all over her body; her breasts and other parts of her body were slashed with a blade and her nipples brutally squeezed and pulled while at the same time the torturers introduced their dirty hands into her vagina and stuck a variety of metal objects inside her. Later on she was submitted to electric shocks, then hung by the knees from a horizontal plank, with hands and ankles tied together (the dreaded *pau de arara*). She fainted, and when she recovered, her five tormentors started threatening her with rape. Her father and her brother were brought in and the captors started forcing the father and daughter into having intercourse. L. de las N.A.M., screaming in terror, fainted again. She was revived with slaps, thrown onto a mattress on the floor, and raped by many men—she cannot recall exactly how many they were. She describes herself (after the massive rape) as "waking up soiled ["impure," her chastity taken away from her by force] and bleeding." What she describes as "waking up" is the realization that the culturally-defined dignity of her womanhood had been shattered; she had fought back so bravely, like a caged animal at the mercy of her executioners. Further suffering was inflicted on this brave woman by introducing mice into her vagina. She describes mice as "going berserk inside me and painfully inserting their paw nails in my flesh."

An extension of the notion of degradation of a woman in the "community" of her family is the forced abuse or humiliation of a woman through her peers. As with "family torture," this method produces pain and humiliation in all those forced to participate in this particular type of sexual torment. A naked political prisoner is placed in the middle of a human circle formed by her naked male co-prisoners, many of whom know her. In cases where she is not known personally, she stands as the representative of "one of their own" ideologically. The men are forced at gunpoint to masturbate while looking at the naked body of the woman and having her as a target when they ejaculate. Once again the woman who finds herself in this type of situation, from which she cannot escape, is further degraded in a painfully debasing incident in which male domination not only increases her inferiority as a woman but robs her of her dignity and individuality as a person.

It should be noted that there appears to be a class element and racial component in the most extreme cases of sexual violence. Proletarian women and women with markedly *mestizo* features—the fusion of

European and Indian admixtures—have been even more brutalized than their lighter sisters coming from bourgeois families. It is, however, also important to stress that the fact that in the highly class-conscious society of Latin America, the sexual torture of female political prisoners has cut across class lines. The common denominator has been the definition as enemy by the fascist military governments, whether the "security threat" comes directly through the woman's political activism—real or supposed—or through the identity she is seen to derive from a male who is politically active.

Torture of the Female Psyche

Although, as is quite evident by now, it is impossible to separate, physical abuse from psychological abuse, the state torturers have designed methods specifically aimed at the mental torment of their prisoners, methods that underscore their domination and control. The harrowing of the psyche of these women is used by their tormentors as complement to the sexual violence that their bodies are undergoing. Psychological torture leaves scars that are almost impossible to heal. A woman's sympathy and empathy for others is played upon; her deep sense of herself as nurturer is manipulated and torn. The following situations and cases show different aspects of sexual/gender violence.

Many women have reported how painfully humiliating it is to have their physiological processes, basically elimination, controlled and observed by their torturers. They were not allowed to go to the bathroom when they needed to go but when their guard felt like taking them. Once in the bathroom, they had to eliminate in front of the torturer, who was aiming all the time at them with a shotgun. He would not even turn his head aside.

Many survivors of torture, while in sexual slavery at the mercy of their authorized torturers, describe the agonizing impact that the sobbing and crying of other women being raped in the adjacent room or a few feet away from them had on the moral integrity that they were trying to preserve in order not to break down. Psychological torture is delivered with false news of the death of family members and/or by threats of having a loved one disappear. A woman professor of mathematics was thrown against a wall and, with a revolver against her forehead, her torturer—a marine—shouted, "Talk, talk, for once and for all, because you are going to be executed and you will never see your small daughter again."

Psychological suffering is also administered by purposely having female political prisoners become aware or witness the rape of women in advanced stages of pregnancy—seven to eight and a half months.

Infliction of extreme psychological cruelty is most often reserved for those women who have dared to take an active role, in their own right, toward the improvement of socioeconomic conditions in their countries. Women given this special attention include political leaders from now banned workers' unions, activists in syndicates and committees consisting of white-collar and professional workers in the fields of health, education, and community welfare, and women who have participated in key political movements.

Elba Vergara's case provides but an illustration of the kind of psychological brutalization female political prisoners are forced to endure. (Denuncia 1975:167-69) A member of the Socialist party, Elba Vergara had been President Allende's secretary for many years. She was fifty-one years old at the time of her arrest, fifteen months after the Chilean military's bloody coup.

Upon her arrest, Elba was taken to a friend's home, a young woman with a three-year-old son. One of the captors took the child by the ankles and walked over to the balcony of the nineteenth floor apartment, threatening to drop him head first if Elba did not give them the information they wanted. The mother of the boy shouted, "Throw him down! But we won't confess to anything." This was Elba's introduction to what would be the special nature of her ordeal.

Taken to one of the "torture houses," Elba was interrogated for seven hours. This relentless interrogation continued for eight days. Still refusing to cooperate, Elba was forced to witness the sadistic murder of two young men she had known during the time Allende was in power. She was taken to a room called the blue room, a small area lit by only two blue bulbs. Her blindfold was removed. Four hooded executioners broke into the room, shouting, "Bring in the actor." A covered body was wheeled in on a stretcher. One of them, then turning to Elba, said, "Sit down. Here you are going to see the representation of a bad actor. You have to help him remember his lines."

They uncovered the naked body of a brutally disfigured young man. His torture had been so severe he could not speak. Elba was asked if she recognized him. She said, "No." She did, in fact, recognize the young man. He had been a chauffeur for a member of the Allende government.

"You are telling us that you don't know him. We shall see whether you know him or not." They took one of his hands and pulled out his fingernails. Elba continued to insist that she could not identify the man. They tore off the one ear he had left at that point. They cut his tongue out. They punctured and emptied one of his eyes. This ordeal lasted three hours. He died then.

A second man was now brought into the "little blue room." He, too, had already suffered horribly. This time the executioners took five hours to kill him in their efforts to force Elba to speak. She still would not give them the information needed.

This extreme psychological torture was designed to torment, terrorize, and break Elba to annihilate her morally, through a sadistic attack on her humanity and the deep maternal aspect of her socialization as a Latin American woman. As the courageous Elba Vergara herself said referring to the first young man tortured and killed before her,

> He could have been my son. The son of any mother in the world. Somebody with whom one had been twenty days before, when he was healthy, fine ... and then they kill him under your very eyes. It is probably worse than any physical torture aimed at oneself.

This kind of psychological torture, this torment through torture of another, involves both the immediate horror and the devastation wrought from helplessness and the long agony resulting from the pretense of choice given a woman.

The use of children by these state torturers and the manipulation of the woman's caring and nurturing role takes many forms. As in the case of Elba Vergara, many women have had to endure having their own children or the children of female friends and political comrades tortured in their presence.

L.V., it is reported by a friend, had her four-and-half-year-old son tortured in front of her. She and her husband, both captured, were then further tortured and killed.

The young offspring of women and men who are sought by a dictatorial regime for their clandestine activities against the government and the children of women and men considered a threat to the "internal security" of the government have been kidnapped by force from their homes. These children are placed in so-called Homes for Children run by the armed forces; they are hostages used to exert pressure on their parents. Most often, a message will reach the mother of the child with an ultimatum: if she does not turn herself in to the security forces, the little girl or boy will remain in captivity and undergo torture or be placed "under the vigilance of sexual perverts who prefer children."

The bureaucratic torture machines of Argentina and Chile use both threats of torture of children and the actual torture of children to further heighten a woman's suffering while still physically brutalizing her. Examples already on the record include:

Tamara, a child of three, was tortured in Chile. Her mother, now in exile, described the treatment her daughter received in detention:

> They undressed my little daughter and whipped her with a leather whip. They put her in a barrel with ice water and held her head under the water until she almost drowned. They threatened to rape her and whipped her again. This was repeated four times a day for four days. (Children 1979:15)
>
> N.B.L., a young mother, was kidnapped by Argentinean Task Force No.3, Military Personnel, November 1977. The task force made her son "Facundo cry in the operating theater"—torture chamber—next to the one in which she was being tortured.
>
> Christina was abducted along with her mother, M. del C.J., by a special task force in October 1978. M., during her own interrogation, was forced to listen to her young daughter's screams. (Testimony 1980:18-19)

Evidence has been on record and continues to mount showing that babies and children are not safeguarded from torture; their torment is sadistically aimed at their mothers.

Under the threat of having a child tortured or "disappeared," mothers have sometimes confessed the hiding place of their husband or *compañero.* Here again is a most diabolical form of psychological torture: The Latin American mother placed in a situation of conflict between her role as wife/lover and her role as mother will almost always opt for her "sacred" maternal duty of protecting the vulnerable child. In addition to living with the brutal assault her body has taken while under interrogation, she must live now, as well, with the "guilt" of having revealed the whereabouts or activities of her husband. There is shattering moral pain brought about by the disintegration of her family. This is the cruellest attack upon a woman's psyche; it shows us so clearly how the torture of these dictatorial military regimes pierces to the essentials of female sexual slavery. The woman must not only suffer in every part of her being; she must also be faced with a shame that is called a "choice" and feel herself a "collaborator" with her torturer, no matter what she does or does not do.

Kathy Barry, in exposing the pervasive patterns and practice of female sexual slavery, begins to weave those threads of connection, showing how slavery extends beyond the individual and further enslaves her. We see this with shocking clarity in how the female is used in the selected ways in which she is tormented as a political prisoner. This is especially and painfully so when it affects and abuses a woman's nurturing role. The split consciousness of this cultural sadism not only tries to smash a woman in and through the center of her being but also zealously spans generations. We do not need to wait thirty years to test a hypothesis of possible damage to the children of V.L., who watched her repeatedly raped, nor the children of V.P.R., left huddled in terror, nor the children who underwent the torment of the detention centers. We do not need to wait to ask about the unutterable complexities of damage done to those who both witnessed and served as examples.

The state torturers must spread their terror both throughout the community and across generations. The military state sadistically literalizes patterns of female sexual slavery. It is important to speak specifically to the facts of those women taken when pregnant.

When a pregnant political prisoner does not die on the torture table or lose her baby after beatings on the abdomen, being kicked, raped, and tortured with electric shock—under the supervision of a doctor—she is returned to her cell, under the same conditions as the rest of the prisoners.

Following her subjection to the pattern of torture described, a young Argentinean woman gave birth to a son. She was tied to a bed by her hands and feet during a five-hour labor, receiving medical attention just as the baby was born; for the duration of their incarceration, the infant was made to sleep on the floor of the cell. Amnesty International doctors examined the woman and the child following their release from prison. Miraculously, the baby appears to show normal mental and physical development. The mother suffers from impaired memory, headaches, inability to concentrate, nervousness, and dizziness. (Children 1979:19)

Amnesty International has documented numerous cases of the disappearance of mothers and children, where the child was either born in prison or abducted with the mother. (1980, 1981) In Argentina, the greatest number of pregnant women and mothers of infants and schoolchildren "disappeared" between 1976 and 1980. During this period, pregnant women were taken to ESMA—the principal Naval Training College in Buenos Aires—which was earmarked as the maternity unit for secret detention camps in the capital city district. All pregnant women who survived interrogation were attended at ESMA by a doctor from the naval hospital. After the birth, the mothers were usually "transferred" and the infants sent to official or clandestine orphanages for adoption by childless couples in the armed forces.

"Transfer," according to surviving witnesses, is the name given to massive assassination in Argentina. Guards tell prisoners at a detention camp that they will not be allowed to take their few possessions or additional clothing as they will be issued uniforms at the next detention center. In actuality, they are killed or become *desaparecidos*—missing—the word used to describe thousands of Argentineans who have never been heard from again, and whose bodies have not been returned to their families for burial.

Hundreds of Argentinean women have given birth and been "transferred." Their babies have been reported as "missing" by grandparents and surviving relatives. The toddlers and older children abducted with their mothers have never been seen again. The grandmothers of these missing babies and children, who have also lost their own daughters and sons, have formed an association, *The Grandmothers of the Plaza de Mayo,* an offshoot of *The Mothers of the Plaza de Mayo.* [3]

Evidence and documentation concerning the *sale* of some of these children, both in Latin America and abroad is just surfacing.

Female sexual enslavement, one of its most hideous forms, is the most salient characteristic of the oppressive military dictatorships in many Latin American countries. It is one of the most difficult crimes against women to punish and eradicate because the oppressors, the torturers, the persecutors, and executioners of women are all members of the authoritarian state, the military state, that has done away with all the basic human rights to which individuals are entitled.

The military state depends on the oppression and exploitation of the poverty-stricken masses of Latin Americans; it is against the full participation of ethnic minorities in national affairs because it is racist. The military state is also the epitome of sexist patriarchal ideology and therefore against the largest minority, women, who have been made to retreat to their traditional role of reproducers and nurturers of the younger generations.

The military state endorses an economic exploitation of the bulk of the population and the natural resources of the country it purports to represent by protecting the economic interests of the wealthy families belonging to the upper-class and by serving as a watchdog for the investment of multinational corporations. Profits for some are reaped faster when the constitution of a country is ignored; when the congress that is to guarantee the democratic process is closed indefinitely, its politicians banned from participation in government affairs; and when strikes and criticisms of the government are made illegal, a cause for punishment and imprisonment.

If the segment of the population that dares criticize the totalitarian military state is female, the punishment is administered through female sexual slavery in torture. The subservient, dependent, passive, and unequal position in society that women experience as opposed to men in a patriarchal society is exacerbated in torture. The courageous women who have managed to survive this brutal appropriation, colonization, and objectification of their bodies, as well as the psychological suffering derived from the cruelly premeditated deprivation of their human womanly dignity have set an example of bravery for us all. They have also handed us the banner of struggle by surviving, by not succumbing at the feet of their tormentors, by transcending their sense of shame and humiliation and offering their personal testimonies to make known the criminal acts of the military state. Their cry is for justice, for the elimination of sexual slavery in torture, for the diffusion of the awareness of its existence and its monstrosity so that it may be stopped, so that it will never happen again.

Thousands of women in countries of the Southern Cone—Peru, Argentina, Chile, Uruguay, Bolivia, and Paraguay—have dared struggle for a more just socioeconomic order. Many of them have died. Thousands have disappeared and thousands are still fighting dictatorships. By so doing, they have acquired an identity of their own; they have become full persons in their own right and thus challenged the passive, submissive, dependent role assigned to women based on the conservative religious archetype of the Virgin Mother that the patriarchal institutions have imprinted through the socialization of all women. These are women who, by their direct actions, are transforming the cultural content of *Marianismo, Mariology.* They have contributed, and are contributing, to rapid and radical changes in the societies to which they belong; they are also creating new female models for the younger generations to follow. This is the legacy of the women political prisoners who have survived sexual slavery in torture. It is also the example that has been presented to us by the women commanders of Nicaragua—Doris Tijerino and so many others—who played an instrumental role in ousting the Somoza regime and who are now involved in the reconstruction of their country. It is also the example set forth by many members of the new Catholic Church in Latin America, whose religious leaders have thrown in their lot with the poor, the persecuted, and the oppressed. The blueprint for the socialization of the traditionally passive Latin American female is changing rapidly. No one as yet has more eloquently described this root change than Sister Martha, who sees the sexism on which Nicaraguan society is founded and speaks about it—about women looked upon as objects of sexual satisfaction, required to be submissive to their husbands, and to obligingly take care of household duties and the children.

But, Sister Martha says, Nicaraguan women now want to change this situation because:

> they have taken an active part in the Revolution not only to achieve freedom for the people but also to achieve their own freedom as women. Today, Nicaraguan women hold Mary, the Mother of God, as their first model for promoting this revolution. She, too, carried to the world a message of liberation ... Mary isn't the sugar-sweet stupid woman reactionary Christians so often make her out to be. At the age of fifteen—the same age as Doris María Tijerino—she took an active part in the liberation of her people. She doesn't speak to individual moralistic changes, but of the reorganization of the social order into one which there are no rich and poor, powerful and humble. And so, faced with this new dawn filled with great hopes and with Christian and revolutionary responsibilities, Nicaraguan women must follow the path begun by Mary of Nazareth and Doris María of Matagalpa. We have but one alternative: *To be women of hope working for the consolidation of our revolution.* (Randall 1981:162)

As one investigates the torture of female political prisoners in Latin America, many connections, sometimes enlightening, though also horrifying, and widespread, both geographically and temporally, come to mind.

I have noted parallels between how women political prisoners have been brutalized in torture in the Southern Cone of Latin America and the black female experience in the United States before the Civil War. Slave masters on plantations terrorized and "tamed" their women slaves by subjecting them to sexual exploitation and oppression through rape, forced breeding, and sadistic floggings during which black women were stripped naked and publicly whipped. Pregnant women were made to lie on the ground, over holes dug to receive an abdomen full with child, and were flogged with whips or beaten with a paddle. (see Davis 1977; Hooks 1982)

Written evidence and "graphics" surviving from the European Middle Ages also describe tortures of women strikingly similar—in fact, in many details identical—to those used by the state torturers in Latin America. The same parts of the body are attacked, in the same ways—technologies were simply somewhat different. Pregnant women met with special attention. The Virgin, here too, was often mounted in torture chambers by the state torturers, despite the intimate relationships between church and state.

With the death throes of the European Medieval world view came a pervasive torture and murder of women. This time, we were called witches, and the church and state then defined witchcraft as a *crimen exceptum*, a crime distinct from all others, the rules of proof suspended, as were all holds on torture. These threats to the public security met with highly refined, highly similar torture techniques. Perhaps a most significant parallel here is the extension and perpetuation of female enslavement through torture. Young female children were threatened and/or tortured into confessing against their mothers; young girls were forced to watch their mothers tortured and then often burned at the stake without the usual dispatchment by an executioner. (Lois Brynes, of Clark University, drew my attention to these parallels.)

Women now working on issues and problems of women survivors of the Nazi holocaust, note many, too many, connections— and particularly powerful ones—with the situation of women in Latin America—gender defined issues. As males were in hiding, mothers and their children were often picked up for "interrogation;" mothers were threatened with the murder of their daughters, the daughters threatened with being forced to watch the torture of their mothers. "They seemed to have a sense of exactly what would terrorize you the most." (Tamara March, *Reflection from a Shattered Mirror*, w.i.p). In these survivors, we see clearly the long-term impact of heinous, authorized torment. We also see the psychic complexities of being one who survives, not only in terms of memory and of what is passed to and through the next generation, but of the subtle, insidious torture of "blaming the victim," for even the sympathetic analyzers use grounds for discussion that imply some ineffable sort of option. These modes of schematizing patriarchy, as it reveals itself under stress, only serve to perpetuate myth systems in their external manifestations and devastating internalization.

Related to what may be described as the final psychic torture through the theme of collaboration in one's family's, community's, or even one's own destruction is the "token torturer" (see, e.g., Mary Daly, *GynEcology*). My interviews reveal that there are women with the bureaucratic apparatus who have duties related to torture. A closer examination of their role reveals that they are in low-level, powerless positions. They are not in charge or ordering torture, when and how it should start, if and when it should end; they are not involved in developing the equipment that is used, nor in the apparently predictable, imaginative sessions that design torment for women. The women involved in these state institutions play supplementary roles to and for male officials. Therefore, it is important to learn more about how women are used by the military state for these supportive activities in torture, which women are selected, and the effect this subordinate collaboration has on these women.

Just as we should look twice, as feminists, at the shaven heads of so-called collaborators, we should strongly object to the common male stereotype of the Teutonic fascist woman guard in a concentration camp. She is most probably a figment of the patriarchal imagination, as she by no means devises and runs the state's torture machines.[4]

The Comadres of El Salvador: A Case Study

Mariclaire Acosta

The story told here by a Salvadoran woman shows how she and others have become involved in the political process while their country was in the midst of revolutionary conflict and massive repression, such as characterizes El Salvador today. This essay is based on testimony given during the Duarte regime, when disappearances increased dramatically. I conducted a number of interviews with Miriam, a leading member of the Committee of Mothers and Relatives of Political Prisoners, Disappeared and Assassinated Persons of El Salvador. This committe, a human rights organization formed by the relatives of the victims of repression (mostly female), is commonly known as the Comadres.

The interviews took place in Mexico City, where Miriam now lives and works as a representative of the Comadres. We met once a week for a period of a little over a year, in order to record her life-history and involvement in the political struggle of her country.

The first section of the essay discusses the impact of State terrorism on Miriam's life and goes on to explain how the disruption of her normal routine and the stigmatization of her family forced her to appeal to an organized group to seek the psychological and political support necessary for her survival. The reader will observe how Miriam's concern for her personal situation develops into an awareness of the plight of other women, collective solidarity, and eventually the full recognition of her political role as a member of the Comadres. The Comadres, a group sustained by the ideology of motherhood, aims to open a political space by denouncing the repressive nature of the present Salvadoran government.

In a sense, the story revealed in this testimony is similar to other experiences of women throughout Latin America who have either founded or participated in organizations akin to Comadres. These have flourished in the past several decades in response to the massive human rights violations committed by different military regimes in the region. The motivation of members of organizations similar to the Comadres is most often identical to that of Miriam.

The essay's second section leaves the realm of the personal and describes the history and development of the Comadres. This group began as an association of the victims of political repression and eventually became a full-fledged organization with international recognition. It is devoted to the defense of fundamental human rights, with an impressive array of strategies and methods designed to counteract the effects of State terror on Salvadoran society. Another important aspect of the Comadres is to force the successive governments of the country to account for the tens of thousands of political killings and disappearances which have taken place since 1972.

The final section of the testimony describes the situation of the Comadres during the the Duarte government as a human rights group playing a leading role in the mobilization of mass support for social change and seeking an end to the civil war that has raged in that country since 1980. The Comadres demand a negotiated peace settlement between the contending political and military forces, represented on one hand by the U.S. backed Christian Democratic Duarte government, and on the other, by the FDR-FLMN, a coalition of political-military organizations involved in guerrilla warfare.

In the course of my research, several questions developed concerning the changes the Committee has undergone since its foundation. Although the Comadres is not a politically ideological group but a human rights organization associated with the Catholic Church, there is no doubt that it has begun to play an important role in the political process of its country.

Both in its strategies, as well as in the political rhetoric, the Committee has moved away from traditional demands of organizations of its kind to a broader conception of the role of human rights and their importance in a revolutionary context (McLeod, 1986). The Committee plays a leading role in the mobilization of the country's urban population against war and in favor of peace and social justice.

During the 1970s, women appeared on the political scene all over Latin America, organizing and conducting a series of social movements articulated around labor and consumer demands, human rights issues, and various problems posed by gender, age-group and ethnic identities. (De Barbieri and Oliveira, 1986) However, the reasons explaining how and why women in Latin America are beginning to mobilize for a large share of political power continues to be explored. (De Barbieri and Oliveira, 1986; Chuchryk, 1986; Bonder, 1983)

The first group of this sort to emerge publicly appeared in Bolivia in 1972, followed by a similar organization in Chile during the year 1974. Since then, many similar organizations have sprouted up throughout the region, the most widely known being perhaps the Mothers of Plaza de Mayo, which appeared in Argentina in 1977, during the period of military dictatorship in that country when terror was at its peak.

Most of these organizations employ similar strategies and share the same origins. They all represent a popular response to counteract the effects of organized State terror on their respective societies. They have many things in common: they all emerged as apolitical grass roots movements led by female relatives of the victims of repression, who took up an organized search for their loved ones, and gradually moved on to more "political" activities under the banner of human rights.

In 1981, these different groups formed a federation, FEDEFAM, (Federación de Familiares de Detenidos Desaparecidos). Since then, FEDEFAM has undertaken the leadership in the struggle for human rights in Latin America, emphasizing the need for the true observance of these rights.

In periods of acute depression, these organizations of victims' relatives have played a fundamental role in easing the hold of organized terror over the population and in mobilizing support for the broader issues, such as respect for the rule of law and fundamental human rights. They are movements considered subversive by the government because they undermine the power of State terrorism by creating a pole of active resistance to organized fear. (H. Vidal, 1982) Whether they are capable of changing the balance of power in their respective countries is another matter. This possibility seems to be related to other factors, such as the political process itself, as well as the role of other activists. In the case of the Comadres, the facts that they have the support of the Catholic Church and that there is an ongoing revolutionary movement in El Salvador have been very important in their transition from a human rights group to an organization committed to change. This has not necessarily been true in other situations, such as the case of the GAM (Grupo de Apoyo Mútuo) in Guatemala, or the Mothers of Plaza de Mayo in Argentina, (McLeod, 1986; Tiffenberg, 1984) where the church has allied itself with the government in power.

In the particular context of this interview, women were clearly *thrown* into the political arena by circumstances that made them victims of the State terror still practiced today in El Salvador. Although many women are somewhat involved in politics, only a core group are active political leaders. What sets these political leaders apart from other women? Could it be the particular manner in which they suffered from repression? Or rather, does the answer to the question lie elsewhere, such as in their particular life histories or in the involvement of their husbands, sons, and other male relatives? Does their participation in politics stem from a family tradition learned in childhood? Questions such as these arose in the course of my interviews, as well as some answers to them.

It would be misleading to claim that all of these questions are covered in the following testimony. Yet, of all the life-histories that I collected, this one best portrays how and under what conditions the movement was started and how the group has evolved since then. It also includes how the Comadres view themselves and their new role in the human rights arena. The description has great value because it represents the voice of a protagonist and her own visionary perspective of the movement. It also provides a moving account of the effects of State terror in Latin American societies and of how different social groups and institutions have reacted to it.

I have deliberately omitted from the account the story of my source's life before entering the Mother's Committee. This is because I believe the key to comprehending the nature of female political participation is found in the events that shape the women's destiny, pushing them to make contact with and become active in groups like the Comadres.

Testimony

They call me Miriam. I am 41 years old, and I joined the Mothers' Committee in 1979 when my husband was kidnapped and disappeared by security forces in San Salvador during the Duarte government. He was a student and a photographer, and because of his political involvement, he was sent to prison where he spent several months. Barely a few weeks after he was released he disappeared. I found his corpse in a body dump on the outskirts of the city some time later. He was terribly mutilated, but I recognized him, and thanks to God, I was able to give him a decent Christian burial. I was very lucky. Very few women in my position have found the bodies of their loved ones.

He was my second husband; we were together for six years and had two girls and a boy. Only the girls survived. The little boy died shortly after birth. Since I had another child, a boy, from a previous marriage, we brought up a total of three children. We were happy together. I used to work as a clothes vendor in different markets around the countryside. We lived with his family. After he was sent to jail, all that changed. My mother-in-law was so frightened, and since she had already lost another son, murdered by the Death Squads, I promised her I would leave the house and set out on my own with the children.

I was able to find lodgings not far from where I lived before. In those days, the year 1979, things were terrible in El Salvador. Terror was rampant. Many people were kidnapped by the animals, which is what we call the Death Squads, and killed. Their bodies were mutilated and then burned in the refuse dumps for the pigs to eat.

For my own protection, I had to change my name and not let my new neighbors know that my husband was a political prisoner. His detention had been in the newspapers because they accused him and his companions of all sorts of crimes. The children were very small—except the boy, who was twelve—and they also learned to keep their mouths shut. We could trust nobody. The National Guard and other security forces had a lot of stool pigeons and collaborators around, and if the neighborhood found out my real situation, we could be classified as "subversives" and God knows what could happen.

It was during this period that I decided to go to the Mothers' Committee and seek help. I knew about them because of Monsignor Romero's—the Archbishop of San Salvador—preachings. So I went to the

Archbishopric, where I knew they had a small office, to state my case. I was also lucky enough to be able to talk to Monsignor Romero personally, and he denounced my husband's capture in his Sunday homily.

He gave me strength to go on, and the Mothers' Committee did a great deal to help me. They kept in touch with the political prisoners even when their families were forbidden to see them, so I was able to find out about my husband and send him food and other things. They also gave me some economic support to ease my situation for the time being.

When my husband was released, I never thought I would have to join the Committee. As far as I was concerned, the whole thing was over...

Of course we had to move again and find a place to live where nobody knew us. We found a small room in a suburb of San Salvador, close to one of the markets where I had clients.

The kidnapping came two months after my husband's release. It was on the day of my little girl's birthday. He had insisted on celebrating it, so I had a cake and some little gifts ready. We waited up all night, but he never came back. Of course, I knew what had happened, but there was little I could do. We were sharing lodgings with other families in that house, and naturally they were very curious to know why he hadn't come back. I pretended that he was having an affair and cried to them that he had probably chosen that very same day to visit his mistress. They were sympathetic and consoled me, but I knew what had really happened, so early in the morning, before sunrise, I took the children and ran, leaving my belongings behind.

I knew that the Mothers' Committee was the only place to go. I didn't dare go to my mother-in-law's or anywhere else. It was too dangerous for them so I went back to the Archbishopric. The Committee kept track of the kidnappings, and a few days later they confirmed what I already knew: that my husband had been taken by the Death Squads and was disappeared.

At the Committee, I found the strength and consolation that I needed. It was the only place where I could really be myself and express my tremendous grief and suffering. The rest of the women were wonderful. Everyone there had also suffered a loss, so it was easier to make oneself understood. With them, I could feel safe. Since I was desperately searching for my husband, I was assigned the task of visiting the body dumps with other women who were also looking for their husbands and sons. It was a terrible time. I had nowhere to leave my two little girls, so after work, I would take them with me to identify bodies. They were terribly frightened and aside from the frightful things that we would encounter, they were also afraid that the National Guard would find out about us and kill us. My eldest girl has had a heart condition and many psychological problems since then. The smallest one was still a baby, so it wasn't so hard on her. They used to cry a lot, and I would feel my heart bursting with pain. I was fortunate enough to find his body. It was a great relief. After that, I would take the children to visit their father at his grave.

After this experience, I decided to stay on with the committee. It was the only place where I felt I belonged. I was assigned other various tasks that were compatible with my occupation of selling in the different markets of the region. This went on for several years until one day I was sent here, to Mexico, to represent the Committee, almost two years ago. I brought my two girls with me, (since the boy married at seventeen), but unfortunately I have been unable to keep them with me since I work all day and have nobody to help me look after them in this enormous city. I sent them back some months ago to live with another mother in El Salvador, where I know they are safe and looked after well. I miss them very much, as well as my companions in the Committee. I am very lonely. I do not like Mexico at all. Nothing: the people, the food, nothing. Everything is awful. But I have a duty to fulfill, and that is to tell the world about our struggle for peace and justice in our country.

We are the mothers of the people. We started looking for our children and loved ones, and now we do for others what they can't do for themselves. That is why, after a while, one becomes insensitive to pain, fear, and even death. I don't know what it is, but we take on a spiritual strength that helps us when we have to look for unidentified bodies among the coffee bushes. We have been joined together in our pain. This group of mothers has renounced the love of life in order to keep up our struggle and to share the joy or pain of a people at war. One becomes conscious of this through suffering and grief.

There are seven hundred of us now in the Committee, mostly women. We come from all social classes, but mostly we come from the poor classes, because those are the ones who have been hit hardest by the repression. Our numbers increase every day, and now we even have incorporated some mothers of soldiers who have disappeared in action. You see, since we fight for the people as a whole, we called upon all the mothers of El Salvador to join, and these women have come to us because their sons were buried in a common grave, nobody knows where.

The Committee works in the following way. First we have several groups that perform different tasks, such as investigating the denunciations brought to us and keeping a record of them. We also have a group that writes bulletins and press releases and broadcasts daily for 20 minutes on YSAX, the Church station. This program is called *Desde la prisión* (from prison), and it gives news about the political prisoners with whom we are in touch every day. This group also organizes the monthly masses in commemoration of Monsignor Romero's assassination, our bi-weekly sit-ins at the Ministry of Justice, and other marches.

Another group keeps up the contacts and relationships with the labor unions, political organizations, government offices, and the press. Every two weeks we hold a press conference with foreign and national correspondents. This committee is also the one that organizes the representation of Comadres in Costa Rica, Mexico and Canada.

There is another group that gives material aid to the families of the victims as well as to the prisoners themselves. We manage to give them a weekly ration of rice, beans, sugar and milk. We are very interested in working with the displaced people who live in the shantytowns of San Salvador and all over the country. The mothers in this group seek them out, investigate their cases, obtain legal support, if possible, and give them whatever material aid they can.

All of our decisions are made collectively. Our task is to go everywhere, to tell the people, denounce what goes on, and give talks. There is much work to do, for instance, investigating the clandestine jails or picking up information in the streets, parks or buses.

Our task is to bring the truth about what really goes on in El Salvador to the people. That is what we do. Every two weeks we organize a "sit-in." In these public demonstrations, each one of us carries a poster with the photograph and details of her disappeared relative. In every "sit-in," the denunciations that have come to us during the past two weeks are read out loud, as well as the position of the Comadres on a series of issues such as the dialogue between the government and the insurgents, the bombings of the civilian population that the government carries out, and the forced recruitment of soldiers. Every poster carries the legend "They were taken away alive; we want them back alive."

Most of our sit-ins take place in the Cathedral, in downtown San Salvador. Some also take place in front of the U.S. Embassy, the Legislative Assembly, or the Ministry of Justice.

I think that women tend to join the Committee more than men do because we are the givers of life. You see, we give our children life. When they are kidnapped or murdered, as mothers or relatives we naturally try to find out what happened. Sometimes, when a mother finds out that her captured son was not involved in political affairs, she asks herself "But if my son was not involved, why did they kill him?" Maybe he was unlucky enough to be killed at a road barrier, or they may have taken him out of his house by force because a neighbor suspected him. So not all those who die are "subversives" like they make us want to believe. Many innocent people die. This is when a mother suddenly becomes conscious of these things, and says to herself: "Why should I not die? If my son died for nothing, if I also have to die; then it will be for something worthwhile, something that I shall have done. Something more important." This is how many women acquire their consciousness.

Sometimes a woman knows that her husband or son participated in something political, like a labor union, for example. Then she may decide to take up his cause, and she says: "If my son died, it was not because he wanted to harm anybody, but because he saw how others were being exploited and ignored. Maybe they needed a better salary and nobody listened to them." This is how her pain and suffering become the will to fight and to tell the people what is really happening.

Sometimes it takes a long time for a woman to join our struggle. I'll give you an example: a woman comes to the Comadres to denounce the disappearance of her son. Well, we go with her to the police, who always deny he is there. Then we go to the Red Cross (the International one) and then to the Human Rights Committee (the one of the people, not the one of the government), and denounce his capture everywhere. We try to give some consolation and share with her whatever we have in the Committee: food, clothes, and shelter. We try to make her feel that she is not alone and write press communiques and open letters to the newspapers trying to publicize her problem. Then it is not the mother alone who has the problem, but the whole Committee. She knows she is not alone because, after that, somebody visits her every week to give her information and asks her to join and take part in our activities and give testimony. After a while, you begin to notice the change in her. She starts reacting and no longer just stays at home to cry. She feels better, is more animated, and wants to go on living. This is when her consciousness begins, and after a while, she joins us in our visits to the embassies and jails.

Our Committee was founded on Christmas Eve, 1977. Previous to that year, we were just women who were desperately searching everywhere for our sons and relatives. We would go and see Monsignor Romero, the

Archbishop of San Salvador, and share with him all our grief and despair. He became the shepherd of his people. The women knew that Monsignor Romero was with them. So one day he invited a group to supper on Christmas Eve, along with some other priests, and proposed to them that they start the Committee. He compared these women to the Virgin Mary and told them that they had to join their voices in order to be heard. It was then that he offered the radio program, which we still have, and the first denunciations were broadcast. Monsignor was the founder of the Comadres. He told the mothers not to fight for only one of the victims, but for the people.

For a time, the mothers met in the Archbishopric, until the Committee was able to find an office of its own. But before that, because of security reasons, the Committee met in the fields or in out-of-the-way places. When I joined, it was still like that. In order to hold a meeting, we would pretend to go on an outing in the surrounding countryside. We would choose a place and sit under a tree. There, we would write out our communiques and discuss various ways to make our voices heard. Everybody would pitch in. When the meeting ended, we would leave in groups of threes in order to avoid suspicion. The Monsignor's support was very important to us in those days. We used to communicate all our decisions to him. He lent us his bank account, so that our first financial aid was given to us through him. The money was used to buy things for the political prisoners, like medicine and food, and also to pay for our press releases.

At first, we would just go together to the barracks and police stations to inquire about the victims. Since that didn't work we realized that we had to make the largest number of people find out in the shortest period of time that someone had been captured. If a kidnapping is publicized immediately, the person has a better chance of survival. So little by little, we realized that we had to be more active and visible. That was when we decided to start "taking" our public places, like churches or government offices. The point of these actions was not only to take the place in a nonviolent way but also to make sure that it was full of people, especially children. This way, they became our "hostages," and through them we acquired some strength to make the government hear our voices.

In order to do a sit-in at a church or a public office, we had to plan very carefully. We would break up into small groups, and some of us would enter the place, say a church, and announce to those inside that they were our hostages until the government agreed to hear our petitions, which we read to them. In the meantime, another group of women would stay outside to watch as well as to mobilize the public and explain what was happening. Another group had to figure out a way to get food and drink to the people inside, and others would conduct the negotiations with the government. We decided on this tactic of taking "hostages" because the press began to refuse to publish our bulletins. It was very risky. One time, we decided to take the Red Cross offices for three months. It was terrible.

Often we were thrown out violently by the security forces. Then, a group of us would start a commotion in the street to draw attention to our cause. After the Red Cross, our most important action was the "taking" of the Cathedral.

After some time, things began to ease up, and we again had access to the newspapers and other media. After a while, the Committee decided to link up with the rest of the world. This was in 1978, and a delegation was sent to Mexico.

Some time later, we were strong enough to have our own offices. By 1980, when the leaders of the Electrical Workers Union (STECEL) were captured, we had an office and held our first press conference there. At the time, we decided to go to the barracks of the National Guard where prisoners were held, to pressure the Guard to let the prisoners go. I was among the chosen ones. We had to leave our documents at the entrance, and they made us carry an ID card around our necks. We finally saw our companions in a large room, on the floor, all tied up like animals. The Guards jeered at us and asked why didn't we form a group to protect their human rights against the guerrillas.

Anyway, after this incident, we decided to go to the schools and factories to ask for food and clothes for the new prisoners. This was a way to spread the word a bit further. It worked, and we found all sorts of ingenious ways to enter the factories without arousing suspicion. Once, when a member of the Committee was captured, we decided to spread the news by stuffing fliers into some egg-crates that we took to the markets.

Little by little, we discovered international support. That was when we began to travel. Now we are known outside El Salvador and have offices in Mexico, Costa Rica and Canada. Two years ago, we were awarded the Robert F. Kennedy prize in the United States, but only one of us was able to collect it. The State Department denied the other two delegates visas. Recently we were given another prize, the Bruno Kreisky award in Austria.

We have travelled all over the world telling people about our work and about our grief, but mainly asking them to help us end this war that is causing us so much grief and pain.

We have paid a high price for all of this activity. Many of us have had to leave the country. Our families have been destroyed, and many of us have been captured, tortured and even killed. The latest case was only last May, when María Teresa Tula was kidnapped by a Death Squad and raped and knifed in Cuscatlán Park. A few weeks later, she was captured again and sent to jail, where her baby was born. Fortunately, the strength we have gained was large enough to force the National Guard to release her. Everyone came to our aid, and people are no longer afraid to protest. But as long as this war goes on, incidents like this are common in El Salvador, and our Committee is not immune to them.

We will continue to fight and struggle wherever we can: in the streets, abroad, everywhere, to make the voice of the Salvadoran people heard. They have tried to silence us by murder and death, but they will never succeed. We are the voice of the people, and we have given the people back their courage and strength to tell the truth. Even if they murder us down to the last one, we will still speak the truth.

Yet, we do not merely seek the truth about repression. We have come a long way over the last nine years. Now we also want a liberated people, a people with the freedom to express whatever they want and to be equal. We want a country where children can have their milk, their food, a roof over their head and a doctor to look after them.

We want a free country, a country free to choose its own representatives, who can appreciate the rights of their citizens and look after their people. The people of El Salvador are at war because they are tired of being exploited. If they ever win this war, better leaders have to emerge, leaders with more awareness of what is really needed. Those who govern now are the rich, and they can't care about us because they have never suffered hunger and cold. They don't know what it's like to be illiterate like me or to have to sleep on the sidewalk. They despise the poor because they have never put themselves in those persons' place. They do not care about them as persons, only about their work.

So this is why there is a war. There is no way out. It is the only thing left to the people: rebellion against suffering and hunger. The people are tired of death and being hungry.

War is the result of all this, and the Comadres want the war to end. We demand that the government and the guerrillas start a dialogue. We are on nobody's side. We need peace, we want peace, and it has to be peace with justice. As a Christian organization, we want this war to stop because we cannot go on like this any longer. That is why we want negotiation. If Mr. Reagan of the United States sends money to the government to continue the war instead of for the thousands of orphans or widows, then we have to hold him responsible for all the deaths and suffering. When a country is at war, not only those who are in combat die; a whole people dies.

That is why we want peace. For it to be real peace, it has to be accompanied with justice. That is, a peace where people's rights will be respected. Our real struggle is for human rights. And for us, human rights are the rights to work, to go to school, to join a union, to say what we want ... These are the rights of the people. Human rights are part of life ...

• • •

Miriam's testimony offers a detailed account of how a popular strategy against massive repression appeared and became consolidated in El Salvador.

Leaving aside the fact that the political context of that country is very particular since El Salvador is involved in a civil war and a revolution is in the making, the mothers' movement for human rights described by her is very similar to others which have made their appearance in Latin American countries dominated by militarism. Thus, Comadres is only one part of a broad social movement for democracy, compromising practically the whole region. (FEDEFAM: 1986).

This movement is a genuine grass roots response to the effects of militarism and the destruction of social relations and structures implicit in the Doctrine of National Security (Acosta: 1984). The groups all share a highly important merit: the ability to curtail the effects of organized terror on their society and to reveal the destructive impact of militaristic governments on the social body. This is no small feat. It requires a degree of heroism which can only be explained by the extreme suffering of these women. In a sense, they have been driven out of their normal lives by forces which they do not understand at first, and gradually, as their struggle to regain normality develops, they realize the extreme abnormality of the situation. This is their great strength: they are able to de-legitimize, by virtue of their grief, the ideological base upon which authoritarian governments stand.

Clearly the development of mothers' movements for human rights signifies the emergence of women as a new political force in Latin America. But does this mean that these women have discovered a feminine way of doing politics? Will these movements break down traditional gender-domination structures? Are they feminist? Their participants claim that in the process of their political activity, they have acquired a consciousness of themselves as persons, which they did not have before (Chuchryk: 1986; Bonafini: 1985), and have also innovated political strategies and types of action that are specifically feminine (Moscardi: 1986). This is clearly seen in Miriam's testimony. Giving aid and relief to political prisoners and their families and adopting children can be seen merely as an extension of the mothering role. However, the political content of this activity is radically different from normal charitable action: the Comadres have to mother a whole people because the institutions that normally do so in society have proven their inability.

In any event, the impact of these organizations on Latin American societies and politics is still an open question and must be dealt with on a country-to-country basis. However, one fact is evident: mothers' movements for human rights are here to stay, and will continue to play an important role in the political process.

Children and Human Rights

Children and Human Rights in Latin America

Elena O. Nightingale
and
Rachel E. Wurf

James P. Grant, executive director of UNICEF, notes that "The care and protection of children is a practice and an ethic rooted deep in the wisdom and culture of all societies." (Castelle, 1989) While this may be fundamentally true, many countries all over the world ignore or abuse the rights of children. This is true for Latin America, where widespread political unrest, and the resulting governmental instability and terrorism lead to the disruption of daily life for citizens of many countries. This essay explores the human rights abuses to which children and their parents are subjected in certain Latin American countries, and discusses what measures can be taken to eradicate such abuses and to preserve and protect children's basic rights.

Different nations place greater value on certain human rights. Historically, socialist countries have placed greater value on economic and social rights, for example, while the United States of America has placed greatest value on political rights and civil liberties. Some repressive governments have claimed that in order to promote economic, social and cultural rights they have had to deny political and civil rights.

Despite differing perceptions of the relative value of particular human rights, most countries have paid little attention to the specific rights of children. The concept of children's rights did not even originate until the early part of the twentieth century. The United Nations Convention on the Rights of the Child, adopted by the U.N. General Assembly on November 20, 1989 and signed by sixty-one countries on January 26, 1990, provides a framework for governments and other adults regarding their responsibilities to children. The Convention defines a child as every human being below the age of eighteen. Exceptions to this definition are made if, by the laws of a particular country, a child attains majority at an earlier age. The Convention categorizes the rights and needs of children according to three main areas:

- **The Right to Survival** through the provision of adequate food, shelter, clean water, and primary health care.
- **The Right to Protection** from abuse, neglect and exploitation, including the right to special protection in times of war.
- **The Right to Develop** in a safe environment, through the provision of formal education, constructive play, advanced health care, and the opportunity to participate in the social, economic, religious and political life of the culture—free from discrimination. (Castelle, 1989)

The Convention also deals with children's social, economic, cultural, civil, and political rights. Like the Universal Declaration of Human Rights, the Convention sets common standards to strive for. Yet governments and regimes all over the world fail to protect the rights of children.

In Latin America in 1970, 26 million children under six years of age lived in absolute poverty. By 1980, the total had risen to 35.5 million, and the projection for the year 2000 is 51 million. (Jupp, 1990) Children living under these conditions clearly suffer from the denial of their most basic human rights.

A vast number of children also suffer from more intentional abuse. Amnesty International has documented the use of torture against children in Peru, Guatemala, Argentina (Amnesty International-USA,1990b) Chile and Ecuador (Amnesty International-USA, 1988) among other countries. In these countries, children are often arrested and detained. In South Africa, until 1988, children were specific targets of detention and even torture! In El Salvador, children younger than 18 years of age have been recruited into the armed services, and Defense for Children International-USA notes that there have been "reports of hundreds of under-age children being forcibly recruited into the armies of Central America ..." (Defense for Children International-USA, 1989)

Latin American children also suffer from devastating human rights abuses. "Disappearance" of one or both parents, which occurred frequently during the "dirty war" in Argentina, family disruption, hunger, and lack of education all take their toll on children.

Torture is the most extreme and vicious form of human rights abuse, and when children are tortured, the heinousness of this crime is impossible to ignore. Torture is the *deliberate* infliction of pain by one person on another. The essential feature of torture is that at least two persons are involved: a perpetrator and a victim. The perpetrator has physical control over the victim, and torture is both purposeful and systematic. The difference between torture and child abuse, for example, is that torture is not a matter of individual aberration, but is instead state-sanctioned violence for political purposes.

Children may be tortured to extract information about their parents, other family members, or their friends and neighbors. Amnesty International told the story of Alberto Alarcón, an eight-year-old boy who lives with his father in Tungurahua in Napo province, Ecuador.

> One morning in May 1987, soldiers burst into his home and attacked him and his father. Alberto was thrown over a roll of barbed wire and beaten. His head was held under water until he almost drowned. The soldiers repeatedly asked him about a rifle they said a neighbor had stolen. (Amnesty International-USA, 1988)

Children may also be tortured to force their parents to speak, or to do what the torturer wants. Nothing works as well as being forced to watch a young son or daughter being tortured. Children are also tortured by being forced to watch the torture of their parents. On May 14, 1988, an eleven-year-old Peruvian boy witnessed the following events:

> Soldiers wearing black ski masks, armed with heavy weapons ... made his father lie on the ground ... one kicked him while another hit him with the butt of a gun. He clung to his father and told the soldiers that his father was innocent, but the sol-

diers frightened him away with a cattle whip ... He didn't want to look after he heard a man cry out when they were stepping on him; [a boy] ... told him ... that they had killed his father, and he was frightened and hid his head because he didn't want to look; he didn't see his father again. Later, the soldiers told them to get away and he ran, along with the women, some of whom told him that they had cut off his father's head. (Amnesty International-USA, 1990a)

Children are also tortured to frighten and intimidate the entire community because if the community knows that even children are not exempt from torture, it becomes obvious that there is nowhere to hide, that there is no way out. Amilcar Méndez, the founder of Consejo de Comunidades Étnicas "Runujel Junam" (CERJ)[1] (Amnesty International-USA,1989), has reported threats and harassment against himself, his family and members of CERJ. For weeks his home was under continuous surveillance by heavily armed civilian-clad officers. Approximately one month after he had received anonymous phone calls warning him that his home would be searched, his fifteen-year-old niece, Iris Yomila Reyes Urizar, was captured by the head of the military detachment in San Andrés Sajcabaja, El Quiche. She was raped while in custody. (Amnesty International, 1990b)

Similar incidents have occurred in other Latin American countries. The case of Joelito Filartiga is well-known. The seventeen-year-old son of a noted physician in Paraguay, Joelito was taken from his home by the police in 1976, tortured and murdered, simply because of his father's work with the poor in Paraguay. After Joelito's death, a peasant told his father:

> You may not understand Doctor, what is happening to you ... But we do understand. Your son was killed, not because he was the son of Filartiga, but because he was the son of one serving us, the poor people. The punishment is not just for you, but it is also for us, the poor. (Claude, 1982)

The Filartigas eventually brought the man responsible for Joelito's murder to trial in New York City, and he was convicted.

Often, soldiers or secret police of repressive regimes are not the only ones who participate in torture. Governments frequently enlist the aid of physicians in this process, sometimes coercing uncooperative physicians into assisting by threatening the physicians or their families. Physicians have examined detainees prior to torture, monitored torture, taken part in torture itself, developed torture techniques, falsified medical information on detainees, revealed confidential information of their patients to the authorities, and, most importantly, have remained silent in the presence of torture.

In Uruguay, a school conducted a "practical course in torture" attended by officers from several Central and South American countries. The object was to accustom the students to taking part in torture. The course doctor, Dr. Roberto Scarabino Caravodosi, would revive victims so they could be tortured again. Army doctors in Chile and other countries have also monitored torture victims so they would not die and could be tortured again. (Quilliam et al., 1986)

During torture and detention, beatings and kicks on the head are the most common abuses. These may lead to permanent brain damage, seizures and intense headaches. For girls, even very young ones, rape is the most common abuse. The consequence of rape ranged from sexually-transmitted diseases and serious injury and mutilation of the reproductive organs to sterility and inability to form a trusting and loving relationship with any man.

The long-term effects of severe trauma on children depend on the age of the child. In general, the younger the child, the more serious the damage to the development of mental health. The reactions to trauma are also dependent on the stage of development of the child. The response of younger children may be serious repression and withdrawal, while school-age children may respond with depression or by acting out. In any case, the traumatic experience may adversely affect children's future relationships, even with their own children.

Attempts to break the will of a child will clearly have serious psychological effects on that child, but the damage is even more severe when a double violation of a child's trust occurs—that is, violation by adults and by the State.

In Chile, from the time when Augusto Pinochet seized power in 1973 until the democratic elections, children grew up in a climate of fear. For this generation, there is a widespread lack of trust in those institutions that ostensibly protect the citizen—the military and the police. A child growing up in this environment can have no sense of security and safety. Even if the child is not physically harmed, the emotional damage done by waiting for a parent to return can be devastating. The husband of Monica

Chislayne Llanca Iturra, who "disappeared" in Chile in September 1974, when her son was two years old, tells of his son's pain:

> The years passed, and the child grew up and asked for his mother. I had to answer truthfully: "The soldiers took her away but she will come back." And the child longed for his mother to return and used to say, "When Mummy comes, we'll raise chickens," or "We'll buy such and such a thing." But suddenly one day he surprised me and said, "Daddy, I think the soldiers killed Mummy"; now he won't talk about it. He's 13. (Amnesty International-USA, 1988)

During the second half of the 1970s, many Argentinean children suffered not only from the detention of their parents but were abducted with them by security forces. Others were born in detention, and separated from their parents shortly after birth. The emotional trauma of children who have suffered such grave human rights abuses is immeasurable. What will happen to those children who have grown up in repressive regimes? Children whose trust in adults and authority in general has been eroded may eventually become violent towards their families or towards the political regime in power.

Only harm can come from a society that brutalizes children. If they survive, without effective treatment, these children will bear the scars of the way they were treated for their entire lives.

To treat children in Chile who have survived the horrors of torture, the Foundation for the Protection of Children Harmed by the State of Emergency (PIDEE) was created by a group of volunteers in 1979. The foundation provides medical, psychological, educational and legal assistance to children who have been tortured, forced to watch their parents being tortured, or hurt by the disappearance of loved ones. These children have sometimes lost the ability to speak. They suffer from headaches, anxiety and insomnia. They also suffer from confusion and shame. They do not understand why this was done to their parents, who were not criminals. Some have spent time in prison with their parents because they had nowhere else to go. One female political prisoner in Chile whose 18-month and three-year-old children spent a year in prison with her asked to give up the children because prison life was destroying them.

The therapeutic approach at PIDEE includes individualized play therapy, art, music and drama therapy as well as family and group therapies. Some children live at the Center while undergoing treatment. The staff is stretched to the limit, but the children benefit greatly. Ideally, pediatricians, child psychologists, psychiatrists, social workers and nurses should work together to rehabilitate the children using several kinds of treatment. Yet, in countries where torture continues, treatment centers operate under threat of closure and arrest of the staff.

Within the past five years, countries have begun to recognize the importance of giving special attention to children who are growing up under repressive regimes. The adoption of the UN Convention on the Rights of the Child is a crucial attempt to raise global awareness of children's human rights using international law as a starting point. The Convention, the first of its kind, sets legally-binding and universally-accepted minimum standards for the treatment of children.

Defense for Children International-USA, a human rights organization devoted entirely to children, considers the Convention to be "one of the most important pieces of human rights legislation in recent history." (Defense for Children International-USA, 1990)

The Convention will become part of the international law only when twenty member nations have ratified it. Thirty days after such ratification, the Convention will take effect only in those countries that have ratified it. While ninety nations had signed the Convention as of May 10, 1990, only three had actually ratified it up to that point. It is important to note that the United States has not yet signed the convention. Among those Latin American countries signing the convention were Belize, Bolivia, Brazil, Chile, Colombia, Costa Rica, Ecuador, El Salvador, Grenada, Guatemala, Mexico, Nicaragua, Panama, Paraguay, Peru, Surinam, Uruguay, and Venezuela. Of these nations, Belize and Ecuador have both ratified the Convention. (Defense for Children International-USA, 1990) The countries which have signed the Convention are not legally bound to its stature, but indicate by doing this that they accept the Convention's principles and will attempt to seek its ratification.

While the Convention is certainly indicative of tremendous progress in the area of human rights for children, it remains controversial. According to Thomas Hammarberg, "The Convention sets the age limit for recruitment to combat service as low as fifteen, and thereby indirectly legitimizes the use of fifteen- and sixteen-year-olds as combat soldiers." (Hammarberg, 1990) As we have already seen, this is a particular problem in Latin America. *The New York Times* reported that in El Salvador, the military "forcibly enlists 12,000 youths a year, often snatching teenagers as young as fourteen from poor and rural families ..." (*New York Times*,

1989)

If the Convention is successful, children and adults all over the world will become aware that children are protected under international law. The document will be the standard-setting device of international human rights, and governments will be held accountable for upholding these standards. Most importantly, ratification of the Convention will raise children's rights on the global political agenda. Hammarberg agrees. "The rights of children should not be subject to petty political disputes; it has to be recognized that firm political measures are needed. The full implementation of the Convention will require political determination. (Hammarberg, 1990)

As it stands, the Convention has yet to be ratified. International human rights organizations are working to encourage ratification by offering information and training to those who work with children, establishing national commissions to coordinate governmental and non-governmental involvement in the ratification process, and taking other actions to increase knowledge about the Convention. In September, 1990, the first World Summit for Children will be held at the United Nations, at which many heads of State and key government representations will participate. Javier Pérez del Cuellar, the Secretary General of the UN, said that the summit's purpose is to engender attention and commitment to the survival, protection and development of children. (Jacobs, 1990)

Child advocacy groups, such as the United Nations International Children's Fund (UNICEF), have begun to address abuses of children's human rights on an international scale. Already, GOBI-FFF[2] programs promoting international child health have had a large impact, and at times, have even been able to overcome political considerations in the interest of child health.

While in the past many professionals have remained silent about human rights abuses, the mindset of many is changing rapidly. In Chile, the major medical association, the Colegio Médico de Chile, changed from turning a blind eye to becoming very active in protesting torture and exposing those physicians who took part in such acts. (Stover, 1987) In Brazil, the Archdiocese organized a project in which a million pages of documentation of torture of detainees derived from military documents, were copied clandestinely, microfiched, sent out of the country and published. Documentation, international exposure and condemnation of human rights abuses have proven effective.

To further this end, a global effort to focus attention on the rights of children has begun. The United States' American Academy of Pediatrics has recently established a committee specifically devoted to the human rights of children. Amnesty International has a new campaign on children and provides updates on the human rights situations in Latin America and other regions. Yet, these efforts, while an excellent start, have not proved to be enough. Improved means of gathering accurate information on torture and improved treatment methods for torture victims, particularly children, are urgently needed. Education about human rights abuses of children through publication in professional journals is crucial, and dissemination of this information must be expanded.

No matter how much hope we hold for the future of our increasingly interdependent world, if the children who will inherit the world are damaged by growing up under repressive and abusive circumstances, that future will be bleak for everyone.

"Children in the Storm": Psychosocial Trauma in Latin America

M. Brinton Lykes

A boy of 12 presented his collage to the group of children gathered. Amidst the twigs and flowers he had glued to his paper to represent the Guatemalan countryside, he had pasted a newspaper clipping of a plane and another of a soldier. His caretaker, an Indian woman who serves as "mother" to the house of 15 Guatemalan children who lost one or more of their parents in the violence of the early '80s, indicated in discussion after the Creative Workshop for Children that, although this young boy had not discussed the incident that led to his coming to the orphanage three years earlier, that is, the murder of his parents and the razing to the ground of his home, she imagined that it was still very present to him. "When I ask him why he draws helicopters or soldiers, he tells me that it is because he likes them. When I see the soldiers and the guns in the collage that he has done, I think that it is probably because he remembers what happened to his parents, that he is still thinking about it." (Guatemala, 1990)

In recent years, psychologists and other mental health workers have begun to document the effects of state-sponsored violence and civil war on civilians and to develop specific clinical and community interventions to address these issues. Such work represents a response to the demands by community members and leaders who document symptoms and behaviors that do not respond to medical intervention and/or persist over time. There have also been demands by families and friends of the disappeared, people imprisoned for political reasons, and those assassinated in military or para-military activities for both accompaniment in their political struggle and relief from the torment such experiences have left behind. Parents and caretakers increasingly report that children do not seem able to "bounce back" from a parent's death or from displacement. This essay describes some of the problems encountered by children in situations of war and/or state-sponsored terror in two Latin American countries and the development of one response called Creative Workshops for Children, an international, interdisciplinary program organized by mental health workers from Argentina, Guatemala and the United States.

Argentina and Guatemala

In Argentina, during the "dirty war" that spanned the last military dictatorship from 1976-1983, a succession of military "juntas" engaged in a brutal and bloody campaign of repression during which as many as 30,000 people, over 80% of whom were between the ages of 16 and 35, were detained and disappeared. The military presented themselves as the defenders of "tradition, family and property," and any criticism of their rule was seen as subversive behavior that needed to be crushed in order to protect the nation. This "war" required that Argentine society be restructured through a "Process of National Reorganization," in which Western and Christian values would again become preeminent.

During the past decade, between 50,000 and 100,000 Guatemalans have been murdered and at least 38,000 have disappeared. Over 400 rural villages were destroyed, and the Guatemalan army's scorched earth policy forced hundreds of thousands who survived to either flee to another part of the country or to leave Guatemala altogether. The primary victims of this "partial genocide" were Indians living in rural communities.

The Doctrine of National Security and "low-intensity warfare" [sic] were the ideological underpinnings for this extreme violence. Torture and disappearance were used extensively in hopes of reducing popular resistance, not only through killing leaders and community organizers but through controlling the entire population. The latter was achieved by creating situations of generalized insecurity and fear. These objectives are furthered through psychological tactics and have direct psychological consequences. For example, in Guatemala, torture, disappearance and murder are denied or redefined by the government and the press as deaths from "common crime." Victims are urged to "forget the past" so that the future may be more rapidly constructed. Argentine laws, such as the recent Presidential Pardon of convicted military leaders, permit assassins to walk the streets with the children of those they killed. Traumatic events that have undermined the very existence of thousands of human beings thereby receive no social validation, thus restricting the social reality in which these events occur to private memories. Fact is internalized and supposed reality is a fiction.[1]

Psychologists working with survivors of torture and disappearance describe these phenomena as central elements of a strategy for suppressing popular dissent, a central objective of "low intensity warfare." By attacking people's ability to distinguish what is true from what is not true or what they know based on personal experience as opposed to the "official story," the government attacks their sense of self, their knowledge of who they are.

Since the mid-1970s, mental health professionals in Chile, Argentina and Uruguay have collaborated with human rights groups organized by family members of political prisoners, the disappeared, and the murdered, that is, direct victims of government-sponsored terror.[2] These psychologists, psychiatrists and social workers are organized as voluntary psychosocial assistance teams or in non-governmental, often church-affiliated, social service organizations. They have provided critical services, including individual and group psychotherapy and community education and resource development. They have also rethought the very nature of the trauma experienced and the necessary forms of treatment and prevention needed for work in contexts of state-sponsored repression.

Systematic psychological assistance work in Central America began more recently. It is being developed by health promoters, leaders of communities, and grass roots organizations who are extending primary health care education and prevention strategies to promote mental health among affected populations. They have benefitted particularly from the re-conceptualization of trauma as a psychosocial rather than intra-psychic phenomenon coming from their own experiences of ongoing trauma; they are correcting misconceptions which describe selected symptoms and behavioral indices as evidence of "post traumatic stress disorder." This re-conceptualization thus describes a psychosocial phenomenon that constitutes, in the words of Salvadoran psychologist Ignacio Martín-Baro, the "concrete crystallization of dehumanizing social relations of exploitation and structural oppression."[3] Psychosocial trauma is not an unusual event in context of war; rather it is an everyday part of life in situations where the slaughter of individuals, the disappearance of loved ones, the fear to speak, and extreme polarization of social life have come to be accepted as normal, despite their clear abnormality.

A broad-based solidarity network emerged in 1987 to support those working to understand and confront the psychosocial consequences of state-sponsored terrorism. The network was organized to support communication and the exchange of information concerning (1) the effects of repression, (2) clinical and community activities in research and in prevention, focused on the recovery of those individuals, communities and social structures that have been affected and (3) local and global issues relevant to action among groups working in the area of mental health and human rights. One outgrowth of this communication has been collaborative work with child survivors.

Child Survivors of State-sponsored Terror

Children are among the most vulnerable victims of these repressive strategies. The Argentine military, for example, understood well the value of children in their struggle. Approximately 8,000 children lost one or both parents and more than 400 had disappeared themselves, thus terrorizing "suspected" families. Other children were made to witness torture sessions of their parents to force them to identify people and to provide information helpful to torturers. In other cases children themselves were tortured in front of their parents as a way of getting the parents to talk.[4]

The Argentine military developed a particular strategy of taking children born in captivity and giving them away as "war booty." Their reorganization of society required that children of "subversives" be removed from their families and given to "good" families (i.e., children of the military or of the upper classes).[5] General Campos, head of the police of the province of Buenos Aires when numbers of children were kidnapped there, said "... Personally, I did not eliminate any children. What I did was to give some of them to charity organizations so that they would find new parents for them. Subversives educate their children into subversion. That has to be stopped."[6]

Consequences of war for Central American children are equally grim. In Guatemala, more than 50% of the internal refugees and more than 60% of those in Mexico are children and adolescents. In addition, between 100,000 and 250,000 Guatemalan children lost one or both parents. Child soldiers have been identified in the ranks of both the URNG and the Guatemalan military. The Army has been repeatedly accused of forcibly "recruiting" poor children from rural areas long before they reach eighteen, the age of obligatory military service.

Many of the children remaining in or returning to Guatemala are forced to live in militarized zones. These are communities where most aspects of life are under direct or indirect surveillance, where most males will participate in "Civilian Patrols," and where re-education programs are typically required. Hundreds of other children barely survive on the streets of Guatemala City, robbing to support their meager existence, sniffing glue to dull their hunger pains, and struggling to avoid becoming victims of the ever-increasing violence in this Central American capital.

War has a particularly brutal effect on the development of children who are forced to construct a sense of self within contexts of seemingly permanent psychosocial trauma, of "normal abnormality." Although individual children respond in quite distinct ways, a small number of studies suggest that children in situations of institutionally-structured violence generally experience higher than usual levels of fear, anxiety, insecurity, and aggressiveness. They frequently have difficulties in expressing themselves corporally and/or emotionally, often experience nightmares, and exhibit both psychosomatic symptoms (chronic head and stomachaches, allergies, tics) and regressive behaviors such as bed-wetting. These symptoms and behaviors have been identified repeatedly by caretakers of Guatemalan Indian children in both orphanages and rural villages. In addition to these symptoms, some Argentine child survivors have been described as having highly-developed intellectual lives but as being emotionally immature.[7]

Ignacio Martín-Baro suggested that children in war situations face numerous existential dilemmas. They must decide between action, (i.e., joining the war as a child-soldier or fleeing). They must either aggressively adopt a socially-stigmatized identity, as, for example, guerrilla or union leader or accept the shutting down of options that can lead to an experience of alienation. They also face the "choice" between structuring a view of the world in terms of one of the polar realities in a situation where one is either friend or enemy and where ambiguity is not tolerated (polarization) and "being torn apart" by that very polarization.[8] Further, in Guatemala, the rupture of the traditional structure of Indian life that emphasizes community, where nature is considered sacred and people believe in an integral relationship between themselves and the land, contributes to creating a vulnerable population of children seriously at risk.

Alternative Strategies for the Promotion of Mental Health

Mental health workers seeking to intervene in such situations are not satisfied to treat individual level trauma. Their personal experiences and political commitment to accompany other survivors have led them to develop ways of addressing both the distorted relationships between social groups that construct and sustain the "normal abnormality" of State-sponsored terror and the effects of these relationships.

For example, Argentina's Movimiento Solidario de Salud Mental[9] developed creative workshops for children, essentially a therapeutic space for those directly affected by organized repression, their families, and the community as a whole. Through a group process, these mental health workers seek to offer a community experience as an alternative to the "traumatized abnormality" that prevails in a situation of State-sponsored repression. Using techniques of play, body movement, dramatization, drawing and creative storytelling, they engage children in a process of communication and self-discovery. In this context, with strengthened skills, the child can encounter some of her/his difficulties, express some of his/her emotions and, through a group process, establish and develop ties with others. Through specifically designed dramatizations, children learn to express aggressiveness within clearly-delineated boundaries and can begin to articulate their own understanding of the ways in which they have been violated.

One particular year-long workshop included children returned from exile and survivors of disappeared parents and ex-political prisoners. The coordinators developed a strategy for responding to and working with several behavioral issues they observed in ongoing groups, including aggressiveness, hyperactivity, and a resistance to respect limits set by the coordinator. They proposed that the group "play with disorder," that is, that they create havoc within a limited physical space, knowing that out of chaos can come creativity. The group was invited to destroy mounds of newspaper and other materials gathered in their workshop space. After a lengthy period of energetic play, the children spontaneously began to wrap themselves in the paper and cloth that they had ripped to shreds. They were then invited to create something from that which they had destroyed. Each chose a different figure, and with colors, papers and their own creativity they constructed costumes. Then they presented themselves as imaginary figures and persons who are marginalized in contemporary Argentine society: crazies (who are constrained in mental institutions), a transvestite (who is hidden from wider society), a martian and a monk (strangers from far away countries). Thus, in their play and in their dramatizations, the group was able to work with the behaviors identified and to socialize some of their feelings and experiences of being marginalized as survivors.

Drawing and playing have similar functions in the life of the child as do words in the life of an adult—ways to create, to imagine, to represent, and to express oneself. Through play and imagination, the child develops a sense of him/herself and the capacity to communicate with others. Ongoing work with several groups of children indicate that such workshops are important tools in the child survivor's continuing process of recovery and reintegration into the social order.

Guatemalan rural health promoters have found these experiences helpful as they develop community-based resources for work with child survivors of violence in their country. Training programs for Guatemalan health promoters as leaders of creative, integrated workshops with children are being developed by an interdisciplinary team of members from Argentina, Guatemala and the United States.[10] Significant cultural and historical differences led to the construction of a participatory methodology that draws heavily on the strengths and traditions of each participating team member. For example, Argentine and North American collaborators are learning how the rich Indian community structures of organization and religious practices that include dramatization, story-telling, and the use of masks facilitate health promoters' adaptation and implementation of certain techniques.

Guatemalans are discussing Western psychosocial models of child development and ways of "hearing" children's deepest feelings, which are not easily accessed through words. Through intense dialogue and shared practice, the team is developing more adequate theory and practice for work with rural children with strong indigenous roots and relatively little exposure to Western educational experiences. These workshops are organized as supplements to ongoing development and health projects and are designed to create a community-based context of care for Guatemalan children.

Last winter, approximately twenty-five health promoters, child caretakers, diocesan workers and educators gathered from various parts of rural Guatemala to participate in an introductory-level training workshop. Some participants worked with children at the time; others were in development programs that work with entire families and were beginning to develop specific health and mental health work with children. An Argentine actor from the MSSM joined me in coordinating this week-long training that began with developing a shared understanding of the situation of Guatemalan children with a particular focus on their mental health problems. The workshop was first and foremost participatory, for unless we can play as adults, we cannot learn to play with children. We engaged in multiple physical activities (including body movement techniques) to get to know ourselves, our physical environment, and each other. We used drawing, story-telling, collage, and dramatization to identify some of the effects of the violence in our own lives and to share experiences. Through this, we developed concrete strategies for working with children experiencing the effects of living in situations of ongoing economic and political repression. The participants then returned to their communities to work with children. This introductory workshop now forms part of a program that envisions the advanced training of a small group of Guatemalan health promoters who will coordinate a project in psychosocial assistance for Guatemalan children.

The techniques used in the workshops draw on the cultural traditions (i.e., oral story-telling and dramatization) and resources (i.e., nature, plants) of the indigenous communities within which they are being developed. This offers additional resources to those who collaborate in the development of mental health in their communities. Our objective is not that the child accumulate information or develop artistic skills. Instead, the goal is, in part, that he/she enhance natural means for communication that will facilitate the expression of physical and mental tensions. The other part of the goal is to facilitate the child's capacity to construct an identity that is not exclusively subject to the dehumanizing and traumatizing reality of war. Children can thereby recover some of the values that are part of their families' realities.

One health promoter indicated that with these techniques she can now better understand what children in her community think and feel. Another promoter said that the workshops provide a set of tools and a context wherein he can more fully respond to the questions of children. These children continue to ask "why" their parents were killed and their crops and homes destroyed. "Children do not forget," he added.

Through their own self-expression, these children can at least partially encounter the truth of their own stories, of the violence that so deeply impacts them on a daily basis. Those who work with children in these contexts continue to find that the denial of a reality that children cannot forget only leads to a further deterioration of their capacity to confront the present. Their work is designed to accompany a process of child development that enables these children to actively participate as subjects in the construction of their future. The hope is that they will later be able to contribute actively to the future of their country.

Psychosocial Assistance: Necessary But Not Sufficient

Despite their perceived value, those of us working in these workshops and with other forms of psychosocial assistance recognize their clear limits. The effects of State-sponsored violence, war, economic inequality, and institutional racism with which these children are living are rooted in political and economic relations and can only be definitively resolved in that arena. One concrete example is that of more than 400 children kidnapped during the 1976-1983 Argentine dictatorship. Many of these children have benefitted personally by some of the programs described here. However, groups such as the Grandmothers of Plaza de Mayo continue to demand the restitution of all of these kidnapped children to their families of origin as the only truthful and just response to the repressive acts committed against them.[11] Furthermore, the failure of the Guatemalan and Argentine governments to bring those guilty of the heinous crimes against their people to justice is one more example of the impunity with which governments in Latin America operate today. Ignacio Martín-Baro spoke of countries, such as Uruguay and Argentina, that have in one form or another replaced military by civilian rule. One of the most difficult problems facing developing "democracies" in Latin America today is, he argues, "the necessity of dealing with the sequelae of the political repression carried out earlier by governments of 'national security'." Martín-Baro suggests that "just as personal traumas require therapy so that they can be worked through and overcome, our Latin American societies require the socio-political therapy of a just reparation for the genocide committed in the name of national security, and indeed, of Western civilization."[12]

Despite these very real limits, international collaboration among mental health workers is both a source of new psychological theory and practice and an impetus to reexamine our social responsibilities. As one Guatemalan workshop participant observed: "These techniques that we have learned will help us to help children, to work directly with them. Sometimes with adults we can't change them ... but children represent the future of Guatemala and a mentally healthy childhood is going to lead to a Guatemala with emotionally healthy adults who will be able to construct a better, more stable, more balanced society."[13]

Chile: the Loss of Childhood

Jennifer G. Schirmer

It is as though I had no childhood. I look for it, but I can't find it.
—Roberto, 20-year-old son of
political prisoner executed in Chile in 1975.

Repression had repercussions far beyond its immediate victims. The files of PIDEE—Protection of Youth Damaged by States of Emergency, an organization founded in 1979 and dedicated to healing childhoods shattered by political repression in Chile—give evidence of this.

These files are about children and youths scarred by torture, detention, disappearance, execution, or exile of a close relative during the many states of emergency in Chile since 1973. Some of the 3,000 youths who have been treated at PIDEE over the last six years have themselves been directly subjected to beatings, torture and imprisonment, and they have undergone severe trauma. But the majority have witnessed the brutal invasion of their home by armed men who threaten, beat up and often carry off a member of the family. They suffer the anguish of this sudden absence in terror of permanent loss. As children, they have no means by which to defend themselves or to understand what has happened.

When looking through the reports, one sees how repression destroys childhood. All these children have shown extreme behavioral shifts from being "normal," "happy," "playful" and "obedient" to being aggressive, irritable and fearful with constant crying, restlessness, nervous tics, stuttering and an extreme dependence upon adults (usually the mother or grandmother). Many have eating problems (either a loss of appetite—and extreme anorexia—or overindulging—and obesity), difficulty sleeping (bed-wetting, nightmares of soldiers and death), or fall behind in schoolwork (poor memory, forgetting how to read, dyslexia, inability to concentrate). Some of the children of the exiled have nightmares of being totally abandoned. There is an extreme fear of the dark among these children, as well as a fear of uniforms.

> Juan (3 years and 8 months old), who was extremely frightened by his mother's violent arrest at home, began stuttering when he saw drawings of a traffic cop allowing a schoolboy to cross the street: "Is he being taken a prisoner? A small boy and a cop? Why do they want to take him a prisoner?" And when he saw a drawing of plainsclothesmen with a police van entering a barrio, he described them as: "a soldier walking and another killing."

Many of these children complain of headaches (a symptom similar to torture victims), and some of the children even take on the same pains of their parents who were beaten and tortured.

> When [Lisa] was 4, her father was arrested ... While in prison, he was subjected to severe torture, including being punched in the stomach by several men simultaneously. Since then, he has suffered severe stomach pains. During his first four months in prison, [Lisa] was not allowed to visit him, and she developed severe anorexia. Since that time, she has stomach pains and anxiety. She has difficulty concentrating and has become increasingly introverted.

Such children say they feel alone and isolated in a society that has adapted to long-term military rule and the need for secrecy. Neighbors, employers and teachers tend to shun these families for fear of reprisal. Classmates may see the PIDEE children as orphaned misfits, and through jokes and jibes, there is a rejection by most friends which is exacerbated by the child's own irritability, constant crying and aggressiveness. A sense of confusion is introduced by the difficulty of the child to understand why their relative has been so violently abused, even though the child may repeat what she/he has been told by adults: "Because they think in another form than those in the government, I'll never see mama or papa."

Not knowing whom to trust in school, these children usually say nothing, becoming more introverted, and internalizing the self-censorship practice by adults in repressive societies. Nine-year-old Alfonso says,

> I don't get together with the other kids [in school]. I don't speak. I keep quiet in school and everywhere. I speak alone. I think alone.

Some adults, because of their own anxiety and inability to confront the child's anguish, avoid talking about the event, thus confirming to the child the need to maintain a circle of silence about the repressive act. This avoidance of the subject has been shown to make the child's anguish even more extreme. Conversely, details of torture and detention can also augment the child's extreme anxiety and feeling of powerlessness. Interestingly, this self-censorship is found more often among youths of the detained/disappeared than among those of the internally exiled (*relegados*).

During play therapy at PIDEE, children talk a lot about death, the absence of the father, unemployment and jail; in fantasy, often it is the child who tries to liberate his or her imprisoned parent; in dreams they speak about the painful incident repeatedly, or they envision the detained/disappeared returning home. Some of the children also have anger and strong desires for revenge:

> I want to take revenge because they hit my mother... I know that I can't take revenge, but I do it in my imagination ... (Alfonso, age 9).

> (I get angry) when I see the soldiers in the police van ... When they place the bombs, it makes me angry they can't blow themselves up ... I want to take the same machine gun and shoot them until there are no more bullets ... and at times, it makes me angry that they don't sack this government (Claudio, age 11).

In their play and fantasies, the children display an extreme preoccupation with their family, such as "I'm worried that my mother will be alone" or "that he'll never be able to return ever again, that they've disappeared him" or "(my father) suffered a lot and lost a lot of weight (during his detention)." Given this preoccupation, there is often an excessive sense of guilt among these children, as though they themselves were responsible for what occurred. This "precocious or premature adulthood" may occur among children (especially young boys) who try to take the place of the detained father in the family: "With things the way they are, I can't think like a child. I have to be a man." (Fidel, age 12)

The mother, too, may be absent, either emotionally or physically. She may herself have been detained and/or tortured, or be in search of work or in search of a disappeared husband. The vision of the mother in all these children's eyes is one of solitariness, sadness and worry.

Emotional preoccupation with the family may also be explained by the economic violence Chilean families have experienced for several years. High unemployment (30 percent in Santiago and 70-80 percent in the barrios) has made it hard for some families to stay together. Families become separated by the search for work. Some family members may move in with relatives (usually the grandparents) while others seek whatever temporary work (*pololos*) she/he can find. Such continual movement and changes in the family-member roles adds to the anguish of the child.

Among younger children (under 10 years of age), there appears to be a regression, an attempt to return to a phase of development where reality was more pleasant. Indeed, in all these children and adults, there is an idealization of both the absent relative and the "happy" past.

The intensity and duration of these children's emotional and physiological disturbances depend very much on the intensity of repression to which they and their family members have been subjected. During the first years of the dictatorship, there were mass executions and many political prisoners in concentration camps. Between 1975 and 1977, disappearance became the means of political repression. By the 1980s, anonymous kidnappings, mass arrests, and "shootouts" between hundreds of soldiers (backed by helicopters) and lone "suspects" had become the new strategy. By 1982-1984, 851 cases of torture during detention were reported to the Chilean Human Rights Commission. The repression continues, with a combination of these tactics.

A child's ability to return to normal childhood is dependent upon a loss of fear that the act will be repeated. A belief that the violence has been finalized is fundamental to the development of a basic sense of security. Unfortunately, many of these children have, more than once, witnessed the violent invasion of their homes and the beating up and dragging away of a parent.

For children or prisoners condemned to death in some indeterminate future, their emotional equilibrium is so strained that they have an intense desire to put an end to it. Eight-year-old Rodrigo, whose father has been condemned to death:

> I believe that it is preferable that they kill him before he continues suffering in jail ... It is preferable that they kill him rather than continuing to wait ...

Similarly, for children of the disappeared, the anxiety of possibly seeing one's relative is constant, perhaps never to be resolved. If the disappearance is resolved (and it is usually negatively), it can be devastatingly depressing. Sonia, now 18 years old, received the news of the death of her father, disappeared when she was eight years old. She says,

> I feel so distrustful now when I walk on the street ... Whatever noise or person frightens me... I turn on all the lights and search throughout the house. I am afraid. I feel very insecure. I remember my father and get a lump in my throat.

Therapy: No Defense Against Continued Violence

Through the combined therapy of individual and familial interviews, play, cultural workshops and "psychopaedagogy" at PIDEE, most of these children have begun to develop a capacity to adapt to a new situation in life. They become close to others with similar shattering experiences and feel less stigmatized and isolated. Yet this does not mean an end to their anguish or fear, for the political and economic repression continues. As one PIDEE psychologist remarked:

> Unlike in most therapy, the external reality in Chile is objectively threatening and dangerous; their fears are not imaginary or unfounded ... Nor can we assure the children that what happened to them will not happen again.

Within such repression there is a loss of boundaries between the external and internal world: the external world violently invades to destroy the family, activating and sometimes reactivating anguish and extreme fear, and the internal world becomes rigid and fragile with a loss of emotional equilibrium and a basic sense of security. These children are not only denied a childhood, but they are children who are forced to continually relive a violent past in their daily lives—lives in which their fears and anxieties and nightmares are indeed real.

The Disappeared Children of Argentina: The Work of the Grandmothers of Plaza de Mayo

Rita Arditti
and
M. Brinton Lykes

"Where are the hundreds of babies born in captivity?" "Where are the disappeared children?" "We are searching for two generations." These are some of the inscriptions on the banners that the Grandmothers of the Plaza de Mayo raise in their public rallies when they reclaim their grandchildren.

Who are the Grandmothers of Plaza de Mayo, and what are their demands? And how does their work contribute to the process of reconstructing history and re-establishing democracy both in Argentina and in other Latin American countries? In 1977, at the height of the military dictatorship in Argentina, twelve women whose children and grandchildren had disappeared began meeting, forming the core group from which the present Association of the Grandmothers of Plaza de Mayo eventually grew (Nosiglia, 1985). Trying not to be noticed, the women met in restaurants, at bus stops, train stations and in other public places. They marched in the Plaza de Mayo with the Mothers of Plaza de Mayo and other human rights groups and presented petitions to the government. They suffered mistreatment, insults and persecution from the military and the police and had to resort to secrecy to protect themselves. They developed a code to be able to speak safely on the telephone about their missing family members: "The White Man" was the Pope; the "pups" or the "notebooks" or the "flowers" were the children; the "girls" or the "young ones" were the Mothers of the Plaza; and the "oldies" or the "old aunts" were themselves.

For the past thirteen years, they have been looking for their "disappeared" grandchildren. The grandmothers have good reason to believe that, in most of the cases, the children born in the camps and the kidnapped children were given as "war booty" to the torturers and killers of their parents. As Nelida de Navajas, one of the Grandmothers put it: "About the appropriated children, we always say, they are like a 'war booty' because just like they stole the TV, the tape recorder, the radio, the refrigerator, they took the children ..." (interview with B. Lykes, 1989)

The Grandmothers estimate that the overall number of disappeared children is about four hundred. In their efforts to find their grandchildren, they visited the juvenile courts to ask for information regarding all adoptions and births of children registered as NN (name unknown), and they made appeals to the community, putting ads in newspapers and distributing posters and fliers with photographs and other information on the kidnapped children. María Isabel de Mariani, who lost her son, daughter-in-law and three-month-old granddaughter during the dictatorship says:

> There is nothing we are not willing to try in order to learn something about the children. When we have some clues that a family is suspected of having unlawfully adopted a child, we start following the family very closely. There have been cases in which one of us has offered her service as a home helper in order to get into a house. In another case, one of the grandfathers posed as a plumber looking for a job. But the biggest help is from the people. We periodically publish information in the newspapers accompanied by the picture of missing children and people come forward with the information about them. When we cannot get close to the children we even use a telephoto lens to follow them from a distance." (*Christian Science Monitor*, October 6, 1986)

One of the problems the Grandmothers faced in their work was that of being able to prove that a child whom they suspected of being one of their "kidnapped-disappeared" children was indeed so. It was not enough to locate the children. They had to prove that they were indeed their relatives. They knew that through blood testing it is possible to establish a biological link between a child and his or her parents. However, in the case of the missing children, the parents were most likely dead, and the biological affiliation had to take place through the grandparents or other members of the family. The Grandmothers asked scientists to develop a test that would establish "grandparenthood." Starting in 1981, they visited research centers like the University of Upsala in Sweden, the Hospital de la Pitié in Paris, and the Blood Center in New York, asking for information that would make possible a test using the blood of the grandparents to prove that a child came from a particular family. (Abuelas de Plaza de Mayo, 1984)

In 1984, a delegation of Grandmothers that was in Washington, D.C., went to the headquarters of the American Association for the Advancement of Science (AAAS) and posed one question to Eric Stover, member of the Committee on Freedom and Responsibility of the AAAS: Did he know if genetic testing could be applied to determine grandparenthood? Stover contacted Mary Claire King, a scientist at the University of California's School of Public Health, who said that yes, a genetic grandparenthood test could be worked out, that it was a logical extension of parenthood testing and, moreover, that she was ready to go to Argentina to help develop the test. Once in Argentina, the Grandmothers suggested to her the hospital where the test could be developed. King developed it and taught it to the research staff of the hospital, many of whom had relatives and friends who had disappeared and were especially sensitive to the issue. (Beckwith, 1987; NOVA)

Grandparenthood testing begins with blood testing of the grandparents (or aunts and uncles) and the child in question. By looking at certain genetic markers, it is possible to establish if certain combinations of the markers were inherited from the grandparents or if they arose by chance. Taking into account the known distribution of genetic markers in the Argentinean population, it is possible to prove that a child comes from a particular family with a certainty of up to 99.95% (Di Lonardo et al., 1984).

It is impossible to know when the last missing child will be found.

Years from now, when the children will be adolescents or adults they may begin to suspect the "official story"of their origin.[1] By then the grandparents and other relatives may be dead. So it became necessary to find a way to keep all the genetic information of these children's relatives. The Grandmothers have worked for the creation of a National Bank of Genetic Data of Relatives of Missing Children. It has been suggested that this bank will also be a weapon against the traffic and trade of children, a serious problem in Argentina.

The Grandmothers have found 50 children: 25 children have been restored to their families of origin; 12 are staying with their adoptive families by agreement between the two families; 6 have been found to have been murdered and another 7 are having their cases discussed in court. Only three children have been found thanks to efforts from the government.

The Restitution Process: Recovering Identity

> "I could not grow, granny, it was as if a hand was squeezing my head." (Said by a child after being restored to her family of origin.)
>
> "Elenita, I have looked for you for so long," said a grandmother to a child born in captivity and now restored to her original family, on the day of her restitution. The child answered: "And I was waiting for you grandmother." (Estela de Carlotto, Grandmother of Plaza de Mayo)

The Grandmothers see their work as part of a process of reconstructing history, of "recovering identity" not only of a child but of the Argentine people. As they put it: "Restitution is an act which is psychically based upon the articulation of truth and justice, where the fullest meaning is simply to cease being disappeared ones." (Abuelas de Plaza de Mayo, 1988)

The Grandmothers explain why a kidnapped child born in captivity should be returned to her or his legitimate family. They put forward seven compelling reasons: 1—because children have a right to recover their identity; 2—because children have a right to live in freedom and dignity without lies or secrets; 3—because children must know their origins; 4—because these children have not been abandoned but have been illegally appropriated; 5—because these children carry engraved in their psyches the sinister conditions of their kidnapping and the tortures of their mothers; 6—because that trauma would impede their normal physical and psychological development, and 7—because only by returning to their "ecological nest" can they grow free, with the love and security that their legitimate families will offer them. (Abuelas, undated leaflet)

Yet, seeking truth and justice in a situation where secrecy and deceit have been accepted as the norm and forgetting the past is official government policy is far from simple. Legal debates and controversy among professionals have arisen regarding the restitution of the children to their families of origin. In March of 1984, Lidia Castagno de Vicentini published an article entitled "The True Parents are the Psychological Parents" in a Rosario morning paper where she analyzed the restitution process. Based on her review of the psychoanalytic and psychological literature of ego psychology, she argued against the return of these children to their legitimate families. Parenthood was described as a cultural and sociological phenomenon, not simply a biological fact. The blood ties that these children have with their grandparents are described as irrelevant in comparison to the almost ten years in which some of them have lived with their substitute families. The restitution of children to their grandparents was felt to reflect biologism, an outdated belief in the primacy of biological ties. More recent research that stresses the importance of the environment and the culture in the child's social construction of an identity was cited as evidence that these children's "true" parents are their adoptive parents.

In an interview published in 1985, Francoise Dolto, a French psychoanalyst who has had a strong influence on Argentine child psychiatry, provided another perspective on this complex issue. She based her remarks on her experience taking care of children that had previously been illegally adopted by the Nazis during the Second World War. She argued that because they had been part of their adoptive families for many years, these children had bonds with these families rather than with their biological families. She concluded that the grandmothers have no real bond with their grandchildren and there is, therefore, no sense in restoring them. These children, she suggested, had already experienced one trauma, and a second traumatic situation, that is, removing them from the families in which they had been living for many years, must be avoided. Having lost their natural parents, why make them now lose their adoptive parents? Although Dolto herself is said to have retracted her position prior to her death, others share her views when they appeal to the "second trauma" as a reason not to restore children.

Proposed interventions relying primarily or exclusively on traditional psychological theories are inadequate to address this situation because they fail to address the political dimension of restitution. Those who argue, for example, that restitution of a child to her/his family of origin reflects a return to "biologism" or creates a "second trauma," divorce the child from his/her socio-historical context and "psychologize" a social problem that exists because state terrorism was unchecked for six years in Argentina. From this perspective, trauma is defined in terms of individual relations between children and their primary caretakers. Although these relations are clearly very important in understanding the individual child's experiences, this analysis ignores the social and political trauma that is at the center of each child's life, the loss of their identity and of their stories. (Arditti and Lykes, 1989; Lykes and Farina, 1989)

The Grandmothers confront the controversy

> "I don't want those who stole my past to be free in my future ... Get it on! No to the *indulto!*" (Written by a restored child. Abuelas de Plaza de Mayo, July/August, 1989)

> "The knowledge of the truth is the best therapy." (Estela de Carlotto, interview with Rita Arditti in Cambridge, MA, October, 1989 after telling the story of Tatiana, a restored child who became calm and relaxed when she learned that her parents had not abandoned her, and that she had been a wanted child.)

The debates concerning restitution continue. The strategy developed by the Grandmothers provides a concrete response to the Argentine situation. The Grandmothers directly confront the familial and societal lie surrounding each kidnapped child, thus reconnecting the child with her/his story and facilitating a process by which she/he can construct his/her identity, a process that is inherently social. They see the development of identity as one that transcends "individual" psychology and that is related to the transmission of values, languages and symbols and to one's insertion in a human group with its own biological and cultural characteristics. This wider universe involves brothers, sisters, cousins, uncles and aunts, and grandparents. The Grandmothers point out that the rights of children are not the only rights that have been violated. Families have been robbed of the possibility of transmitting their values and traditions, of reproducing their social life through the process of acculturation.

The Grandmothers have responded to this horrific violation of all norms of human behavior, which turns children into objects, with a course of actions that is a necessary prerequisite to these children having the opportunity to develop as healthy social subjects. Their work points to a concept of parenting as a socially-based construction *that can only take place in the interests of the child if truth and justice are part of the process.*

The Grandmothers and their assistance teams have identified many important psychological issues related to the restitution process. One such issue, familiar to people working in the adoption reform movement[2] focuses on the consequences of lying and secrecy for children and for community as a whole. To perpetuate a lie can, in itself, lead to extraordinary difficulties when the truth finally emerges (Lifton, 1988). Many of the 400 or so kidnapped children will eventually find out that they were kidnapped, that their parents were killed, that there were family members who could have taken them into their homes, and that they had relatives who wanted them. Further, the experience of the restitution process suggests that the found children, when presented with the information about their origins in a context of love and support, do not become traumatized. Rather they are able to incorporate the new knowledge into their lives. (Herrera and Tenenbaum, 1990) As with any new, significant information, the process of incorporation differs depending upon the age of the child and the context in which it is shared. The Grandmothers and their assistance teams are continually attentive to these realities. The policy of restitution of the found children to their families of origin does not necessarily exclude a continuing relationship with the families that have raised them. Irene Barki's book (1988) documents in detail one such case, (that of Felipe Gatica), in which the "adoptive" mother, who had not been involved in the kidnapping of the child, became part of an extended family arrangement, clearly beneficial to the child.

On a political level, the Grandmothers continue to organize nationally and internationally. An August 1988 press release protesting recent judicial decisions stated:

> The (judge's) plan is to prevent us from recovering more missing children. It is wanting to cancel the guiding thread of

> historical memory: the missing ones who are still alive, our children. It is to deny their captive existence ... It's the definite end for them. But it must be clear that, for the enlightened people as well as for the international community that accompanies the Grandmothers of Plaza de Mayo, restitution is the only valid, amending path. And this is the path we will go on covering.

At the international level, the Grandmothers have worked successfully for the inclusion of a right to one's identity as an article in the final draft of the UN sponsored International Rights of Children resolution.

The work of the Grandmothers strikes at the core of family issues regarding parenthood and identity and raises important ethical questions. They are dealing with some of the basic issues that we all face: What is a family? What is the status of the child? Is there an inalienable right to know one's origins? Insights derived from their work challenge the unspoken assumption that children are commodities to be bought and sold and that adults have a right to their purchase.

The Grandmothers are asserting the right of children to truth, to their individual and collective stories, to their families and to their country. As they themselves put it: "We work for our children and for all of the children of future generations in the world, in order to preserve their identity, their roots, and their history, the fundamental basis for human dignity." (Abuelas, 1987)

Life and Death in El Salvador: A Child's Testimony

César A. Chelala

"The rural guard in the valley where I lived used to come in with guns. They bombed with airplanes and helicopters and many other things. They killed children. The guard had pity for no one. Whomever they found they killed."

These words are part of a conversation that a twelve-year-old from El Salvador, whom I shall call Pablo, had with his teacher, Ms. Gail D. Nystrom, at a summer school program in Costa Rica. The program was organized under the auspices of the International Red Cross and the United Nations, and both children from Costa Rica and refugee children from El Salvador participated in it. The rural guard that Pablo talks about is part of the security forces in El Salvador. Those paramilitary forces have, for the past few years, terrorized the population into not cooperating with the guerrillas in the country. One of their methods is to conduct search and destroy operations, during which thousands of civilians have been killed. Many other thousands have fled their homes and are now living in refugee camps in neighboring countries.

According to official estimates, there are presently more than 300,000 refugees in Mexico and Central America. More than 48% of those are children ten years old or younger, according to Mr. Colón Bermúdez, a Public

Information Officer from the Regional Office in Costa Rica of the United Nations High Commissioner for Refugees. In spite of these appalling numbers, war continues unabated, and the children also continue being its most tragic, defenseless victims.

I talked recently to Ms. Gail D. Nystrom, the coordinator of the Salvadorean Refugee Project in Costa Rica. Ms. Nystrom told me how one day the children were playing in the school grounds when they saw two helicopters in the sky. The children became terrified, especially Pablo. "It took me a long time," Ms. Nystrom told me, "before I could get Pablo to calm down and tell me why he was so afraid." What follows is what Pablo said.

• • •

"When the guard first came to my house, they told my mother that they did not want to see her even for one more second in the house, so my mother went somewhere else. When the guards came back, they were drunk, and they were very angry. They came into our house and killed five members of my family. The Guard killed my grandfather. I was looking at him when the guards came into the house and murdered him. Before the guards came in, my grandfather had told us to hide under the bed. I was there with a little girl from our family. When the guards came in, they started shooting guns like crazy. A bullet hit the head of the little girl, and she died instantly. Aside from that two-year-old girl, the guards killed that same day a five-year-old girl, an aunt of mine, my grandmother, and my grandfather. They killed everybody just using their machetes ... chopped up like that ... I left the house with two cousins who hid under the bed with me and with some women who were in another house farther away, and we ran into the woods.

We were lost for one month in the woods. We drank water from the trees because it was raining. I was wearing shorts and did not have a piece of blanket to keep me warm. I had some sugar that I had brought to be able to give to the younger children, and I still had it when I got lost. It rained and rained, so we got water from the trees and made more sugar water. When it rained in the night, we slept in caves where there were animals.

There were three of us lost. After twelve days of wandering, I could hardly walk and had to crawl. We then found some other people who told us that the guards were nearby, and we had to keep going with them to get farther away.

When the guards found our group, they began to shoot like crazy people. Since they could not see us, they shot everywhere into the mountain, so we kept going farther away. My legs were hurting, and I almost began to cry.

Finally, a group of guerrillas found us and brought us back with other people. They sent us to a place where they had these people protected so that the guards could not find them.

Then, some other guerrillas came to get us from there and take us somewhere else. In this way, we arrived at a place called San Francisco. The next day the guards made a huge invasion there and killed hundreds of people and animals, hens, dogs, pigs … everything was killed there. The guards killed every living thing. We got away just in time.

In El Salvador, the Guard does not spare anyone. They kill teachers, they kill everyone. In the schools, they come in and rip up the notebooks and take the teachers out and kill them. The next day the bodies appear wrapped up in plastic bags, some of them partly eaten by dogs. They are all tied up and have machete cuts on their necks. Sometimes even the family does not recognize their faces or their bodies.

We saw a companion who was killed, and we didn't even recognize his face; he had been hit by a whip. We went to bury him, and then the family came to get him. We showed them where we had buried him. The family went and got him, but the guards were around and the family was afraid, so they hid him under some sacks of rice and told the guards that they were carrying a load of rice."

• • •

Pablo is now living in Costa Rica, with what is left of his family.

Contributors

Mariclaire Acosta is the president of the Mexican chapter of Amnesty International. She is the founder of the branch of *Fem Latin America,* a feminist journal.

Marjorie Agosin is an associate professor of Spanish at Wellesley College. She has done extensive research in the field of human rights, especially on Chile. Among her numerous publications on the subject are *Women of Smoke* and *Scraps of Life.*

Rita Arditti was born in Argentina into a Jewish Sephardic family. She studied biology in Italy at the University of Rome and is currently a professor for a special program called Without Walls based at the University of Cincinnati. She is also the co-author of *Science and Liberation* (Boston: South End Press, 1980) and *Test Tube Women: What Future for Motherhood?* (Boston: Pandora Press, 1984).

Monica Bruno is a Costa Rican student of Spanish literature and physics at Wellesley College. She has translated various articles on human rights in Latin America and has worked extensively with Marjorie Agosin on various anthologies on women and human rights in Latin America.

Ximena Bunster is a Chilean anthropologist and former visiting fellow at the Center for Non-Violent Sanctions at Harvard University. She is also the co-author of *Sellers and Servants* with Elsa M. Chaney and has published numerous articles on women and Latin American culture.

Marifran Carlson holds a doctorate in Latin American history from the University of Chicago. She is the author of *Feminismo: The Women's Movement in Argentina from its Beginnings to Eva Perón.* An independent scholar and self-employed businesswoman, she is active in human rights causes.

César A. Chelala is an Argentine medical scientist and writer, as well as an international consultant on medical issues. Dr. Chelala is the co-winner of the 1979 Overseas Press Club of America Award for the best article on human rights.

Patricia Chuchryk is a sociologist at Lethbridge University in Alberta,

Canada. Her research focuses on gender and employment and on the women's movement in Latin America.

M. **Brinton Lykes** is an associate professor of sociology at Rhode Island College. She is also one of the founders of Red de Salud Mental Latinoamericana, a health organization concerned with the problems of health and human rights in Latin America.

Elena O. Nightingale is special advisor to the president of the Carnegie Corporation of New York. An associate professor of pediatrics and a genetic consultant at the Georgetown School of Medicine, she is co-author with Eric Stover of *The Breaking of Bodies and Mind: Torture, Psychiatric Abuse and the Health Professions.*

Jennifer Schirmer is an anthropologist at Wellesley College. Her research focuses on Women's Human Rights Groups in Latin America, and she specializes in Chile, Argentina and Guatemala.

Endnotes

Introduction

1 For further information on the history of human rights, please see "An Overview of International Human Rights Law" by Hurst Hannum in *Guide to International Human Rights Practice,* Philadelphia: University of Pennsylvania Press, 1986. Also see *Human Rights in the World Community: Issues and Actions,* edited by Richard Pierre Claude and Burns H. Weston, Philadelphia: University of Pennsylvania Press, 1989.

2 Robin Morgan, *Sisterhood is Global,* New York: Doubleday, 1984, p. 1.

3 Ibid., p. 3.

4 There is no written documentation concerning the pensions of men who have disappeared, but from my work with the Association of the Detained/Disappeared in Chile, I verified this information. Also, Patricia Chuchryk speaks of this issue in her essay "Feminist Anti-Authoritarian Politics: The Role of Women's Organizations in the Chilean Transition to Democracy" in *The Women's Movement in Latin America,* edited by Jane Jarquette, pp. 149-184.

5 For further information on these international agreements, see *American Convention on Human Rights,* OAS Report by the General Secretary of the OAS, 1983.

6 See Jarquette's introduction to *The Women's Movement in Latin America* for general information on this subject.

7 See Medina's "Women's Rights as Human Rights: Latin American Countries and the OAS" in *Women, Feminist Identity and Society: The 1980s Selected Papers,* Amsterdam and Philadelphia: John Benjamin Publishing Company, 1985, pp. 63-80.

8 Ibid., p. 64.

9 To my knowledge, the only study to date that deals with torture as a gender issue is the one by Ximena Bunster that appears in this anthology. For further studies on the issue of torture, see the Amnesty International Report, "Torture in the Eighties," London, 1984; Nightingale and Stover, *The Breaking of Bodies and Minds,* New York: Freeman and company, 1985; and the chapter by Matthew Lippman "The Protection of Human Rights: The Problems of Torture" in Claude and Weston. Concerning Argentina, see the National Commissions of Disappeared People's report, *Never Again,* London: Faber & Faber, 1986.

10 The most interesting theoretical study of the way women have created new forms of "making politics" is by the Chilean sociologist Julieta Kirkwood, *Ser política en Chile: Las feministas y los partidos,* Santiago de Chile: FLACSO, 1986. Also see Marjorie Agosin, "Metaphors of Political Ideology: The Cases of Chile and Argentina" in *Women of Smoke,* Toronto: Williams-Wallace, 1988; and

Elizabeth Jenlin, *Los nuevos movimientos sociales,* Buenos Aires: Centro Editorial de América Latina, 1984.

11 For an interesting overview of women's political participation see Jarquette's introduction to *Women's Movements in Latin America.*

12 Bunster has used this phrase in personal conversations as well as in lectures given in the United States in 1988-89. Sara Rudich used the phrase "a women's politics of resistance" in her essay "Women's Resistance: The Example of Chile and Argentina," Barnard Occasional Papers on Women's Issues, Vol. IV, No. 1, pp. 34-55.

13 An indispensable book dealing with the health profession and issues of torture and physical abuse is *The Breaking of Bodies and Minds,* by Nightingale and Stover.

14 See Agosin, *Renée Eppelbaum and the Mothers of Plaza de Mayo,* Toronto: Williams-Wallace, 1989.

"Those Who Die for Life Cannot be Called Dead": Women and Human Rights Protest in Latin America

1 This chant is used by the Guatemalan Mutual Support Group. Personal observation, Guatemala City, (Jan. 1986).

2 A female member of the *Agrupación* , *quoted in* H. VIDAL, DAR LA VIDA POR LA VIDA: LA AGRUPACION CHILENA DE FAMILIARES DE DETENIDOS-DESAPARECIDOS (ENSAYO DE ANTROPOLOGIA SIMBOLICA) 60 (1982) (all translations of Spanish sources are the author's own).

3 A Plaza de Mayo Mother, *quoted in* J. BOUSQUET, LAS LOCAS DE PLAZA DE MAYO 150 (3rd ed. 1983).

4 *Agrupación* is the Spanish term for "solidarity group."

5 There are 11 countries represented with 21 committees of relatives of the disappeared throughout Latin America, most of which are members of the Latin American Federation of Relatives of the Detained-Disappeared ("FEDEFAM") founded in 1981 in San José, Costa Rica. 3 FEDEFAM, ANNUAL REPORT 82 (1987).

6 Cortázar, *Negación del Olvido, quoted in* H. VIDAL, *supra* note 2, at 59.

7 J. SIMPSON & J. BENNETT, THE DISAPPEARED AND THE MOTHERS OF THE PLAZA 169 (1985) [hereinafter SIMPSON & BENNETT].

8 Davis points out that this image was part of the festivities of riotous behavior in seventeenth century Europe. She describes the more positive license offered lower class unruly women rising up as mothers "to tell the truth about unjust

rule" and "to defend the community's interests and standards." N. DAVIS, SOCIETY AND CULTURE IN EARLY MODERN FRANCE 146 (1975). These unruly women, however, were not seen as being responsible for their actions and "it is small wonder that the husbands sometimes thought it safer to send their wives out to do the rioting alone." *Id.*

9 A significant number of rioters against enclosures and for common rights were women in England in the early seventeenth century. As Davis points out, "[w]omen turn up telling off priests and pastors [and] being central actors in grain and bread riots in town and country, participants in tax revolts and other rural disturbances." *Id.*; *see also* Hufton, *Women in Revolution, 1789-96*, PAST AND PRESENT No. 53, at 90, 94-95 (Nov. 1971); *cf.* Kaplan, *Female Consciousness and Collective Action: The Case of Barcelona 1910-1918*, 73 SIGNS 544, 545-66 (1982).

10 M ACOSTA, *Prácticas Represivas y Sus Efectos en la Cultura Política: Algunas Reflexiones*, *quoted in* 1 CUADERNOS CENTROAMERICANOS DE DERECHOS HUMANOS, POR LA VIDA Y LA PAZ DE LOS PUEBLOS CENTROAMERICANOS 5 (1986) (emphasis added).

11 AMNESTY INTERNATIONAL USA, "DISAPPEARANCES:" A WORKBOOK 1-3 (1983) [hereinafter DISAPPEARANCES]; Amnesty International considers that a "disappearance" has occurred when there are reasonable grounds to believe that a person has been abducted by the authorities or with their connivance, and the authorities deny that the victim is in custody. *Id.* On the legal difficulty of establishing death, see Mignone, Estlund, & Issacharoff, *Dictatorship on Trial: Prosecution of Human Rights Violations in Argentina*, 10 YALE J. INT'L L. 118, 121 n.7 (1985) [hereinafter Mignone]; *see also* ORGANIZACION DE LOS ESTADOS AMERICANOS, TERCER INFORME SOBRE LA SITUACION DE LOS DERECHOS HUMANOS EN LA REPUBLICA DE GUATEMALA 89 (Argentinian Spanish language ed. 1985) [hereinafter OEA 1985].

12 *¡Hasta Encontrarlos!*, FEDEFAM No. 17, 1985, at 61 [hereinafter FEDEFAM]. It is estimated that 8,760 people have disappeared in Argentina since 1976, of which approximately 86 percent were 35 years old or younger and 30 percent were women, 10 percent of whom were pregnant. ARGENTINE NATIONAL COMMISSION ON THE DISAPPEARED, NUNCA MAS 284-85 (1986) [hereinafter CONADEP]. Other reports estimate between 15,000 and 22,000 disappeared during this same period. AMERICAS WATCH, THE STATE DEPARTMENT MISINFORMS; A STUDY OF ACCOUNTING FOR THE DISAPPEARED IN ARGENTINA 4 (1983) [hereinafter ACCOUNTING FOR THE DISAPPEARED]. In Chile, the government's campaign between 1973 and 1975 to eliminate all opponents resulted in the separation of 200,000 Chilean families due to arrest, detention, exile abroad or disappearance. As of 1983, the Chilean Commission on Human Rights estimated that there were 1,600 to 2,500 unresolved disappearances, AMERICAS WATCH, CHILE SINCE THE COUP: TEN YEARS OF REPRESSION 125, 133 (1983) [hereinafter AW

CHILE SINCE THE COUP]. The situation in Guatemala is among the worst, with approximately 38,000 disappearances over the past 30 years. BRITISH PARLIAMENTARY HUMAN RIGHTS GROUP, "BITTER & CRUEL . . ." viii (1984) [hereinafter BITTER & CRUEL].

13 U.N. ESCOR, REPORT OF THE WORKING GROUP ON ENFORCED OR INVOLUNTARY DISAPPEARANCES at 107, U.N. Doc. E/CN.4/1986/18, U.N. Sales No. GE.86-10157 (1986).

14 *Id.* at 12.

15 *See* DISAPPEARANCES, *supra* note 11, at 75-118.

16 Regarding the specifics of this law, see *infra* note 45.

17 *See* JELINn, *The Movement: Eclipsed by Democracy?*, 4 NACLA REPORT OF THE AMERICAS 36 (July/Aug. 1987).

18 *See* AMERICAS WATCH, THE VICARIA DE LA SOLIDARIDAD IN CHILE 7 (1987) (regarding the lack of protest in Chile) [hereinafter VICARIA DE LA SOLIDARIDAD]; *see infra* note 70 (regarding repression against human rights organizations in Guatemala); *see* J. BOUSQUET, *supra* note 3, at 42-43 (regarding the lack of protest in Argentina at the time of the formation of the Madres).

19 SIMPSON & BENNETT, *supra* note 7, at 157.

20 *Id.*

21 J. BOUSQUET, *supra* note 3, at 49. At one of the first meetings, the police arrived to challenge the women demonstrating, which was prohibited. Upon hearing their emotional insistence that they were not militants or demonstrators but merely mothers trying to find their children, the police withdrew. *Id.* After the incident, relatives of the disappeared formed the autonomous Commission of Relatives of the Disappeared and Political Prisoners, which proceeded to split into two groups, that of the "Parents," who were seen by some as "communist," and that of the "Madres," who were seen as "overly religious." One of the Madres explained why the women chose to form their own group: "The solidarity among the parents of the disappeared is not very evident. Many of them deny being united with the others. They assert that their children have done nothing wrong, and they don't want their case to be confused with the others 'who have something to be reproached for.'" *Id.* at 54.

Soon after, the Permanent Assembly of Human Rights was founded by members of diverse churches, liberal politicians, and lawyers, including the future president and Radical Party leader Raul Alfonsín, *Id.* at 54-55. Their public support of the relatives of the disappeared helped, although none of these groups was able to give effective protection. *See* H. FRÜHLING, NON-PROFIT ORGANIZATIONS AS OPPOSITION TO AUTHORITARIAN RULE: THE CASE OF HUMAN RIGHTS ORGANIZATIONS AND PRIVATE RESEARCH CENTERS IN CHILE 38 (1985) (available at the Institution for Social and

Policy Studies, Yale University).

22 While the report by the National Commission on the Disappearance of Persons ("CONADEP") entitled *Nunca más* (or "Never Again") documented the disappearance of 8,960 persons between March 1976 and December 1983 (with some 600 disappearances occurring in the months before March 1976), it expressed the belief that the actual number of disappearances significantly exceeded 9,000 since many family members had been afraid to report them. CONADEP, *supra* note 12, at 447. Of these 8,960 disappeared, 30 percent were workers, 21 percent students, 17.9 percent white-collar, 10 percent professionals, and 3.8 percent housewives. There were no fewer than 365 clandestine jails in Argentina during that period in which torture was committed upon almost every victim. CONADEP, *supra* note 12, at 448.

23 See SIMPSON & BENNETT, *supra* note 7, at 153-54.

24 J. BOUSQUET, *supra* note 3, at 59. Many relatives of the disappeared were intimidated from going to the courts by explicit threats or the general climate of terror; others were unable to find a lawyer willing to assist them Signs were posted in the courthouses stating that habeas corpus petitions would not be accepted without the signature of a lawyer—virtually a death warrant for the lawyer. One hundred nine lawyers were kidnapped, their fates unknown by the Argentine National Commission on the Disappeared. CONADEP, *supra* note 12, at 412. Judges, too, were not immune from security forces. In 1981, a few days after an appellate court judge declared the state of siege unconstitutional, he had to flee the country. Snyder, *State of Siege and Rule of Law in Argentina: The Politics and Rhetoric of Vindication*, 15 LAWYER OF THE AMERICAS 517 (1984) (citing R. Fernandez Taboada & J. Vidal, *Quien es Pedro Narvaiz*, SOMOS, Feb. 11, 1983, at 8). At any rate, petitions for habeas corpus before the courts usually accomplished nothing since the various "security forces" invariably denied that the missing person had been arrested or was in their custody. This lack of official acknowledgment of custody meant the court most often declared itself "incompetent" to review cases "as presented," and not a single person was successfully prosecuted in either military or civilian courts for any of the disappearances until the Alfonsín government. *See* Mignone, *supra* note 11, at 122-23; *see also* Snyder *supra,* at 513-517 (regarding habeas corpus petitions during the military regime). Judges were not only unable to secure justice but were often unwilling to do so, with many military judges drawn out of retirement to replace those judges who did not agree with the Junta. Mignone, *supra* note 11, at 124.

25 J. BOUSQUET, *supra* note 3, at 11; SIMPSON & BENNETT, *supra* note 7, at 158.

26 J. BOUSQUET, *supra* note 3, at 55.

27 *Id.* at 56.

28 *Id.* at 61, 69. Among those who signed was an entire workshop from which a

union leader had disappeared; many signatures were from the provinces where repression was very severe. *Id.* at 64. *See* D. FRONTALINI & M.C. CAJATI, EL MITO DE LA GUERRA SUCIA 82 (1984) (regarding the pretext of a "dirty war" by the Argentinian military to create a new political order).

29 *See* J. BOUSQUET, *supra* note 3, at 71.

30 AMNESTY INTERNATIONAL, ARGENTINA: THE MILITARY JUNTAS AND HUMAN RIGHTS—REPORT OF THE TRIAL OF THE FORMER JUNTA MEMBERS, 1985 at 5 (1985) [hereinafter THE MILITARY JUNTAS AND HUMAN RIGHTS]; AMERICAS WATCH, TRUTH AND PARTIAL JUSTICE IN ARGENTINA 43-44 (1987) [hereinafter TRUTH AND PARTIAL JUSTICE].

31 TRUTH AND PARTIAL JUSTICE, *supra* note 30, at 43-44; *see also* J. BOUSQUET, *supra* note 3, at 74-77.

32 The women were last seen at the Navy's secret detention center (ESMA) by survivors. TRUTH AND PARTIAL JUSTICE, *supra* note 30, at 44.

33 *See* SIMPSON & BENNETT, *supra* note 7, at 163.

34 J. BOUSQUET, *supra* note 3, at 81.

35 *Id.* at 99.

36 *See* J. CORRADI, THE FITFUL REPUBLIC: ECONOMY, SOCIETY AND POLITICS IN ARGENTINA 124 (1985).

37 J. BOUSQUET, *supra* note 3, at 103.

38 SIMPSON & BENNETT, *supra* note 7, at 163.

39 J. BOUSQUET, *supra* note 3, at 78.

40 *Id.* at 122.

41 COMISION INTERAMERICANA DE DERECHOS HUMANOS, ORGANIZACION DE LOS ESTADOS AMERICANOS, EL INFORME PROHIBIDO: INFORME DE LA O.E.A. SOBRE LA SITUACION DE LOS DERECHOS HUMANOS EN ARGENTINA 130 n.9 (Argentinian Spanish language ed. 1984) [hereinafter EL INFORME PROHIBIDO].

42 SIMPSON & BENNETT, *supra* note 7, at 167.

43 *See* J. BOUSQUET *supra* note 3, at 131; SIMPSON & BENNETT, *supra* note 7, at 168-69. Meanwhile, a subgroup of the commission of Relatives of the Disappeared, the Grandmothers of the Plaza de Mayo ("*Abuelas*"), had formed to find the 47 disappeared children in Argentina since the coup—eight captured with their parents and 39 assumed born during captivity. J. BOUSQUET, *supra* note 3, at 140. *See generally* J. NOSIBLIA, BOTIN DE GUERRA (1985) (regarding the history of the Grandmothers).

44 EL INFORME PROHIBIDO, *supra* note 41, at 143-44.

45 *See* THE MILITARY JUNTAS AND HUMAN RIGHTS, *supra* note 30, at 5. Article 1 of the law establishes that the person may be presumed legally dead without anyone being notified of such, if he or she had been legally denounced as disappeared between November 6, 1974 (the date of declaration of the state of siege) and September 12, 1979. EL INFORME PROHIBIDO, *supra* note 40, at 139. Article 2 of the law allows the state to initiate a nonadversarial proceeding to declare someone presumptively dead. After the enactment of this law, then, the Argentinian state could declare a disappeared person dead without his or her family being able to oppose it. Once this proceeding was concluded, the families could not try to bring criminal charges or use writs of habeas corpus to find out more information about the disappeared. *See id.* at 147.

46 *See* EL INFORME PROHIBIDO, *supra* note 41, at 143-45.

47 *See id.* at 138-45.

48 *See* J. BOUSQUET, *supra* note 3, at 141-42. The date of this announcement was August 22, 1979. *Id.* at 141.

49 The Junta was seemingly concerned with promoting policies aimed at maintaining the family; for example, they sponsored a public relations campaign to encourage traditional childcare in the home. At the same time, though, some of the Junta's policies, such as the cancellation of an unmarried woman's right to her companion's pension, hit poor women the hardest. *See* JELIN, *supra* note 17, at 36.

50 *See* J. BOUSQUET, *supra* note 3, at 144.

51 J. BOUSQUET, *supra* note 3, at 142-43.

52 *Id.* at 146-47.

53 EL INFORME PROHIBIDO, *supra* note 41, at 143 n.17.

54 *Clarin*, a newspaper of major distribution, carried an advertisement signed by 175 representatives of many political sectors supporting the demands of the relatives of the disappeared. J. BOUSQUET, *supra* note 3, at 177.

55 *See Id.* at 178.

56 *Id.*

57 On November 7, 1981, a 50,000-strong march for "Peace, Bread and Work" brought together blue- and white-collar, employed and unemployed, and marked the beginning of anti-Junta resistance. *See* A. DABAT & L. LORENZANO, ARGENTINA: THE MALVINAS AND THE END OF THE MILITARY RULE 74 (1984) [hereinafter DABAT AND LORENZANO]. In February 1982, the unions joined the Madres of the Plaza de Mayo outside the Presidential Palace for the first time, signaling a nascent popular-worker coalition to protest

the economic crisis and human rights violations. *See id.* On March 30, 1982, the Madres, human rights groups, various political parties, and some 15,000 demonstrators, chanting "the military dictatorship is near its end," fought police all day, showing how unified the resistance had become in controlling the streets. *See id.* at 75.

58 DABAT & LORENZANO, *supra* note 57, at 76.

59 *See* JELIN, *supra* note 17, at 36.

60 *Id.*, DABAT & LORENZANO, *supra* note 57, at 107.

61 For example, the "Resistance March" had 10,000 participants in the Plaza de Mayo on December 10, 1982. DABAT & LORENZANO, *supra* note 57, at 153. There was also the 24-hour March called by the Madres on September 21, demanding "the live appearance of the disappeared," and finally, the "March for Life" called by eight human rights organizations on October 5, 1983, only a few weeks before the presidential elections. AMERICAS WATCH, HUMAN RIGHTS IN ARGENTINA: A REPORT FROM THE CENTRO DE ESTUDIOS LEGALES Y SOCIALES (CELS) IN BUENOS AIRES 1 (1983) [hereinafter CELS REPORT].

62 *See* DABAT & LORENZANO, *supra* note 57, at 149. In a government report, the "Final Document of the Military Junta on the Struggle Against Subversion and Terrorism," published on April 28, 1983, the disappearances were explained as war casualties. *Id.* at 153. Finally, on September 3, 1983, the Junta announced its Law of National Pacification pardoning themselves for crimes committed with a political purpose, including kidnapping, torture and murder, which had been committed during the so-called "dirty war against subversion." *See* THE MILITARY JUNTAS AND HUMAN RIGHTS, *supra* note 30, at 6; CELS REPORT, *supra* note 61, at 13-16.

63 *See Madres de Plaza de Mayo* No. 8, July 1985, at 5, col. 1.

64 *See generally* H. FRUHLING, *La Defensa de los Derechos Humanos en el Cono Sur: Dilemas y Perspectivas Hacia el Futuro* (paper presented at Latin American Association Conference, Boston) (October 23-25, 1986) (on file at *Harvard Human Rights Yearbook*).

65 FEDEFAM, *supra* note 5, at 3.

66 Law 23.492. known as *Punto Final*, or the "full stop" law, was passed on Christmas Eve, 1986 by the Argentinian Congress. THE MILITARY JUNTAS AND HUMAN RIGHTS, *supra* note 30, at 93.

67 Personal collective interview in Buenos Aires (Jan. 8, 1987) (given the sensitive nature of the interviews conducted in all three countries, and the promise of confidentiality the author gave to those interviewed, only the location and date of the interviews are included in this essay). The "due obedience" law, which has had the effect of an amnesty for a large number of potential defendants, was

passed on June 5, 1987, after a rebellion by military officers. It states that defendants were acting in error about the legitimacy of orders given during the "dirty war." While covering torture, murder, and arbitrary arrest, the law does exempt three offenses: rape, theft and the falsification of civil status—the crime by which the children of the disappeared were given false identities and given to other families. *See* TRUTH AND PARTIAL JUSTICE, *supra* note 30, at 68-70. This may prove to be a hopeful sign for the Grandmothers of the Plaza de Mayo that the disappeared children of the "lost generation" may be found.

68 BITTER AND CRUEL, *supra* note 12, at viii; CENTRAL AMERICA REPORT, Mar. 7, 1986, at 6 (publication of Inforpress CentroAmericana).

69 The Guatemalan Human Rights Commission and the Justice and Peace Commission must operate out of Mexico City for security reasons. *See* AMNESTY INTERNATIONAL, GUATEMALA: THE HUMAN RIGHTS RECORD, 137 (1987) [hereinafter AI GUATEMALA 1987]. The 1987 Amnesty report details the difficulties of investigating human rights abuses in Guatemala. *Id.* at 33-37; *see also* COMISION DE DERECHOS HUMANOS DE GUATEMALA—CDHG, REPORT: SPECIAL MISSION TO GUATEMALA TO INVESTIGATE ON HUMAN RIGHTS AND SPECIFICALLY ABOUT INVOLUNTARY AND FORCED DISAPPEARANCES (1983).

70 For a study of the process of terror in Guatemala, *see* AI GUATEMALA 1987, *supra* note 69, at 137. *See generally* G. AGUILERA PERALTA & J. ROMERO IMERY, *ET AL.*, DIALECTICA DEL TERROR EN GUATEMALA (1981).

71 The Committee of Relatives of Disappeared Persons, formed by the Association of University Students, disbanded after its advisor, lawyer Edmundo Guerra Theilheimer, was shot and killed at his desk by plainsclothes police on March 10, 1967. The National Committee for Human Rights of the late 1970s dissolved with the abduction of its director, journalist and psychologist Irma Flaquer. And finally, a "Peace Commission" formed in February 1984 with university rector Eduardo Meyer Maldonado (now Minister of Education) and church, media, and private enterprise representatives disbanded after three months because of lack of government cooperation with investigations into disappearances. *See* AMERICAS WATCH, THE GROUP FOR MUTUAL SUPPORT 2-4 (1985) [hereinafter GROUP FOR MUTUAL SUPPORT]. In May 1987, the Archdiocese of Guatemala City announced that a human rights office, a Solidarity Vicariate, (*Vicaría de la Solidaridad*) would begin to function in Guatemala by December 1987. Its function would be to "denounce but not to accuse." When asked if specific individuals were to be accused of human rights abuses, Archbishop Peñados del Barrio answered, "If there is proof, then we will accuse." As of this writing the Vicariate has not yet opened. *Church to Open Human Rights Office*, GUATEMALA NEWS IN BRIEF, No. 14, 1987, at 5 (publication of Americas Watch).

72 Interview with exiled CNUS leader in Mexico City (Jan. 1984); *see also* 2 M. MCCLINTOCK, THE AMERICAN CONNECTION: STATE TERROR AND

POPULAR RESISTANCE IN GUATEMALA 137 (1985).

73 G. BLACK, GARRISON GUATEMALA 47 (1984); *see also* AMNESTY INTERNATIONAL, GUATEMALA: A GOVERNMENT PROGRAM OF POLITICAL MURDER (1981). This report alleges the existence of a specialized agency, under the direct supervision of President Lucas García's office, responsible for coordinating civil and military security operations, which included routine assassinations, secret detentions and executions. *Id.* at 7.

74 *Id.* at 47.

75 C. KRUEGER & K. ENGE, SECURITY AND DEVELOPMENT CONDITIONS IN THE GUATEMALAN HIGHLANDS v (Washington Office on Latin America ed. 1985); *see also* AI GUATEMALA 1987, *supra* note 69, at 56-65; *see generally* CULTURAL SURVIVAL, INC. AND ANTHROPOLOGY RESOURCE CENTER, VOICES OF THE SURVIVORS, No. 10 (1983).

76 *See* AMERICAS WATCH, CIVIL PAROLS IN GUATEMALA, vi, 24 (1986).

77 During the two-year Mejía Víctores regime some 1,336 forced disappearances were registered. III GUATEMALAN HUMAN RIGHTS COMMISSION INFORMATION BULL., No.9, at 2 (1985). The Guatemalan Human Rights Commission estimates that its figures represent only 30 percent of the true numbers. GUATEMALA HUMAN RIGHTS COMMISSION, REPORT FOR THE 39TH GENERAL ASSEMBLY OF THE UNITED NATIONS ON THE HUMAN RIGHTS SITUATION IN GUATEMALA III, n. 4 (1984). GAM estimates that the two major Guatemalan dailies, *El Gráfico* and *Prensa Libre*, only report 40 percent of criminal acts. *Grupo de Apoyo Mútuo, Boletín Informativo*, No. 2, Sept., 1986, at 10 [hereinafter *Boletín Informativo* No. 2]. *See* M MCCLINTOCK, *supra* note 72. For an overview of the logic of counterinsurgency since the 1960s in Guatemala, *see generally* G. BLACK, *supra* note 73.

78 *See* AMERICAS WATCH & BRITISH PARLIAMENTARY HUMAN RIGHTS GROUP, HUMAN RIGHTS IN GUATEMALA DURING PRESIDENT CEREZO'S FIRST YEAR 2, 32-34 (1987) [hereinafter PRESIDENT CEREZO'S FIRST YEAR].

79 The Peace Commission was started by Rector Eduardo Meyer Maldonado of the San Carlos University. It was to bring together representatives from the church, state, private enterprise, the media, and other interest groups. Within three months, Meyer resigned as coordinator because the Commission received no support from the government and was thus virtually inoperative. *See* GROUP FOR MUTUAL SUPPORT, *supra* note 71, at 4.

80 The Peace Brigades is a non-violent, non-partisan human rights group with offices in the United States, Canada and Costa Rica.

81 N.Y. Times, July 21, 1984, at A12, col. 1. According to Nineth de García, one of the organizers and spokeswoman of the group, "[w]e formed our group because we could not find support in any institution. In just one week, we had

25 relatives. Still, many people were afraid to join us." Christian Science Monitor, Jan. 18, 1985, at 12, col 1.

82 GROUP FOR MUTUAL SUPPORT, *supra* note 71 at 12, 48.

83 *Solidaridad: Con El Grupo de Apoyo Mutuo De Guatemala, El Gráfico*, July 21, 1985; Group for Mutual Support, *supra* note 71, at 48; Personal observations of marches by GAM in Guatemala City (Jan. 1986).

84 *See* DAVIS, *State Violence and Agrarian Crisis in Guatemala: The Roots of the Indian-Peasant Rebellion*, in TROUBLE IN OUR BACKYARD 162-67 (M. Diskin ed. 1983), at 155-71; *see also* M. MCCLINTOCK, *supra* note 72, at 137-38.

85 AMNESTY INTERNATIONAL, DISAPPEARANCES IN GUATEMALA UNDER THE GOVERNMENT OF GENERAL OSCAR HUMBERTO MEJIA VICTORES App. I (1985), *cited in* GROUP FOR MUTUAL SUPPORT, *supra* note 71, at 8.

86 GAM Statement, 1984-1985 [hereinafter GAM Statement] (on file at *Harvard Human Rights Yearbook*).

87 *Id.*

88 On October 12, 1984, GAM staged a 27 kilometer "March for Peace" from San Lucas Sacatepequez into Guatemala City, which ended with a mass for the disappeared in the Cathedral which some 1,000 people attended. This was the first such demonstration in Guatemala City in four years. At the previous demonstration on May 1, 1980, 28 people were kidnapped from the streets around the National Palace and approximately 100 subsequently were abducted or assassinated. GROUP FOR MUTUAL SUPPORT, *supra* note 71, at 12.

89 GAM Statement, *supra* note 84.

90 *Id.*

91 Protests and requests for the National Constituent Assembly to support the GAM were unsuccessful. *See* GROUP FOR MUTUAL SUPPORT, *supra* note 71, at 12.

92 *Id.* at 27. The Christian Democratic Deputy, Roberto Carpio Nicolle, Acting President of the National Assembly (and now Vice-President of Guatemala) said "[t]he problem of Guatemala is much deeper than the disappearance of a loved one." *Abogan por Desaparecidos, El Gráfico*, Nov. 15, 1984.

93 Christian Science Monitor, Jan. 18, 1985, at 12, col 1.

94 AI GUATEMALA, 1987, *supra* note 69, at 141.

95 GAM Statement, *supra* note 85; *see also Piden que aparezcan familiares ausentes, El Gráfico*, Feb. 9, 1985; *Manifestación del Grupo de Apoyo Mutuo Interrumpió Tránsito de Vehículos, Prensa Libre*, Mar. 16, 1985; *¡Ocupan el Ministerio*

Público!, El Gráfico, Mar. 2, 1985. The Commission eventually did issue a three-page report which said very little. *See* GROUP FOR MUTUAL SUPPORT, *supra* note 71, at 55. General Mejía Víctores told the GAM leaders that he didn't know where their relatives were and added "[i]t is difficult to control the violence which reigns in this country . . .[b]ut we must remember that Guatemala is an undeveloped country." *Jefe de Estado Recibe a Grupo de Apoyo Mutuo, La Palabra,* June 22, 1985.

96 GAM Statement, *supra* note 85. Despite the murders and disappearances, the military government denied making a single political arrest or holding a single political prisoner. However, as the former Vice-President Francisco Villagran (now in exile) put it "[t]here are no political prisoners in Guatemala, only political murders." AMNESTY INTERNATIONAL, GUATEMALA: A GOVERNMENT PROGRAM OF POLITICAL MURDER 5 (1981).

97 The body of Edgar Rolando Ramazzini Herrera, 25, was found on November 30, 1984. He had been missing since October 13, 1984. According to Nineth de García, "[h]is body was left in front of his house, with his entrails removed and his eyes gouged out. He was so unrecognizable that even his wife couldn't identify him." GROUP FOR MUTUAL SUPPORT, *supra* note 71, at 25. The tortured body of Rudy Gustavo Figueroa Muñoz, who had also disappeared on October 13, 1984, was found about a week later. *Id.*

98 *Id.* at 38.

99 *Mejía Víctores: Apoyo Mutuo Está Ligado a la Subversión*—transcript from *Teleprensa,* March 14, 1985, *cited in* GROUP FOR MUTUAL SUPPORT, *supra* note 71, at 36.

100 His tongue had been cut out, burn marks suggested the use of a blow torch, and the back of his head was crushed. AI GUATEMALA 1987, *supra* note 69, at 141-142. The doctor who signed the forensic report (citing liver damage as the cause of death) himself disappeared under mysterious circumstances eight days later. *Id.* The six policemen who are believed to have committed the act were found dead. GROUP FOR MUTUAL SUPPORT, *supra* note 71, at 41. Several diplomats have stated that they believe military officers were ordering the killing of some soldiers and police officers involved in death squads and torture to prevent evidence from emerging later. N.Y. Times, Dec. 4, 1985, at A8, col 3.

101 The government autopsy report claimed they had died from injuries from a car accident. However, there was evidence that they were tortured and murdered. GROUP FOR MUTUAL SUPPORT, *supra* note 71, at 45-46; IA GUATEMALA 1987, *supra* note 69. at 145-46. When Mejía Víctores was asked at the press conference in November 1985 about the deaths of GAM'S leaders, he explained that Godoy had perished "in a traffic accident." As for Gómez, "[w]ho knows how he died?" Nairn, *Guatemala Votes,* 241 THE NATION 541 (Nov. 23, 1985).

102 *Ministro de Gobernación Rechaza Acusaciones de Apoyo Mutuo, Prensa Libre,*

June 29, 1985.

103 N.Y. Times, March 2, 1986, § 1, at 18, col 1.

104 PRESIDENT CEREZO'S FIRST YEAR, *supra* note 78, at 15.

105 ACAFADE Special Report, No. 3, July 1986 (publication of Guatemalan Human Rights Commission); Cerezo wrote a letter to GAM in which he stated that he would not meet with them until they are "more reasonable." Boletín Informativo, No. 2, *supra* note 77, at 5.

106 *Labbé Gives More Statistics*, GUATEMALA NEWS IN BRIEF, No. 15, 1987, at 4-5. Four hundred and ninety of these relatives later went to the Supreme Court to sign individual petitions and to provide more details to the judge. 30 *del GAM han llegado al juzgado, La Hora*, June 23, 1986.

107 *See* PRESIDENT CEREZO'S FIRST YEAR, *supra* note 78, at 17.

108 GUATEMALA NEWS IN BRIEF, No. 15, 1987, *supra* note 106, at 5.

109 *Labbé Issues New Findings*, GUATEMALA NEWS IN BRIEF, No. 18, 1987, at 5.

110 *Id.*

111 *Widows and Orphans' Fund Stalled*, GUATEMALA NEWS IN BRIEF, No. 15, 1987, at 6. In September 1986, moreover, peasant from Santa Apolonia and San Martín Jilotepque, Chimaltenango, alleged that at an army-ordered meeting in the town square, the First Lady offered 50 quetzales (less than $17) to each family that had lost a relative over the past few years. GAM and ACAFADE (Central American Association for the Families of the Detained-Disappeared) interpreted the gesture as an attempt to buy out families associated with GAM. *Peasants Describe Government Bribery*, GUATEMALA NEWS IN BRIEF, No. 7, 1986, at 6.

112 Boletín Informativo No. 2, *supra* note 77, at 2.

113 GAM *Meets with Cerezo—No Results*, GUATEMALA NEWS IN BRIEF, No. 17, 1987, at 5.

114 VICARIA DE LA SOLIDARIDAD, *supra* note 18, at 5,7.

115 *Id.* at 7.

116 AW CHILE SINCE THE COUP, *supra* note 12, at 126.

117 *Id.* at 3-10.

118 Chilean society became disciplined through dissinformation, suspicions, rumors, doubts and anxiety with a minimum of personnel. H. VIDAL, *supra* note 2, at 10; *see also* Frühling, *Stages of Repression and Legal Strategy for the Defense of Human Rights in Chile: 1973-1980*, 5 HUMAN RIGHTS QUARTERLY 510 (discussing the methods of repression used in Chile from 1973 to 1980);

see also Schirmer, *Legalizing Repression in Chile*, DISSENT (Summer 1983) (regarding the Chilean military's shifts in the methods or repression in 1979 and 1980).

119 H. VIDAL, *supra* note 2, at 72-82.

120 Important Communist Party leaders were captured in clandestine meeting houses while members were detained in public thoroughfares. DINA accentuated its secrecy, avoiding, where possible, eye-witnesses. The bodies which were found this period were monstrously mutilated to impede identification. *Id.* at 78; *see also* Frühling, *Disciplinando a la Sociedad, Estado y Sociedad Civil en Chile 1973-1978*, at 23 (documento presentado a la Primera Conferencia de la Asociación Chilena de Investigación para la Paz (ACHIP), Santiago de Chile, July 2-3, 1981) (on file at *Harvard Human Rights Yearbook*).

121 H. VIDAL, *supra* note 2, at 78-79.

122 *Id.* at 19. Class differences are also overcome on a social level: "They speak to each other with the familiar 'tu' [you] in spite of (maintaining) differences in age and social condition . . .They converse, smoke, drink coffee, and eat together." *Id.* at 17-18.

123 VICARIA DE LA SOLIDARIDAD, *supra* note 18, at 7.

124 *See* Decree No. 2.191 in EDITORIAL JURIDICA DE CHILE, CODIGO DE JUSTICIA MILITAR 277 (1986); AW CHILE SINCE THE COUP, *supra* note 12, at 11.

125 H. VIDAL, *supra* note 2, at 81.

126 *Id.* at 82-83.

127 ORGANIZATION OF AMERICAN STATES, REPORT ON THE SITUATION OF HUMAN RIGHTS IN CHILE 78 (1985).

128 H. VIDAL, *supra* note 2, at 6; *see also* VERDUGO & ORREGO, DETENIDOS-DESAPARECIDOS: UNA HERIDA ABIERTA, 17-26 (1983). Pinochet has said in an interview that the problem of the disappeared was part of an "unconfessable" conspiracy orchestrated by those only interested in slandering Chile. *President Augusto Pinochet: "Estoy Aquí Porque Mi Pueblo Me Pide Que Me Quede,"* COSAS, Mar. 22, 1984, at 13.

129 H. VIDAL, *supra* note 2, at 83.

130 *Id.* at 61-62. As part of this buying of conscience, Señora Lucia Hiriart de Pinochet with her Centro de Madres (CEMA) offered economic assistance to the mothers of the disappeared. One of the *Agrupación* women went to see the First Lady and asked her "as a mother and a woman" to help her find her husband. The Señora never saw her, but her assistants (mostly military wives) who keep offering the woman clothing, shoes, and money, were dumbfounded when the woman heatedly refused to accept the gifts and walked out. *Id.* Like

the Argentine amnesty law, the Chilean law reveals the attempt by the conservative regime to legally maintain patriarchical households.

131 *Id.* at 84.

132 *Id.*

133 Eleven bodes were found in a talc mine. It was determined that they had been killed in 1973. At least some of these people were buried alive. *See generally* M. PACHECO, LONQUEN (1983).

134 *See generally* FUNDACION DE AYUDA SOCIAL DE LAS IGLESIAS CRISTIANAS (FASIC), YUMBEL: CUANDO LOS MUERTOS VUELVAN A SU TIERRA, 10-37 (1982) [hereinafter FASIC].

135 H. VIDAL, *supra* note 2, at 111-112; *see also* FASIC, *supra* note 134.

136 The site of the protest was carefully chosen. It is one of the greatest transit points in Santiago, with nine bus lines uniting all poor neighborhoods. Furthermore, its symbolic significance was considered as it is at the center of the Courts of Justice (which the women viewed as cooperating with the repression), the government newspaper building, and the defunct Congress. See H. VIDAL, *supra* note 2, at 122-28.

137 *Id.* at 150.

138 They were asked questions by female CNI agents such as "What do you get out of this activity? Are you still hot [for your husband]? Do you have any lovers?" *Id.* at 152.

139 *Id.* at 151-52.

140 *Id.* at 152-53.

141 As one *Agrupación* member stated: "To arrive at discussing how many centimeters this way and that way constitutes a violation of the Law of Internal Security of the State, and not its responsibility for the disappeared (which no one wants to discuss), one can see the degree of grotesqueness to which the judicial spheres have come." *Id.* at 156.

142 VICARIA DE LA SOLIDARIDAD, RESUMEN DE PRENSA 16 (1983), (on file at *Harvard Human rights Yearbook*); *Agrupación, ¡Hasta Encontrarlos!* (Dec. 1983) (on file at *Harvard Human Rights Yearbook*).

143 In an interview with the *Agrupación* members in 1984, one member explained that the women had no other alternative than to plan such acts of civil disobedience. "No one has responded to our demands. [The military] has not been made responsible [for their acts]; they have not given one guarantee of human rights to any family in Chile . . . And we are the knife in their side . . . The Courts are a farce . . . We aren't at war. It is *they* who are at war." Interview with *Agrupación* member in Santiago, Chile (Mar. 1984).

144 *See* ROWN, *Chileans are Gaining on Pinochet,* 241 THE NATION 537, 551-52 (Nov. 23, 1985).

145 *See id.* at 551-52.

146 In the years following 1973, there were numerous investigations by the courts into the disappearances; however, virtually all were closed due to insufficient evidence. Only one case, the *desaparecidos* case, which involved ten persons who were arrested in December 1976 by the DINA and never heard from again, remained active. *See* ZABEL, ORENTLICHER & NACHMAN, *Human Rights and the Administration of Justice In Chile,* 42 THE RECORD 454 (May 1987) (publication of the Association of the Bar of the City of New York) [hereinafter Zabel]. While it languished for close to six years, in 1983 Judge Cerda undertook what has been characterized as "one of the most thorough investigations ever conducted by a Chilean judge in a human rights case." *Id.* at 455. The investigation gained momentum in 1984 when a former member of the Air Force intelligence unit gave testimony on the activities of an interservice clandestine unit that had ben involved in eliminating far-left opposition during the mid-1970s. *Id.*

147 ¿Dónde están?, No. 6, 1985 at 37 (publication of the *Agrupación de Familiares de Detenidos-Desaparecidos*) [hereinafter DONDE ESTAN 1985]; *see also* ¡HASTA ENCONTRAR LA VERDAD!, Dec. 1976 (publication of the *Agrupación de Familiares de Detenidos-Desaparecidos*).

148 Among those indicted were three Air Force generals and 14 members of the *carabineros.* ZABEL, *supra* note 146, at 456. According to a source close to the inquiry, the investigating judge had gathered evidence involving many disappearances beyond the ten he had been assigned, and indictments against officers at the highest level were possible. *Id.* at 484 n. 25.

149 *Id.* at 457. Moreover, the Supreme Court issued a disciplinary ruling against the investigative judge, Carlos Cerda Fernandez, stripping him of any continuing power in the case and suspending him for two months at half salary. *Id.* at 460.

150 For example, in 1985 they staged a street protest to proclaim August 30 the International Day of the Detained-Disappeared. *See* DONDE ESTAN 1985, *supra* note 147, at 35.

151 *Madres de Plaza de Mayo,* July 1985, at 18, col 1.

152 *Id.*

153 J. BOUSQUET, *supra* note 3, at 45.

154 GROUP FOR MUTUAL SUPPORT, *supra* note 71, at 57.

155 As one mother lamented, "Can you imagine what it is like to search for a loved one in an apparently 'normal' society that was rapidly transformed for me into

a grey fort, with large doors shut and persons who answered laconically, 'he has not been detained'. . . ?" H. VIDAL, *supra* note 2, at 96.

156 *Id.* at 97.

157 SIMPSON & BENNETT, *supra* note 7, at 159; *see also* AI GUATEMALA 1987, *supra* note 69, at 137.

158 Interview with *Agrupación* members in Santiago, Chile (Mar. 1984).

159 *Id.*

160 *Abogan por Desaparecidos, El Gráfico*, Aug. 5, 1984.

161 J. BOUSQUET, *supra* note 3, at 48.

162 *Id.* at 80.

163 Interview with *Agrupación* members in Santiago, Chile (Mar. 1984). *See also* EL INFORME PROHIBIDO, *supra* note 41, at 131.

164 A Madre *quoted in* SIMPSON & BENNETT, *supra* note 7, at 158.

165 THE GROUP FOR MUTUAL SUPPORT, *supra* note 71, at 50; *see generally* BRIGADAS DE PAZ INTERNACIONALES, June and July 1987 (the monthly newsletter of the International Peace Brigades) (on file at *Harvard Human Rights Yearbook*).

166 SIMPSON & BENNETT, *supra* note 7, at 168; the *Vicaria de la Solidaridad* has withstood physical breach of its authority, both in terms of its premises and its confidential sources of information. *See* VICARIA DE LA SOLIDARIDAD EN CHILE, *supra* note 18, at 41-42.

167 Telephone interview with exiled GAM leader (Mar. 1986)/

168 SIMPSON & BENNETT, *supra* note 7, at 169.

169 *Id.* at 158.

170 A "disappearance office" was also set up in Guatemala in 1982 by General Ríos Montt in the national police headquarters where families could report the details of abductions. The office functioned for several months, drawing hundreds of hopeful families to its doors. Not a single case was solved, and some speculated that the office had been set up for the specific purpose of gathering more information on the relatives and acquaintances of those who had been abducted. The office was abolished with the 1983 coup of General Mejía Víctores. THE GROUP FOR MUTUAL SUPPORT, *supra* note 71, at 3.

171 Georges LeFebvre once noted that the worker "in the crowds of the street momentarily escapes the institutions which socialize his activities." Vidler, *The Scenes of the Street: Transformations in Ideal and Reality*, 1750-1871 in ON STREETS 42 (S. Anderson ed. 1978). But the streets historically conspired against this expression of popular power. For instance, the French conservative

fonctionnaire Jean-François Sobry reflected in 1805 that architecture was an indispensable art for the maintenance of public order, demonstrating to the citizen "the example of order, the happiness of order, the supremacy of order, the magnificence of order, the spectacle of order." *Id.*; *see also* J. SCHIRMER, Taking Political Space: Women's Actions in Europe and Latin America, paper presented at 6th Internat'l Conference of Europeanists. Wash., D.C., Oct 30-Nov. 1, 1987 (on file at *Harvard Human Rights Yearbook*).

172 BERGER, *The Nature of Mass Demonstrations,* NEW SOCIETY, May 23, 1968, at 754-55, *quoted in* Kaplan, *supra* note 9, at 559.

173 Compare with Macchiocchi, *Female Sexuality in Fascist Ideology,* 1 FEMINIST REVIEW 70 (1976) (discussion of Mussolini's "coffins and cradles" role for women).

174 SHATAN, *Genocide and Bereavement* in GENOCIDE IN PARAGUAY 115 (Arens ed. 1976); *see also* DISAPPEARANCES, *supra* note 11, at 109-18 (discussion of psychological impact of the disappearances).

175 *See* ORDERS TO KILL: THE MANUFACTURE OF MURDERERS, 24 CENTRAL AMERICAN REPORT 4 (Sept./Oct. 1985); *see also* PHYSICIANS FOR HUMAN RIGHTS, HUMAN RIGHTS AND MENTAL HEALTH IN CHILE: A MISSION OF INQUIRY 9-12, 16-17 (1985); *see generally* AMNESTY INTERNATIONAL, CHILE: EVIDENCE OF TORTURE (1983) (discussion of various cases of torture, including those of women).

176 *See generally* BUNSTER, *Surviving Beyond Fear: Women and Torture in Latin America* in WOMEN AND CHANGE IN LATIN AMERICA: NEW DIRECTIONS IN SEX AND CLASS IN LATIN AMERICA 297-325 (Nash & Safa eds., 1986); K. THEWELEIT, MALE FANTASIES (1987).

177 Interview with GAM member in Guatemala City, Guatemala (Jan. 1986).

178 It is only since 1981, after five years of silence, tolerance and complacency that the Conference of Argentinian Bishops has begun to criticize the regime: "We must be discerning about the justifications for the anti-guerrilla campaign and methods used in the struggle. The illegitimate repression also shrouded the nation in mourning." DABAT & LORENZANO, *supra* note 57, at 72 (quoting the Conference of Argentinian Bishops' document entitled *Church and National Community*). For a more complete discussion of the role of the Church in Argentina, *see generally* E.F. MIGNONE, IGLESIA Y DICTADURA (1986). The GAM has had a supportive but uneasy relationship with the Church. The Archbishop Peñados del Barrio has publicly stated his willingness to be cautiously supportive. *El Gráfico,* Mar. 7, 1985; *cf.* THE GROUP FOR MUTUAL SUPPORT, *supra* note 71, at 34-35 (documents the Church's criticism of GAM). The Church in Chile has provided much support to the *Agrupación.* The Vicariate of Solidarity, formed in 1976 within the Catholic Church, provided human rights work both a physical and spiritual umbrella. VICARIA DE LA SOLIDARIDAD, *supra* note 18, at 28-29. It is clear that the

institutional support of the Church has helped spare these women the kind of treatment experienced by similar groups in Argentina and Guatemala. *See generally id.*

179 Within the conservative Catholic schema women "neither are history nor make it . . . The mission of the woman is to make men who make history." M. GALLEGO MENDEZ, MUJER, FALANGE Y FRANQUISMO 143 (1983) (quoting García Valdecasas of the Spanish Falange); *see generally* Macchiocchi, *supra* note 173; *see also* C. KOONZ, MOTHER IN THE FATHERLAND: WOMEN, THE FAMILY AND NAZI POLITICS 93-123 (1987) (on the use of maternal symbolism in Nazi Germany).

180 CAPLAN, *Introduction to Female Sexuality in Fascist Ideology*, 1 FEMINIST REVIEW 64 (1976) (examining the connections between Christian ideology of female sexuality and patriarchal authoritarianism); *see also* M. WARNER, ALONE OF ALL HER SEX: THE MYTH AND CULT OF THE VIRGIN MARY 338 (1976).

181 J. BOUSQUET, *supra* note 3, at 45.

182 *See* STEVENS, *Marianismo: The Other Face of Machismo*, in FEMALE AND MALE IN LATIN AMERICA 90-101 (Pescatello ed. 1973).

183 *See* WARNER, *supra* note 180, at 224-35.

184 *See* KAPLAN, *supra* note 9, at 62.

185 THE GROUP FOR MUTUAL SUPPORT, *supra* note 71, at 37.

186 As one prisoner related "[B]efore letting us lie down on the floor to go to sleep, the guards forced us to say 'Our Father' and a 'Hail Mary' out loud, and at the same time they told us 'to give thanks to God for being able to live one day more' and that 'this may not be the last day.' Then we went to sleep." CONADEP, *supra* note 12, at 339 (testimony of Juan Martín, File #440).

187 "It is to remember the sacrifice of Christ, nailed to the cross. We also have our Christ, and we are reliving the pain of Mary. But we are not permitted to console him with our presence. We are also Christians, the same as those who proclaim themselves to be servants of Christianity and yet who are our executioners." J. BOUSQUET, *supra* note 3, at 47.

188 "Where are you, Papa?" *Prensa Libre*, July 21, 1984.

189 H. VIDAL, *supra* note 2, at 60.

Subversive Mothers: The Women's Opposition to the Military Regime in Chile

1 This essay was presented at the XIII International congress of the Latin

American Studies Association in Boston, MA in 1986. Without the assistance of several Chilean women, this paper could not have been written. First, I owe my thanks to those women who allowed themselves to be interviewed, and some did with trepidation. I am also indebted to the friend and colleague, who, with a great deal of difficulty, conducted some of these interviews. Long discussions with another friend and colleague, a long time member of the two organizations discussed in this paper, provided a number of important insights. Although, for the obvious reasons, these individuals cannot be identified, their contributions are gratefully acknowledged.

2 See Arancibia, Charlin and Landstreet, 1984, who suggest that during the first ten years of military rule, four distinct phases of repression can be identified.

3 An article in the Caracas daily, "El Universal," (August 26, 1983) quoted a minister in Pinochet's cabinet as saying: "In Chile no one has disappeared...the lists that have been presented are false and contain the names of persons who wanted to abandon their families and leave the country or names of persons who never really existed." (Cited in del Olmo, 1986:42).

4 There are several of these associations: The Association of the Relatives of the Detained and Disappeared, of Political Prisoners, of the Exiled, and of the Politically Executed. The members of all these groups are primarily women and while I would suggest that the observations made in this essay apply equally to all of these groups, most of the interviews were conducted with members of the Association of the Relatives of the Detained and Disappeared, henceforth referred to as the Agrupación.

5 The data for this essay was collected as part of my doctoral research (see Chuchryk, 1986) and by a Chilean research assistant (July-August, 1986).

6 A study done by Silva in 1986 (p.146) placed their membership at 380.

7 In August, 1983, I was permitted to attend a meeting of the *cabezas de grupo*. I conducted a group interview which lasted roughly one and a half hours, at which time I left so that they could conduct their regular business without an outsider present.

8 MEMCH 83 was formed to coordinate women's activities as part of the mobilization around the Days of Protest (beginning May 11, 1983) in response to pleas made by Olga Poblete and Elena Caffarena, two of the original members of the Movimiento Pro-Emancipación de la Mujer Chilena (1935), at a meeting organized to launch the publication of a collection of documents authored by the leaders of the first MEMCH. The intention of MEMCH 83 was to create a united women's front against the military government. The specificity of the women's situation was not considered a fundamental part of this opposition, although several of those elected to the founding committee were well known Chilean feminists. Later on, however, demands such as equal pay and the right to work for women were incorporated into the MEMCH 83 platform. Indeed, on November 29, 1983, MEMCH 83 organized a women's demonstration, not

only to oppose the military regime, but also to demand peace and women's rights.

9 In Chilean political structure, to be political has generally meant to be partisan. There is a long-standing historical precedent, however, for women's groups in Chile to reject partisan labels and attempt to maintain autonomy from political parties. See Kirkwood, 1982.

10 There has been much discussion internally whether or not this kind of work is paternalistic. They have concluded, however, that even if only one family has one of its needs looked after, then the members of that family can continue their struggle more easily.

11 In October, 1986, Amnesty International initiated its Carmen Bueno campaign designed to draw attention to the issue of the detained-disappeared in Chile. Carmen Bueno disappeared in 1974.

12 The notion of women as being typically conservative is not limited to Latin America. See McCormack (1975) for a useful analysis and discussion of the political science literature which attempts to document this.

13 This is pointed out by del Olmo (1986:43).

14 For a greater discussion and analysis of EPF see Crummett, 1977; Chaney, 1974 and Mattelat, 1975.

15 For a much more complete discussion of the SNM and CEMA-Chile see Munizaga, 1983, Larraín, 1982; Lechner and Levy, 1984 and Chuchryk, 1984.

16 It is also important to emphasize that motherhood does not exempt women from torture, imprisonment, and sometimes death. See Bunster-Burotto, 1985.

17 This was true also of the Women's Patriotic Front, an organization of workers, housewives, professionals, students and union activists formed in 1972 to support Allende, and the 19th and 20th century feminists who based their arguments on the moral imperative of motherhood (see Lavrin, 1986 and Kirkwood, 1982). For a discussion on how women have traditionally conceptualized their political roles as extensions of their domestic roles, see Chaney, 1979.

18 This is consistent with Chaney's 1979 exposition.

19 See del Olmo, 1986:43, who suggests that this is not an unusual consequence.

20 See also Delsing et al., 1983:32, who made similar observations.

21 For a full discussion see Chuchryk, 1984.

22 For a complete discussion dealing with Chilean women and the transition to democracy, see Chuchryk, "The Feminist Anti-Authoritarian Politics: the Role of Women's Organizations in the Chilean Transition to Democracy" in Jane Jarquette, ed., *The Women's Movement in Latin America*, Unwin-Hyman:

Boston, 1989.

Bibliography

Arancibia, J., M. Charlin and P. Landstreet, "One Decade of State Repression in Chile: A Preliminary Analysis" in Arch Ritter (ed.), *Latin America and the Caribbean: Geopolitics, Development and Culture-Conference Proceedings.* Ottawa: Canadian

Association for Latin American and Caribbean Studies, 1984.

Barnes, Jon, "Appendix: Human Rights and the Pinochet Decade," in Phil O'Brien and Jackie Roddick, *Chile: The Pinochet Decade,* London: Latin American Bureau, 1983.

Bunster-Burotto, Ximena. "Women and Torture in Latin America" in June Nash and Helen Safa (eds.), *Women and Change in Latin America,* South Hadley, Mass.: Bergin and Garvey, 1985.

Chaney, Elsa, *Supermadre: Women in Politics in Latin America,* Austin, Texas: University of Texas Press, 1979.

Chaney, Elsa, "The Mobilization of Women in Allende's Chile" in Jane Jarquette (ed.), *Women in Politics,* New York: John Wiley and Sons, 1974.

Chuchryk, Patricia, "Politics, Process and Ideology: The Politicalization of Women and Women's Roles in Chile Since 1973" in Landstreet and Nef (eds.) *By Reason of force: Social Science Perspectives on Contemporary Chile,* Toronto: CERLAC-LARU, York University, (Forthcoming).

Chuchryk, Patricia, "Protest, Politics and Personal Life: The Emergence of Feminism in a Military Dictatorship, Chile, 1973-1983." Unpublished Doctoral Dissertation, York University, Toronto, Canada, 1984.

Círculo de Estudio de la Mujer, "La Mujer en el Discurso Oficial de Pinochet," "Un Pequeño Romance," "Algunas Ideas de los Factores que Influirían en el Comportamiento Conservador de la Mujer Campesina," Santiago: mimeo, 1980.

Crummett, María de los Angeles, "El Poder Femenino: The Mobilization of Women Against Socialism in Chile" in *Latin American Perspectives,* IV (4), 1977Delsing, Riet, Andrea Rodo, Paulina Saball and Betty Walker, "Tipología de Organizaciones y Grupos de Mujeres Pobladoras," Santiago: Documentación, Estudios, Educación, SUR, Documento de Trabajo No. 17, April, 1983.

Dinges, John, "The Rise of the Opposition" *NACLA Report on the Americas,* 17 (5), Sept./Oct. 1983."¿Dónde Están? Entrevista con Mujeres de la Agrupación de Familiares de los Detenidos-Desaparecidos," *Revista Furia,* Chile, No. 3, March,

1982.

Elliot, Carolyn M., "Theories of Development: An Assessment" in *Signs* 3 (1), 1977.

Henault, Mirta, "Argentina: Mujeres de la Resistencia" in *Fem*, Mexico, 37, Dec./Jan. 1984-85.

Kirkwood, Julieta, "Ser Política en Chile: Las Feministas y los Partidos," Santiago: Programa FLACSO, Documento de Trabajo No. 143, 1982.

Larraín, Cristina, *Catastro de Organizaciones Femeninas del Gobierno*, Santiago: Instituto Chileno de Estudios Humanísticos, 1982.

Larraín, Cristina, *Diagnóstico de Organizaciones Femeninas*, Santiago: Instituto Chileno de Estudios Humanísticos, 1981.

Lavrin, Asunción, "The Ideology of Feminism in the Southern Cone, 1900-1940," The Wilson Center, Latin American Program, Washington, C.C., Working Paper No. 169, 1986.

Lechner Norbert and Susana Levy, "Notas Sobre la Vida Cotidiana III: El Disciplinamientode la Mujer," Santiago: Programa FLACSO, Materia de Discusión, No. 57, July, 1984.

Lernoux, Penny, *Cry of the People*, Penguin Books, 1982."El Lugar de la Mujer en el Mundo de Pinochet" in *Revista Furia*, Chile, No. 3, March,1982.

Mattelart, Michele, "La Mujer y la Línea de Masa de la Burguesía: El Caso de Chile" in María del Carmen Elú de Leñero (ed.) *La mujer en América Latina*, Vol. 2, Mexico:Sep-setentas, 1975.

McCormack, Thelma, "Toward a Non-Sexist Perspective on Social and Political Change" in Millman and Moss Kanter (eds.) *Another Voice: Feminist Perspectives on Social Life and Social Science*, Garden City, N.Y.: Anchor Books, 1975. "La mujer chilena se mobiliza activamente en la lucha general para la libertad y la democracia" in *Chile-America*, No. 54-55, June, July, 1979.

Munizaga, Giselle, "El discurso Público de Pinochet, 1973-1976," Buenos Aires:CLACSO, 1983 del Olmo, Rosa, "Women and the Search for the Detained-Disappeared Persons in Latin America" (translated by J.L. Newton). *Resources for Feminist Research* 15 (1), March, 1986.

Santa Cruz, Adriana, "Movimiento de la Mujer: Cauce a una Aspiración Justa," *Análisis*, (59), July, 1983.

Silva Donoso, María de la Luz, *La Participación de la Mujer: Las Organizaciones de Mujeres*, Buenos Aires: Friedrich-Naumann-Stiftung Foundation, 1986.

Surviving Beyond Fear: Women and Torture in Latin America

I wish to acknowledge the women who have survived sexual slavery in torture and have found the strength to bear witness, and the women who did not survive the torture but who did contribute and are contributing toward change for all of us. My special admiration and feeling of gratitude goes to my friend V. de N. or V.N. for her inestimable contribution to this essay in sharing with me her painful experience in various torture centers in her own country. Her courage and her strength not to give up, to continue living, as well as her efforts to adapt to a difficult situation in exile, supporting herself and her children, provided an inspiration for all of us. Perhaps her greatest contribution is the fact that she has not lost faith in her political ideas, which seek the liberation of her people. On the contrary, her horrendous experience of torture seems to have made her commitment even stronger.

I also wish to thank those persons active in and through human rights organizations who cannot be named out of concerns for repercussions.

Kathleen Barry's work on female sexual slavery allowed me to make coherent, if not rational, the patterns of torture designed for women political prisoners. I am particularly indebted to her for insights concerning expansion of the concept of political terror as torture and the extension of slavery beyond the individual, thereby further enslaving her.

I am grateful to Lois Brynes for lengthy discussion on the issues addressed in this essay and for her theoretical insights—particularly notions of "option" and collaboration and connections made with women to the Middle Ages and women who survived the Nazi holocaust. I am especially grateful for her labors as editorial consultant, which meant "diving into the wreck" of these horror again and again.

I would also like to acknowledge the constructive criticisms of the draft of this essay offered by Cynthia Enloe and her generosity in sharing with me her expertise on militaristic institutions, as well as her analyses of the effects of militarization in countries controlled by military elites.

Finally, I am grateful to Elizabeth Gervais who put this essay into readable form.

1 *Mariolatry* (by any other name) and its attendant conceptions of Madonna/Whore—*Mors per Evam, vita per Miriam*—is indeed *global*, in the socialization of women, in the schematization of women in patriarchy. It is simply more superficially apparent in Latin America, through the entrenched dominance of Catholicism.

2 A definition of torture may bring certain atrocities to the surface, but at the same time, it keeps us from allowing other equally heinous facts to come into focus. As feminists, we must understand and make understood the political torture involved in living in a state of terror and ask who the tormentor may

be. As feminists, we must refuse the neutralization of limitation by definition; we must ask if it is more a torment to have a torch held to your skin or to be covered with napalm.

3 The Mothers of Plaza de Mayo circle in silence for half an hour daily wearing white headscarves and bearing the photos of their "missing" ones. For Mother's Day of October, 1981, over five thousand women filled the square. The Grandmothers of Plaza de Mayo share a small office and their placards with the Mothers' group, but petition on their own for the approximately eight hundred missing children of "disappeared" parents. The Grandmothers believe that their grandchildren are in official and clandestine orphanages or that they have been adopted in Argentina and in neighboring countries. Some of Argentina's "missing children" have been found in Uruguay, Brazil and Chile. Unfortunately, too few have been found, see *Buenos Aires Herald*, July 11, 1981; the *Manchester Guardian*, November 28, 1981; *Connexions: An International Women's Quarterly, No. 7, Winter 1983.*

4 This essay was previously published in *Women and Change in Latin America*, edited by June Nash and Helen Safa, New York: Bergin & Garvey, Publishers, Inc., 1985.

Information gathered through direct communication, reports quoted in the OAS Report on the Situation of Human Rights in Uruguay, and my own analysis of hundreds of recorded cases of human rights violations in Chile, Argentina, and Uruguay, show that all female and male detainees have been tortured with the different methods described below.

Incommunicado detention: This is a type of punishment where the prisoner is placed in isolation, usually hooded or with eyes closed by a blindfold, in a room with no light or ventilation. Women report having been isolated from ten days up to four months.

Wall-standing: The prisoner is ordered to remain standing in a fixed position, sometimes with arms upraised or holding weighty objects, with legs kept well apart, for hours or days. Sometimes wall-standing takes place nude and in the open air. Many women have been forced to stand, handcuffed and blindfolded for two to three consecutive days without food and without sleep. Sometimes they have been forbidden to go to the bathroom.

Beatings: There are a variety of ways in which prisoners are beaten: karate, with sticks, with iron objects, with rubber bludgeons, fistcuffs, brass knuckles, kicks, and so forth. Many prisoners have lost teeth and suffered fractured ribs and ruptured eardrums. Women prisoners are usually slapped on the face with open palms and punched in the stomach making them lose their balance and fall; they are kicked until they stand up again. It is common for women prisoners to faint under this agonizing treatment; they are "revived" by a cold shower, followed by electric shocks.

Electric prod: Electric current is applied to the most sensitive part of the prisoners' bodies—gums, lips, eyes, genital organs, breasts. If the torturers are careful and expert, 200 volts exactly are used as 220 volts are regarded as fatal.

Parrilla eléctrica (Electric grid): Here the prisoner is tied naked to a metallic bed-like frame with arms and legs open. This facilitates the application of electric shocks.

The submarine: The prisoner is repeatedly immersed upside down, in a tank of water—generally mixed with vomit, blood, or urine—until on the verge of asphyxiation. May times the prisoner dies during this torture.

The dry submarine: This method of torture involves the slow asphyxiation of the prisoner by wrapping the head of the tortured person in a plastic bag or sack.

Stocks: The prisoner, generally nude, is tied to four stakes in the ground—always in the open air—so that arms and legs are completely separated.

The horse: (This specific type of torture is designed for men). The nude prisoner is made to mount a sawhorse which keeps him from touching the ground. His arms are held open, and the sawhorse is moved backward and forward beneath him so that the individual being tortured feels as if he were being sawed in half. This results in serious injury to the genital organs.

Pau de arara: The person being tortured is hung by the knees from a horizontal plank, with hands and ankles tied together. This procedure cuts off the circulation of the blood; the body turns livid and the individual being tortured faints.

Drugs: Pentathol, especially, is administered to produce a relaxed semi-hypnotic state in the prisoner whereby he or she offers little resistance, and information is easily obtained.

Violent sexual acts: There are many and varied cases where torturers violate detainees and when mutilating devices are inserted in the vagina and anus. At times male detainees are sexually violated.

Bibliography

Amnesty International, *Children,* London: Amnesty Publications, 1979.

Amnesty International, *Testimony on secret detention camps in Argentina,* USA.: Amnesty International Publications, 1980.

Amnesty International, *Amnesty International Report 1980,* London: Amnesty Publications, 1980.

Amnesty International, *Amnesty International Report 1981,* London: Amnesty International, 1981.

Amnesty International, *Amnesty International Report 1982,* London:

AmnestyInternational, 1982.

Amnesty International, *Matchbox,* USA.: Published by Amnesty International USA, 1981.

Barry, Kathleen, *Female sexual slavery,* New York: Avon Books, 1979.

Comisión Interamericana de Derechos Humanos, *Informe Sobre la Situación de los Derechos Humanos en Chile,* Washington D.C.: Secretaría General de los Estados Americanos, 1974.

Comisión Internacional de Investigación de los Crímenes de la Junta Militar en Chile, *Denuncia y Testimonio,* Helsinki: Comisión Internacional de Investigación de los Crímenes de la Junta Militar en Chile, 1975.

Comisión Interamericana de Derechos Humanos, *Informe Sobre la Situación de los Derechos Humanos en Argentina,* Washington D.C.: Secretaría General de los Estados Americanos, 1980.

Connexions/An International Women's Quarterly, "Las Abuelas-Search for the Missing" in *Connexions, An International Women's Quarterly.* Winter, No.7, 1983.

Davis, Angela, "Reflection on the Black woman's role in the community of slaves" in *The Black Scholar,* Vol. 3, No. 4. December, 1971.

Elu de Lenero, María del Carmen, (Ed.) *Perspectivas Femeninas en América Latina,* México: Sep-Setentas, 1976.

Enloe, Cynthia, "The Military Model," "NATO: What is it and why should women care?"and "NATO: The lesson machine" in W. Chapkis, Ed. *Loaded Questions Women in the Military,* Amsterdam/Washington, D.C.: Transnational Institute, 1981.

________, *Does Khaki become you? The militarization of women's lives.* London: Pluto Press, May 1983 and Boston: South End Press, August, 1983.

Hooks, Bell, *Ain't I a woman. Black Women and Feminism,* Boston: South End Press, 1982.

Inter-American Commission on Human Rights, *Third report on the situation of human rights in Chile,* Washington D.C.: General Secretariat of the Organization of American States, 1977.

________, *Report on the situation of human rights in Uruguay,* Washington, D.C.:

CIDH General Secretaría of the Organization of American States, 1978.

________, *Ten years of activities 1971-1981,* Washington D.C.: General Secretariat of the Organization of American States, 1982.

Latin American and Caribbean Women's Collective, *Slaves of slaves, the challenge of Latin American women,* London: Zed Press, 1980.

Lernoux, Penny, *Cry of the people,* New York: Doubleday & Company, 1980.

Nash, June and Helen I. Safa, Eds. *Sex and class in Latin America,* New York: Praeger Publishers, 1976.

Randall, Margaret, *Sandino's daughters. Testimonies of Nicaraguan women in struggle,* Vancouver: New Star Books Ltd, 1981.

Schoultz, Lars, *Human rights and United States policy towards Latin America,* Princeton, New Jersey: Princeton University Press, 1981.

Stevens, Evelyn P, "*Marianismo:* The other face of *machismo* in Latin America." In Ann Pescatello (Ed.) *Female and male in Latin America,* Pittsburgh: University of Pittsburgh Press, 1973.

The Disappeared Children of Argentina: The Work of the Grandmothers of Plaza de Mayo

We would like to thank the Grandmothers of Plaza de Mayo whose untiring work in the name of justice continues to be crucial to the ongoing efforts within Latin America to recover from the brutal experiences of state terrorism and to our own understanding of the rights of children. In particular, we would like to acknowledge the contributions of Estela de Carlotto, Nelida de Navajas, Elsa de Oesterheld and María Isabel Chorobik de Mariani to our thinking about these issues. We also thank Juan Jorge Fariña of the Movimiento Solidario de Salud Mental, Buenos Aires, with whom one of us has worked during the past several years and whose ideas have sparked lively conversation and debate.

1 "The Official Story" is an Argentinean film telling the story of a high school teacher whose daughter, adopted at birth, was stolen from a family of "detained-disappeared."

2 The adoption reform movement promotes openness and honesty in adoption practices in the U.S. and Canada. The American Adoption congress, an umbrella organization of adoptees, birth parents, adoptive parents, adoption agencies and individual professionals is the leading organization working to change adoption practices. They can be reached at: AAC, P.O. Box 44040, L'Enfant Plaza Station, Washington, D.C., 20026-0040.

Bibliography

Abuelas de Plaza de Mayo, "Niños desaparecidos en la Argentina desde 1976," May,1984.

Abuelas de Plaza de Mayo, "Abducted Children in Argentina," September, 1987.

Abuelas de Plaza de Mayo, *Missing Children who Disappeared in Argentina between 1976 and 1983,* Buenos Aires, 1988.

Arditti, Rita and Brinton M. Lykes, "The Missing Children of Argentina," in *Sojourner,* 14(5), 1989, pp. 17-19.

Barki, Irene, *Pour ces yeux-la,* Paris: Editions La Decouverte, 1988.

Beckwith, Barbara, "Science for human rights: using genetic screening and forensicscience to find Argentina's 'disappeared'," in *Science for the People,* January-February, 1987.

Castagno de Vicentini, L., "Los verdaderos padres son los padres psicológicos" [The true parents are the psychological parents.], in *La Capital,* Rosario, Argentina, March, 1984.

Comisión Nacional de los Desaparecidos, *Nunca Más: The Report of the Argentine National Commission on the Disappeared,* New York: Farrar, Strauss & Giroux, 1986.

Di Lonardo, A.M., P. Darlu, M. Bauer, C. Orrego, and M-C. King, "Human Genetics and Human Rights: Identifying the Families of Kidnapped Children," in *American Journal of Forensic Medicine and Pathology,* 5(4), pp. 339-347, 1984.

Dolto, Francoise, Interview summarized in the journal *PSYCHE,* Buenos Aires, 1985.

Frontalini, D. and M.C. Caiati, *El mito de la guerra sucia* [The myth of the Dirty War], Buenos Aires: CELS, 1984.

Herrera, Matilde and Tenenbaum, *Identidad: Despojo y Restitución* [Identity: Dispossession and Restitution], Buenos Aires: Contrapunto, 1990.

Lykes, M. Brinton. and Juan Jorge Fariña, "Can the Unofficial Story Have a Happy Ending?" in *LINKS Central American Health Report,* 6(1), 1989.

NOVA, *The Search for the Disappeared,* 1986. A PBS show. The transcript of the one-hour show is available for $4 from NOVA, Box 322, Boston, MA. A videocassette or 16 mm. film can be purchased from Coronet Film and Video, 108 Wilmot Rd., Deerfield, IL 60015, 1-800-621-2131.

Partnoy, Alicia, *The Little School: Tales of Disappearance and Survival in Argentina,* San Francisco/Pittsburgh: Cleis Press, 1986.

Simpson, John and Jana Bennett, *The Disappeared and the Mothers of Plaza de Mayo,* New York: St. Martin's Press, 1985.

Suárez-Orozco, Marcelo M., "The Treatment of Children in the 'Dirty War': Ideology, State Terrorism and the Abuse of Children in Argentina," in Nancy Scheper-Hughes, ed., *Child Survival,* Holland: D. Reidel Publishing Co., pp.227-246, 1987.

Chile: The Loss of Childhood

Bibliography

Alamos, Loreto, "Repercusiones Psicológicas en Niños Víctimas de la Represión Política." Documentos de Trabajo, PIDEE, 1986.

Cohn, Jorgen, "Children and Torture." The Danish Medical Group, Amnesty International, Copenhagen, 1982.

Constable, Pamela, "Children Bear Scars of Repression." in *TheBoston Globe,* 22 December, 1985.

The Comadres of El Salvador: A Case Study

Bibliography

Acosta, Mariclaire, "La violación generalizada de los derechos humanos como política de gobierno: notas sobre el caso latinoamericano" in *Revista Mexicana de Sociología,* No.1, January-March, 1984, pp. 335-355.

Amnesty International, *Disappearances, A Workbook,* New York: Amnesty International, 1981.

Barbiere, Teresa de and Orlandina de Oliveira, "Nuevos sujetos sociales: la presencia política de las mujeres en América Latina" in *Nueva Antropología,* No.30, Mexico, November,1986, pp.5-30.

Barry and Preusch, *The Central America Fact Book,* New York: Grove Press, 1986.

Bonafini, Hebe de, *Historias de vida,* Buenos Aires: Fraterna, 1985.

Bonder, Gloria, "¿Cuál mujer? ¿Cuál política?" in *Fem,* Mexico, June/July, 1986, pp.5-11.

Chuchryk, Patricia, *Subversive Mothers: Women's Opposition to the Military Regime in Chile,* presented at the XIII International Congress of the Latin American Studies Association, Boston, October, 1986.

FEDEFAM, "Los desaparecidos: paz, justicia y democracia " during a regional encounter in La Paz, Bolivia, July 1986.

McLeod, Morna, *GAM-COMADRES: Un análisis comparativo,* Mexico: CITGUA, 1986.

Moscardi, Alicia and Piera Oria, *Mitos viejos, luchas nuevas, transformación o ruptura de la cotidianeidad en la lucha de Madres y Abuelas de la Plaza de Mayo?,* Buenos Aires, 1986.Serie Cuadernos, 1986.

Tiffenberg, Ernesto, *Sufrimiento y evolución del movimiento de Madres de Plaza de Mayo el contexto de los nuevos movimientos sociales,* Mexico: UNAM, 1984.

Vidal, Hernán, *Dar la vida por dar la vida: la Agrupación Chilena de Familiares de*

Detenidos-Desaparecidos, Minneapolis: Institute for the Study of Ideologies and Literature, 1982.

"Children in the Storm": Psychosocial Trauma in Latin America

1 See M. Brinton Lykes & Ramsay Liem, "Human Rights and Mental Health in the United States: Lessons from Latin America" in *Journal of Social Issues,* No.46 (3), 1990, pp. 151-165, for a fuller elaboration of these points.

2 See Elizabeth Lira, *De la Solidaridad a la Reparación Social: El quehacer Psicológico en las Dictaduras y en los Procesos de Democratización del Cono Sur,* Presentación, XV Congress, Latin American Studies Association, 1989.

3 Ignacio Martín-Baro, "La violencia política y la guerra como causas del trauma psicosocial en El Salvador " in *Revista de Psicología de El Salvador,* 23, pp. 123-141.

4 Ernesto Sábato et al., *Nunca Más: The Report of the Argentine National Commission on the Disappeared,* New York: Farrar, Strauss, Giroux, 1986; Marcelo M. Suarez-Orozco, "The treatment of Children in the 'Dirty War': Ideology, State Terrorism and the Abuse of Children in Argentina," in Nancy Scheper-Hughes, ed., *Child Survival,* Holland: D. Reidel Publishing Company, 1987, pp. 227-246.

5 Ibid

6 Cited by Irene Barki, *Pour ces yeux-la,* Paris: Editions La Decouverte, 1988, p. 241.

7 See among others, Movimiento Solidario de Salud Mental, *Terrorismo de Estado: Efectos Psicológicos en los Niños,* Buenos Aires: Editorial Paidos, 1987; Raija-Leena Punamaki, "Psychological stress responses of Palestinian mothers and their children in conditions of military occupation and political violence" in *The Quarterly Newsletter of the Laboratory of Comparative Human Cognition,* 9. pp. 76-84; Ciencia y Tecnología para Guatemala (CITGUA), in *Los dibujos de los niños refugiados,* Mexico City: Cuaderno 17, Año 6, November, 1989.

8 See Ignacio Martín-Baro, "Guerra y trauma psicosocial del niño Salvadoreño," Ponencia del Seminario-Taller, *Tratamiento y Recuperación Post-Traumática del Niño,* San Salvador, 1988, (English translation by Anne Wallace presented by Adrianne Aron at the American Psychological Association Annual Meeting, Boston, MA, August, 13, 1990.

9 The Movimiento Solidario de Salud Mental (MSSM), the psychological assistance team of the Commission of Families of Detained and Disappeared for Political Reasons, is a non-governmental organization founded in 1982 to

develop alternative theory and practice in mental health, with a clear emphasis on mental health and human rights. Since its beginning, the MSSM has developed diverse programs that include clinical services, research, community prevention and teaching. The general focus of all programs reflects a belief that structural social change is a precondition to the development of mental health for oppressed sectors of society. The MSSM's approximately 40 members include psychologists, psychiatrists, experts in social communication, actors, teachers and researchers.

10 Descriptions of these workshops as well as a training video describing this work are available from the author.

11 See, for example, Abuelas de Plaza de Mayo, *El secuestro-apropriación de ninños y su restitución,* Buenos Aires, 1989; Rita Arditti and M. Brinton Lykes, "The missing children in Argentina" in *Sojourner,* No.14 (5), 1989, pp. 17-19; M.Brinton Lykes and Juan Jorge Farina, "Can the unofficial story have a happy ending?"

12 *Derechos Humanos: Todo es según el dolor con que se mira,* Santiago de Chile: ILAS 1989 and *Commonweal,* No., 117 (6), 23 February, 1990.

13 We invite interested readers to help develop similar work by contacting our international Network in Mental Health and Human Rights (Mental Health Committee/BCHRCA, c/o McGuinn Hall 413, Boston College, Chestnut Hill, MA 02167.)

Children and Human Rights in Latin America

1 CERJ is the Council of Indigenous Communities, an organization founded to protect the rights of Guatemala's indigenous people.

2 GOBI-FFF stands for Growth chart to monitor a child's nutrition; Oral rehydration therapy for victims of diarrheal disease; Breastfeeding; Immunization against six common childhood diseases; Food supplements for pregnant and lactating women; Female education and Family spacing.

Bibliography

_______, *Abducted children in Argentina,* Argentina: Abuelas de Plaza de Mayo, 1989.

Amnesty International-USA, *Amnesty International Focus on Children,* 1988.

Amnesty International-USA, *Guatemala: Recent Human Rights Developments,* May, 1989.

Amnesty International-USA, Boy witness, *Amnesty International Newsletter,* 20 (5), May, 1990a, p.6.

Amnesty International-USA, *Children's Campaign*, 1990b.

Castelle, K., *In the child's best interest: A primer on the UN Convention on the rights of the child*, New York: Defense for Children International-USA, 1989.

Claude, R.P., [Interview with Dr. Joel Filartiga, Washington D.C.] in E. Stover, and E. Nightingale (eds.), *The breaking of bodies and minds: Torture, psychiatric abuse and the health professions*, New York: W.H. Freeman and Company, March 19, 1982, p. 94.

Defense for Children International -USA, *Convention action*, Defense for Children International-USA Convention Clearinghouse: New York, 1990.

Defense for Children International-USA, "Using Children as Soldiers: What is the Opinion on congress?" in *The Children's Tribune*, Jan. 9, 1989, p. 1.

Hammarberg, T., "The UN Convention on the rights of the child—and how to make it work," in *Human Rights Quarterly*, 12 (1), 1990, p. 104.

Hannum, H., *Guide to International Human Rights Practice*, Philadelphia: University of Pennsylvania Press, 1986.

Jacobs, D. (ed.), *Action for children*, 5(1), 1990.

Jupp, M., "The UN Convention on the rights of the child" in *Human Rights Quarterly*, 12(1), 1990, p. 133.

Kuper, L., *Genocide: Its political use in the twentieth century*, New Haven: Yale University Press, 1981.

Lifton, R.J., *The Nazi doctors: Medical killing and the psychology of genocide*, New York: Basic Books, Inc., 1986.

Quilliam et al., *The torture report*, London: British Medical Association, 1986.

__________, "Salvador Army Fills by Force," in *New York Times*, April 21, 1989,p.A3.

Stover, E. and M. Nelson, "Medical action against torture," in E. Stover and E. Nightingale (eds.) Op. cit., pp. 110-113.

Stover, E., *The open secret: Torture and the medical profession in Chile*, Washington D.C.: Committee on Scientific Freedom and Responsibility, American Association for the Advancement of Science, 1987.

United Nations, *Universal Declaration of Human Rights*, Adopted Dec. 10, 1948, GA Res., 217A, (III), U.N. Document 11/810, 1948.